The Korean War: Challenges in Crisis, Credibility, and Command

America in Crisis

Editor: Robert A. Divine

H. W. Brands: *Into the Labyrinth: The United States and the Middle East, 1945–1993*

H. W. Brands: *Since Vietnam: The United States in World Affairs, 1973–1995*

Robert A. Divine: *The Reluctant Belligerent: American Entry into World War II*

George C. Herring: *America's Longest War: The United States and Vietnam, 1950–1975, 3/e*

Burton I. Kaufman: *The Korean War: Challenges in Crisis, Credibility and Command, 2/e*

Walter LeFeber: *America, Russia and the Cold War, 8/e*

H. Wayne Morgan: *America's Road to Empire: The War with Spain and Overseas Expansion*

Daniel M. Smith: *The Great Departure: The United States and World War I, 1914–1920*

Gaddis Smith: *American Diplomacy during the Second World War, 1941–1945*

The Korean War: Challenges in Crisis, Credibility, and Command

SECOND EDITION

Burton I. Kaufman

Virginia Polytechnic Institute and State University

The McGraw-Hill Companies, Inc.

New York   St. Louis   San Francisco   Auckland   Bogotá   Caracas   Lisbon
London   Madrid   Mexico City   Milan   Montreal   New Delhi   San Juan
Singapore   Sydney   Tokyo   Toronto

McGraw-Hill

A Division of The **McGraw·Hill** Companies

This book was set in Palatino by Ruttle, Shaw & Wetherill, Inc.
The editor was Lyn Uhl;
The production supervisor was Diane Ficarra.
The cover was designed by Joan Greenfield.
Project supervision was done by Ruttle, Shaw & Wetherill, Inc.
R. R. Donnelley & Sons Company was printer and binder.

Cover Photo: detail of Korean War Memorial, Washington D.C., courtesy
Liaison International.

THE KOREAN WAR
Challenges in Crisis, Credibility, and Command

1 2 3 4 5 6 7 8 9 0 DOC DOC 9 0 9 8 7 6

ISBN 0-07-034150-8

Library of Congress Cataloging-in-Publication Data
Kaufman, Burton Ira.
    The Korean war : challenges in crisis, credibility, and command /
Burton I. Kaufman. — 2nd ed.
        p.   cm. — (America in crisis)
    Includes bibliographical references and index.
    ISBN 0-07-034150-8
    1. Korean War, 1950–1953—United States.   2. United States—
Politics and government—1945–1953.   I. Title.   II. Series.
DS919.K38   1997
951.904'2—dc20   96-22664

About the Author

BURTON I. KAUFMAN is Professor of History and Humanities and Director of the Center for Interdisciplinary Studies at Virginia Polytechnic Institute and State University (Virginia Tech). Before coming to Virginia Tech in 1988 he taught at the University of New Orleans and Kansas State University. His books include *Trade and Aid: Eisenhower's Foreign Economic Policy, 1953–1961* (1984); *The Presidency of James Earl Carter, Jr.* (1993); and *The Arab World and the United States: Inter–Arab Rivalry and Superpower Diplomacy* (1995). He is presently working on a book about the impact of the Suez and Panama canals on the modern world.

For Scott

Contents

INTRODUCTION   *ix*

INTRODUCTION TO THE SECOND EDITION   *xiii*

1. The Outbreak of Hostilities   1
2. War and the Climate of Crisis and Conspiracy   32
3. The UN Offensive and Chinese Intervention   51
4. The Recall and the MacArthur Hearings   89
5. Negotiations   115
6. Prisoners, Propaganda, and Politics   145
7. New President, New Initiatives   170
8. Peace Without Victory   193

CONCLUSION   *210*

SUGGESTIONS FOR FURTHER READING   *218*

INDEX   *233*

Introduction

President Harry S. Truman wrote in his *Memoirs* that he regarded his decision to send American troops into Korea in June 1950 as his most important as president.[1] Certainly the Korean war was a turning point in the Cold War that has dominated international diplomacy since 1945. According to State Department expert Charles E. Bohlen, "[i]t was the Korean War and not World War II that made [the United States] a world military-political power." The historian John Gaddis has commented that "the real commitment to contain communism everywhere originated in the events surrounding the Korean War."[2]

This is a history of the United States' involvement in the Korean war, including the reasons behind Truman's fateful decision to commit American troops to Korea after North Korean forces invaded South Korea on June 25, 1950. The book covers the major military decisions and events of the war, but it is primarily a study of foreign policy and not a military history. To the extent that it deals with the military history of the war its emphasis is on the nexus at which foreign policy decision-making in Washington and military decision-making in Korea and Tokyo interacted with each other. Thus, its focus is more on the White House, the Pentagon, and the negotiating tables at Kaesong and Panmunjom than in the foothills and mountains of Korea.

By placing the conflict in a broad domestic and international setting and by discussing the various political pressures on the White House, both at home and abroad, I have also tried to provide the necessary context for understanding the decision-making and diplomacy associated with the war. In this respect, I have attempted to make clear the constraints under which the Truman administration operated, first in terms of its initial decision to commit American troops to the war, then in its determination to cross the 38th parallel and "roll back" Communist expansion, and, finally, in its resolve to fight a limited war following the entry of the Chinese Communists into the conflict in November 1950. Similar considerations continued to influence American policy for the remainder of the war, and they are also discussed at considerable length.

The three basic themes of the book are those of crisis, credibility, and command. The first two are interrelated. The White House's decision to send troops into Korea and then to continue fighting a war there for almost three years can be fully appreciated only in terms of the crisis atmosphere that was so apparent in Washington during the late 1940s and early 1950s, an atmosphere underscored by the Red Scare and McCarthyism at home and by the fear of Communist expansion abroad. Likewise, the Truman administration committed American forces over an extended period in a country little known to most Americans before the summer of 1950 because it viewed the conflict in terms of maintaining American credibility abroad and its own credibility at home.

The third theme of the book has to do with what D. Clayton James has called a "crisis of command," and it relates to the problems of command in the first major conflict of any consequence (barring perhaps the War of 1812) in which the United States had to accept terms of settlement less than those of total victory. This was a bitter experience for many of America's military leaders, and I attempt to provide the reader with a sense of the problems they faced and the frustrations they endured in trying to conduct such a war. Without trying to rehabilitate the common image of General Douglas MacArthur as a military leader obsessed with his own sense of destiny and by a reckless disregard for higher authority, I try to view the war from his perspective and that of his two successors in Tokyo, Generals Matthew Ridgway and Mark Clark. I argue the need for a more sympathetic understanding on the part of foreign policy-makers in Washington of the military imperatives of fighting a war.

There are a number of people who gave me sage advice while I wrote this book whom I would like to thank. Naomi Schneider, formerly with Alfred A. Knopf, did an expert job in editing the first half of this book, always forcing me to be clear and precise. The series editor, Professor Robert Divine of the University of Texas at Austin, was extremely helpful and sympathetic in his remarks to me. My former colleague Professor Joe Hawes, now at Memphis State University, read the entire manuscript carefully and told me to move from merely writing a competent book to writing one that was also interesting. I have tried to follow his advice. My colleague and good friend Professor Al Hamscher, a true craftsman, helped me through some rough organizational and stylistic hurdles. I'd like to thank the reviewers of the second edition: Roger Dingman, Mesa State College, and Mark Lytle, Bard College. But I dedicate this book to the entire history faculty at Kansas State University, as fine a group of dedicated teachers, scholars, and just good colleagues and friends as anyone could want. The reader will forgive me if I mention them by name: Kent Donovan, Clyde Ferguson, Marsha Frey, Buddy Gray, Al Hamscher, Robin Higham, Ken Jones, Jake Kipp, George Kren, Bob Linder, John McCulloh, Don Mrozek, Don Nieman, Roy Page, Homer Socolofsky, Lynn Stoner (now at Arizona State University), Dent Wilcoxon, and Sue Zschoche.

Notes

1. Harry S. Truman, *Memoirs by Harry S. Truman: Years of Trial and Hope, 1946–1952* (New York, 1956), 390.
2. Charles E. Bohlen, *Witness to History, 1919–1969* (New York, 1973), 303; John Lewis Gaddis, "Was the Truman Doctrine a Real Turning Point?" *Foreign Affairs,* 52 (January 1974), 386.

Introduction to the Second Edition

In this second edition of *The Korean War: Challenges in Crisis, Credibility, and Command*, I have retained the major themes of the first edition, which, I believe, remain as valid today as they were when I first wrote the book a decade ago. However, this edition differs from the first in two major ways. First, it is substantially shorter than the first edition; indeed, it is as much an abridgement of the first edition as a revision. I have done this by eliminating much of the detail of the first edition without, I hope, weakening its major themes and points. Second, I have tried to incorporate the abundance of new scholarship on Korea that has been published over the last ten years. I have much more to say in this edition about such matters as the geopolitical context of the Korean war, Soviet and Chinese policy with respect to the war, and the consideration given by the United States to the use of nuclear weapons during the war. For their insights into these and other matters, I am grateful to such fine scholars as Roger Dingman, Rosemary Foot, and Michael Hunt. I wish to thank, especially, Roger Dingman, who wrote a lengthy, thoughtful, and extremely useful critique of the first edition. Although I have not followed all of Roger's recommendations, I have been guided by them throughout the preparation of this edition and have incorporated most of his suggestions into the text.

I dedicate this book to my son, Scott, a fledgling historian who at the time of the book's completion is an ABD at Ohio University. I can think of no greater compliment that a son or daughter can pay to a parent than to want to follow in his or her footsteps. Scott has paid me that compliment. But more than that, Scott acted as my editor, carefully reading the first edition and savagely eliminating extraneous material. I relish the opportunity to reciprocate.

CHAPTER ONE

The Outbreak of Hostilities

The Korean conflict of 1950–1953 involved a great power struggle between the United States and the Soviet Union superimposed on a civil war between North and South Korea. It came amid a climate of crisis in the United States highlighted by fear of Communist aggression throughout the world and compounded by apprehension about internal Communist subversion reaching the highest levels of government. In the five years preceding the outbreak of hostilities in Korea, relations between the United States and the Soviet Union had soured and then become poisoned. Misperceptions and misunderstandings of one superpower by the other had hardened into myths that aggravated real grievances. Fearful of a worldwide Communist conspiracy and faced with a regional political order largely in chaos as a result of Japan's defeat in World War II, the United States had been sucked into the vortex of Asian politics. American officials had formulated policy for Korea that badly estimated the consequences of their actions and failed to comprehend fully the political implications of Korea's social and political structure. Out of similar anxiety Washington responded to news of the North Korean invasion of South Korea on June 25, 1950, with deliberate speed now that it believed the Soviet Union had shown its true intentions in terms of world domination.

Relations between Washington and Moscow had not been good since the Communists first came to power in 1917. Along with other Western countries, the United States had intervened in the Russian Civil War in 1918, and Washington had not even recognized the Soviet Union until 1933. For its part Moscow made repeated calls in the 1920s and 1930s for world revolution and the destruction of American capitalism. Americans were also shocked by news of purges within the Soviet Union in the 1930s and by the Nazi-Soviet Pact of August 1939, which led to Germany's invasion of Poland the next month.[1]

Out of the expediency of needing to defeat a common enemy after Germany turned on Russia in 1941, capitalist America and communist Russia had fought together during World War II, and for a time in early 1945, when the leaders of the wartime coalition met at the Crimean resort of Yalta on the Black Sea, it seemed possible that a lasting friendship might develop between the two powers. With Germany facing imminent defeat, the leaders of the Grand Alliance—Roosevelt, Stalin, and Prime Minister Winston Churchill of England—concentrated on planning for the peace that would follow the war. Among the agreements they reached at Yalta was the Declaration on Liberated Europe, in which the Allies pledged to hold free elections in countries freed from the Axis powers. The Soviet Union also promised to reorganize the pro-Communist government of Poland along more democratic lines and to enter the war against Japan within three months after the Germans surrendered in Europe.

Even at Yalta, however, there were some very substantial differences between the United States and the Soviet Union. Unquestionably the most serious of these concerned the future of eastern Europe, particularly the status of Poland. Despite the Declaration on Liberated Europe, Stalin was determined to maintain tight control over the region and to prevent Poland from being used as a corridor of invasion from the west. Having established a Communist government in Poland, he refused to expand it to include representatives of a pro-western government or to hold elections in Poland, despite promises to the contrary. He also insisted on moving Poland's boundaries to the west, annexing territory along the Russo-Polish boundary in the east, and compensating Poland by taking territory from Germany in the west.

Americans felt betrayed by Stalin's determination to carve out a sphere of influence in eastern Europe and by his refusal to carry out the promises he made at Yalta. This was particularly true of the country's large ethnic eastern European population, many of whom still had families there. Very quickly there began to develop an image in the United States of an untrustworthy former ally, not all that different from Nazi Germany in terms of its totalitarian government and expansionist ambitions, and needing to be treated with a combination of toughness and deep suspicion. Without such a policy, a growing number of Americans believed, Moscow would attempt aggression throughout the world.

Certainly Harry Truman, who succeeded to the presidency on Roosevelt's death in April, 1945, shared much of this view of the Soviet Union. Although he did not fully abandon Roosevelt's policy of seeking accommodation with Moscow in favor of a "get tough" policy until early 1946, Truman disliked and distrusted the Soviets. An indication of Truman's attitude toward the Russians was his famous meeting of April 23, 1945, with Soviet Foreign Minister Vyacheslav Molotov, who was on his way to the opening of the United Nations in San Francisco. In their meeting Truman allegedly berated Molotov "in terms of one syllable" and responded to Molotov's protests that he "had never been talked to like that in [his] life" with the comment, "Carry out your agreements and you won't get talked to like that [again]."

From Moscow's point of view, however, the American position was both unfriendly and hypocritical. Americans talked about an open world and the elimination of spheres of influence but maintained their own sphere of influence in the Western Hemisphere. They spoke of free elections in eastern Europe but supported dictatorships in Central and South America. They sought to dictate the form of government in Poland, which bordered on the Soviet Union, but had not consulted Moscow or made much of an issue about representative government when administrations were being established for Greece and Belgium. From all this it was easy for the Russians to conclude that the United States was pursuing the same policy of hostility toward the Soviet people that it had always pursued and that the capitalist nations of the West were seeking to "encircle" the Soviet Union for the purpose of eventually overthrowing the communist form of government.

In other words, within a very short time after the western coalition had met at Yalta to map out the peace that would follow the war, the coalition had begun to unravel. Traditional distrusts had surfaced once more, and new misperceptions had developed about Soviet aggression, on the one hand, and American counter-revolutionary activity, on the other. Some of the drift away from wartime partnership to peacetime confrontation was already evident at the Potsdam Conference of July 1945. At this, the last of the "Big Three" wartime meetings, held after Germany had surrendered but before the Japanese had been defeated, President Truman made clear his anger at the Soviet Union for not abiding by the Yalta agreements on eastern Europe. He also disagreed with Stalin on a number of other issues, including a common policy for Germany, and he left Potsdam determined not to allow the Soviets to participate in the control of Japan.

One of the issues that Truman discussed with Stalin was the postwar status of Korea. This was not the first time the Allied leaders had considered this matter. For forty years, ever since the Russo-Japanese War of 1904, Korea had been under the complete control of the Japanese, who had attempted to destroy all semblance of its national identity. But at the Cairo conference of November 1943, President Roosevelt, Prime Minister Churchill, and Generalissimo Chiang Kai-shek of China had stated their determination "that in due course Korea shall become free and independent." The Soviet Union adhered to this agreement at the Tehran conference the same month, and at Potsdam the wartime partners reaffirmed the Cairo statement, making it clear that Japan would not be allowed to retain Korea.[2]

What Roosevelt had anticipated at Cairo, however, was a multi-power trusteeship, including the United States, the Soviet Union, China, and Great Britain, which might last as long as forty years. He believed that Korea needed to go through a period of apprenticeship before receiving full independence. At the same time, the American President opposed occupation of Korea by a single nation, fearing that might lead to the same kind of great power rivalry for the control of Korea that had contributed to the Russo-Japanese War and, for that matter, to the Sino-Japanese conflict ten years earlier. Washington wanted to avoid the mistakes of the 1930s when no checks were placed on Japanese expansion in Asia and German aggression in Central Europe. Also, Roosevelt was not naive in dealing with the Russians, and while he stressed the importance of Soviet-American cooperation, he realized at the same time that Soviet occupation of Korea might threaten the American position in the Pacific and further enhance Soviet power in Northeast Asia at a time when Japan could no longer act as an effective counterweight to Soviet influence. As for the United States, it was simply not willing to assume the responsibility of a single trustee.[3]

However, the White House failed to make concrete arrangements for the postwar occupation of Korea, in part because of Roosevelt's policy of postponing decisions on postwar political matters so long as the fighting continued and in part because of his tendency to procrastinate over difficult problems. This was particularly regrettable given the deterioration in Soviet-American relations that soon took place. In fact, by the time the war ended on August 15, 1945, hard-liners within the State Department were already arguing that Soviet occupation of the Korean peninsula would threaten American security interests in the Far East. By no means did everyone within the State Department share this view, and America's military leaders at the Pentagon consistently maintained that Korea would have no strategic value in case of a general world conflict and that American forces could be better used elsewhere.[4]

Nonetheless, Truman listened to the hard-liners in the State Department. Still overwhelmed by the duties of his office and faced with a surfeit of foreign policy problems, particularly the growing strain in relations with Moscow, the President agreed to a proposal aimed at preventing a Soviet take-over of Korea by accepting a zone of occupation in the country south of a line at the 38th parallel. The line, which was based on convenience rather than on any historical or geographical rationale, would divide Soviet and American occupation forces. Now the two superpowers would face each other across a divided land.[5]

In reaching the decision to divide Korea into two zones of occupation, the White House failed to appreciate fully the internal social and political disorder in Korea at war's end or the aspirations of the Korean people themselves. Although divided by ideological and personal disputes, a Korean nationalist movement had been gaining strength since 1919, when on March 1 of that year hundreds of thousands of Koreans took to the streets to protest Japan's colonial rule. But although Korean nationalism remained undaunted by forty years of Japanese occupation, Japan's colonial enterprise had upset Korea's delicately balanced economic and social structure.[6]

As a result, when American occupation forces landed in Korea in September 1945, the country was in a state of political chaos and locked in an internal social struggle. Regardless of political persuasion, Koreans were united on the fundamental issue of immediate Korean independence. But forces on the political left, demanding fundamental change in Korean society, clashed with political elites seeking to maintain privileges enjoyed under Japanese rule. Workers and peasant unions mushroomed, and Communist strength grew. The Korean People's Republic (KPR), an anti-Japanese coalition of Korean nationalists, organized just before the arrival of the Americans, failed to bridge the differences between right and left. Instead, the KPR oriented itself increasingly toward radical change, including land confiscation and redistribution and nationalization of major industries. Except for foreign intervention, it probably would have triumphed politically throughout the peninsula within a few months.[7]

News that the United States would occupy Korea, however, proved the critical factor in organizing the right to ward off leftist attacks on existing privileges. Landowners, manufacturers, and other businessmen (including Japanese collaborators) formed the Korean Democratic Party (KDP), which became the pillar of the right and would remain the single strongest rightist party throughout the American occupation. Offering no well-articulated program of its own, focusing its efforts in Seoul, and having little support in the countryside, the KDP's principal purpose was to resist the groups and programs associated with the KPR.[8]

Officially, American policy was not to recognize any group as Korea's legitimate government but to proceed with the establishment of an American Military Government (AMG). The commander of the American troops, Lieutenant General John Hodge, was thus given few instructions other than that "no organized political groups, however sound in sentiment, should have any part in determining the policies of military government." In fact, though, Hodge had been impressed with the political chaos in Korea even before taking up his new assignment, and after he arrived in Korea in September 1945, he quickly established ties with what he regarded as the forces of political order and stability. In October, he welcomed back to Seoul Syngman Rhee, who had received a Ph.D. in international relations from Princeton in 1910 and had spent the past thirty years in the United States promoting the cause of Korean independence. Not widely known in Korea, Rhee was nevertheless generally regarded in the West as the leading spokesman for Korean nationalism. Proud, obstinate, tenacious, and obstreperous, he was also a political conservative and strident anti-Communist, who condemned what he called "the slavery" of North Korea under the Soviets. Shortly after Rhee's return, Hodge made the first move toward instituting a separate southern government under Rhee and his followers.[9]

(1945)

By December the polarization of Korean politics south of the 38th parallel had gone far. But a chance still existed that a unified and neutralist state could be established in Korea involving a broad coalition of Korean nationalists both north and south of the 38th parallel. An analogue of the leftist movements in the south existed above the 38th parallel. The difference was that the Soviet Union nurtured their development and gave them a great degree of autonomy. Accordingly, they offered the foundation on which a coalition government for all of Korea could be based.

Almost certainly, the Soviets intended that no other power should gain complete control of the Korean peninsula and that any government established in Korea would have to be "friendly" to their interests, which meant maintaining close ties to Moscow. With respect to both these matters, they were well aware of Korea's strategic and economic importance in terms of Russia's own historic interests in Manchuria and Siberia and of their quest for warmwater ports in East Asia; in particular they wanted to secure control over Cheju Island, off Korea's southwest coast, as well as the ports of Pusan at Korea's southeast tip and Inchon on the west coast about twenty-five miles due west of Korea's capital of Seoul. At the same time, they were anxious to establish a buffer in northern Korea to protect their vital port of Vladivostock just a few miles from the Korean-Soviet border.

Perhaps not surprisingly, therefore, the Soviet Union sponsored the development of the Korean Communist Party (KCP) after the war (although, interestingly, only in its own zone of occupation). Moscow also sealed off the flow of goods southward from its zone in order to use the coal, electric power, and heavy industry of northern Korea to supply its needs in the Far East. But the Soviet Union was faced with huge reconstruction problems at home, was more concerned with developments in Eastern Europe than in Asia, and lacked the resources to create a full satellite state in Korea even if that had been its purpose. Within the operating assumption of a dependable regime in Korea, therefore, Moscow was prepared to allow Koreans considerable autonomy.[10]

Accordingly, at the Moscow foreign ministers' conference in December 1945, the Soviets agreed to an American proposal for a joint Soviet-American commission to prepare Korea for the election of a provisional government, which would be followed by a fourpower trusteeship lasting for as long as five years. The Joint Commission was to consult with democratic parties and social organizations throughout Korea. Any provisional government truly representative of the Korean people would have to involve representatives of leftist groups, including the KRP and the Communists, but this did not mean Soviet domination of Korea.

A unified and neutralized Korea was not to be, however. In the first place, strikes, work stoppages, and demonstrations by Koreans of all political persuasions broke out in the south against the Moscow agreement because of its proposal of a five-year trusteeship. The proposal itself became part of a domestic power struggle, with a variety of participants of all political persuasions vying for power. Also, Soviet-American relations, which remained strained despite the success of the Moscow meeting, were aggravated further by the AMG's effort to attribute responsibility for the trusteeship proposal to the Soviets and by Hodge's open support of the movement against trusteeship.[11]

By the spring of 1946, relations between the Soviet Union and the United States had deteriorated to the point where the chances of cooperation between the two powers over such places as Korea had become virtually nil. Any success that might have been achieved at Moscow in repairing Soviet-American relations was effectively nullified in March 1946 when the Soviets refused to follow the British and Americans in withdrawing their troops from oil-rich Iran, despite a 1942 treaty requiring the Russians to leave the country within six months after the end of the war. Not until Washington sent a strong note to Moscow demanding immediate withdrawal of Soviet troops and the Iranians agreed to establish a joint operating company with the Russians (in a treaty later rejected by the Iranian Parliament) did the Soviets agree to pull out their forces.

Meanwhile, in an effort to mobilize the Soviet people for the task of reconstruction after the United States rejected a Soviet request for a $1-billion loan, Stalin delivered a speech in which he talked about the incompatibility of communism and capitalism. About the same time, George Kennan, a State Department expert on the Soviet Union, sent a long telegram from Moscow to Washington warning that the United States was confronted with "a political force committed fanatically to the belief that with [the] U.S. there can be no permanent modus vivendi." Kennan also wrote about the need to contain further Soviet expansionism, while in Washington the State Department came under increasingly heavy attack from

Republican leaders in Congress for allegedly following an appeasement policy toward the Soviets.[12]

All this led President Truman to adopt a "get tough" policy with the Russians, which impacted on the Korean policy of both Washington and Moscow. On the one hand, the administration supported Hodge's program of limiting leftist activity in the south as its purpose became increasingly one of containing Soviet expansion in Korea and less one of providing for Korea's eventual unification and independence. On the other hand, the Soviet Union refused to consult with rightist and moderate elements in Korea about the election of a provisional government for the country, using as a pretext their opposition to a trusteeship. The United States rejected the Soviet position and, in May 1946, the Joint Commission disbanded after failing to resolve the differences between Moscow and Washington.[13]

During the next two years Soviet and American positions on Korea hardened even more, and the partition of the country became permanent. The U.S. Occupation's policy of working closely with the right came back to haunt it. In the spring of 1946 it launched a campaign to bring more moderate leaders into the governing process in the south in the hope of ending its dependency on the right by creating a centrist coalition. Along with a broad program of economic and social reform (particularly land reform) it would appeal to the majority of Koreans and, in the process, isolate extremists of both the right and left while providing the basis for a new middle class. Even Hodge grew tired of the carping demands by Rhee and his group for immediate independence, and he became annoyed at their hostility toward any major economic and social change.[14]

A coalition was, in fact, organized that included moderate leftists and rightists. But it failed to bridge the differences that remained even among its own members, and it fell apart completely after the assassination, in the summer of 1947, of one of its most prominent members, Lyuh Woon-hyung, a moderate leftist with important political ties to the north. By this time, however, the Soviet Union had tightened its grip on the north, establishing a Communist Provisional People's Committee led by Kim Il-sung, a thirty-five-year-old former resistance fighter who had participated in anti-Japanese activities since the early 1930s and had received military training from the Soviets during the war. A second Soviet-American

(1947)

Joint Commission, which had been formed in the spring of 1947, also ended in failure. By this time, too, the AMG had given up its effort to establish a consensus government in the south and was once more backing the extreme right led by Rhee.[15]

In fact, the United States had already begun to consider ways of gracefully withdrawing from Korea without turning it over entirely to Communist control. In the winter and spring of 1947, Washington was clearly in the throes of a dilemma with respect to Korea. For one thing, American foreign policy, based as it was on containing Communist expansion, could not easily risk a Communist takeover of Korea. For another, Washington was faced with acute political and economic crises in Europe and the Middle East. A brutal winter in Europe threatening total economic paralysis and collapse was accompanied by a British announcement that it could no longer furnish economic and military aid either to Greece, whose British-backed government was fighting a Communist-led insurgency, or to Turkey, which many foreign policy experts considered a likely target for Soviet aggression.

Together these two developments created an emergency-like situation in Washington. In 1947 the administration responded by pushing the $400-million Truman Doctrine through Congress and making an open-ended pledge to protect friendly nations from subversion and aggression. A few months later, Secretary of State George Marshall proposed a massive program of economic assistance to Europe, which later became incorporated into the $12-billion Marshall Plan.

In simplest terms, funds were not available to meet the needs of Europe and the Mediterranean areas and at the same time pay for the expensive occupation in Korea, especially when a Republican-controlled Congress was insisting that Truman cut his budget and when the administration had to consider the possibility that it might be called on to aid Chiang Kai-shek in his struggle against the Chinese Communists. Furthermore, a widespread belief already existed among the Joint Chiefs of Staff (JCS) and at the War Department that from a military and strategic standpoint Korea was of little value and that the two divisions in Korea of approximately 45,000 men could be better used elsewhere.[16]

Over the next several months, the administration wrestled with the dilemma posed by Korea. In August 1947, an Ad Hoc Committee on Korea recommended that if no agreement could be reached between the four powers regarding the election of a provisional Korean government, the United States should announce its intention to turn the whole Korean problem over to the United Nations General Assembly. A month later, Acting Secretary of State Robert A. Lovett informed the political adviser in Korea, Joseph E. Jacobs, that it was "extremely unlikely" that the Soviets would take part in a four-power conversation on Korea. In October 1947, Washington presented a resolution to the General Assembly calling for the Soviet Union and the United States to hold elections in their respective zones, no later than March 31, 1948, for the formation of a national assembly and a national government. A United Nations Temporary Commission on Korea (UNTCOK) would be established to supervise the elections and report to the General Assembly. In November the General Assembly approved the American proposal.[17]

The United States now threw its entire support behind Syngman Rhee. Although unstated at the time, the administration's policy was now clearly one of holding elections in anticipation of establishing a separate South Korean government. Washington realized that the Soviet Union, having refused to participate in four-power discussions on Korea, would never go along with an American-sponsored plan under the auspices of the United Nations, which at the time was dominated by the United States. Time was on the side of the Communists. In the south, Communist strength was continuing to grow as politics there became increasingly polarized. In September 1947, Jacobs reported from Seoul that "at least thirty percent of the people in South Korea [were] Leftists, following the Cominterm Communist leaders who would support the Soviets behind the United States lines." Once the United States was effectively removed from Korea, all kinds of possibilities existed for Communist domination of the entire peninsula within a relatively short period.[18]

Policy makers in Washington considered it all the more imperative, therefore, that the United States establish a separate regime in the south resistant to Communist infiltration and subversion and supportive of America's overall foreign policy aims. Given the polarization of Korean politics, the large following that Rhee still commanded on the right, and the fact that he was the only major political leader in the south to favor the establishment of a separate government, the administration felt it had little alternative but to support him despite its previous reservations about his leadership.

Indeed, the White House became rigidly committed to Rhee and to the establishment of a separate anti-Communist government for South Korea.[19]

Other members of UNTCOK, including even America's own allies, Australia and Canada, believed that no elections should be held in Korea unless they could be administered throughout the entire peninsula. But the AMG bitterly assailed this "British bloc" for its "leftist leanings," and in February 1948 the UN General Assembly approved an American-sponsored resolution giving UNTCOK authority to supervise elections "in such parts of Korea as might be accessible to the Commission." Elections were held in May 1948, and although UNTCOK divided once more over their fairness, Rhee won an impressive, if not overwhelming, victory. In July, the newly established legislative assembly easily elected Rhee as the first president of the Republic of Korea (ROK). Although a separate regime, the Democratic People's Republic (DPR), headed by Kim Il-sung, was established in North Korea, the UN General Assembly adopted a resolution in December declaring the South Korean government the lawful government in that part of Korea where UNTCOK was able to observe elections and stating that it was the "only such Government in Korea."[20]

Conditions in South Korea remained very unstable and chaotic, however, and Rhee instituted a program of repression that included the imposition of martial law. Even during the election campaign there had been widespread violence and disorder, especially on the island of Cheju, where guerrilla units associated with the political left attacked towns, burned villages, and kidnapped and killed a number of rightists and police. After Rhee had been in office for a few months, the fighting flared up again and became even more widespread and violent. Before it ended in January 1949, it claimed 30,000 lives, or about ten percent of the island's population.

Meanwhile the rebellion spread to other regions. Two thousand members of the South Korean constabulary mutinied in October 1948 as they were about to embark for Cheju. Leaders of the mutineers explained that they "refused to murder the people of Cheju-do [fighting] against imperialist policy." The next month Rhee imposed martial law over about one-fourth of Korea. But reports of sporadic violence continued to be received in Seoul. The rebellion undermined public confidence in the security forces and widened the gulf between the police and the army. So, too, it showed how weak the Rhee government was to deal with such a crisis. Rhee himself was reported by some observers to be suffering from "incipient senility," while his cabinet was badly torn by political dissension and personal rivalry. Without American support the South Korean leader may not have been able to remain in political power.[21]

Nevertheless, the United States decided to go ahead with its plans for the withdrawal of American forces. Not everyone agreed with this decision. The State Department demurred, pointing not only to the instability of the Rhee regime but also to the military threat from the north. The North Koreans built a large army fully supplied with Soviet arms. Military intelligence estimates of North Korean armed strength concluded that the North was capable of victory if civil war broke out. In the opinion of the State Department, therefore, only the continued presence of the American occupation forces could give the Korean government the period needed to improve internal conditions.[22]

Weighted against this view, however, was a combination of budgetary restraints and the continued insistence by the military that Korea had no military or strategic value in a war in Asia. In addition, Mao Zedong's imminent victory in China over the Nationalist regime of Chiang Kai-shek, despite billions of dollars of aid to Chiang, left the Pentagon even more leery of making military commitments to the Asian mainland. In this regard, most military leaders shared the administration's view that Europe and not Asia was the main area of confrontation with the Soviet Union. They were also convinced that the resources obligated to the Far East should be limited to the island strongholds of Japan, Okinawa, Formosa, and the Philippines.[23]

The military pressed its view before the National Security Council (NSC), and in March 1949 it won a significant victory when the NSC issued its latest directive. Although the NSC recognized that the withdrawal of American troops from Korea, even with the substitution of military and technical assistance, might be followed by a North Korean attempt to overthrow the South Korean government, it stated that the risk existed at all times and that the final withdrawal of American troops should be completed no later than June 30, 1949. Prior to the final withdrawal of these forces, Korea should be given a stockpile of equipment and maintenance supplies adequate to cover six months' replacement and consumption requirements, together with an emergency reserve.[24]

Syngman Rhee, who was determined to reunify Korea under his government, was clearly unhappy with the purely defensive nature of American military aid. Instead, he wanted airplanes, combat ships, and arms to equip an additional 100,000 troops. The United States agreed to the establishment of a Korean Military Advisory Group (KMAG) to help train ROK military forces, but Washington was not prepared to give Rhee the military assistance he needed to attack North Korea.[25]

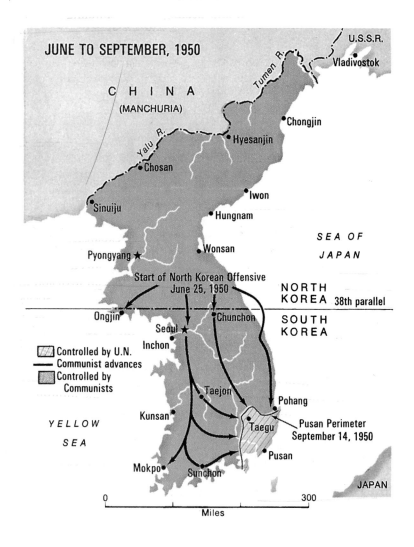

JUNE TO SEPTEMBER, 1950

U.S.S.R.
Vladivostok

CHINA
(MANCHURIA)

Tumen R.

Chongjin

Yalu R.

Hyesanjin

Chosan

Iwon

Sinuiju

Hungnam

SEA OF
JAPAN

Pyongyang ★

Wonsan

Start of North Korean Offensive
June 25, 1950

NORTH
KOREA   38th parallel

Ongjin

Chunchon

SOUTH
KOREA

Seoul ★

Inchon

☐ Controlled by U.N.
— Communist advances
☐ Controlled by
Communists

Taejon

Pohang

Kunsan

YELLOW

SEA

Taegu

Pusan Perimeter
September 14, 1950

Pusan

Mokpo

Sunchon

JAPAN

0   300

Miles

Yet the administration still regarded the country as symbolically important—indeed, the only symbol after the Communist victory in China—of America's willingness to contain Communist expansion in Asia. The problem for the administration was how to keep Korea from following the same course as China without making a major military commitment to Korea. Its solution was to rely on a program of military and economic assistance to the Rhee government and to press the government to avoid the mistakes that had led to the Chinese disaster; this meant stopping its harsh repression of political dissent and dealing with a spiraling inflation caused by its practice of deficit spending and the printing of paper money.[26] Underlying American policy was the assumption that an invasion from North Korea was not likely in the near future and that with sufficient American assistance South Korea could take care of any trouble started by North Korea, although it could not repel an invasion started by the Chinese Communists or supported by them or the Soviet Union. In this context, Secretary of State Dean Acheson delivered a major address to the National Press Club in January 1950 in which he outlined a defense perimeter in the Far Pacific that excluded South Korea. Although Acheson was later blamed for having encouraged North Korea to attack South Korea by his speech, he was merely reaffirming the administration's position that South Korea—and, for that matter, all the Asiatic mainland and Formosa—could be saved from Communist expansion without the use of military force.[27]

Administration policy toward South Korea changed remarkably little in the six months prior to the North Korean invasion in June 1950. During this time the administration continued to speak out against Rhee's repressive policies, and it was instrumental in preventing him from postponing general elections scheduled for May to November. At the same time, State Department officials continued to press the Rhee government for internal reforms—especially more stringent measures to bring inflation under control. Also of growing concern to some American officials was the infiltration of guerrilla forces from the North and evidence of North Korea's military superiority over South Korea.[28]

Yet to most observers in Washington the situation in South Korea on the eve of the North Korean invasion did not seem particularly critical, certainly not as serious as the situation elsewhere. In the May 1950 elections, Rhee's political organization won only forty-eight of the two hundred and ten seats in the new National

Assembly despite the fact that the South Korean leader arrested thirty political opponents in "anti-Communist" raids just before the elections. But Rhee still controlled more seats than any other party, and he was able to piece together a coalition government that had a reasonable chance of survival. The countryside was also relatively tranquil. Despite some fighting near the 38th parallel, guerrilla activity and border clashes actually fell off markedly in the months before the war, and the ROK army enjoyed considerable success in wiping out those bands that did cross into South Korea. So, too, the government was increasingly successful in its ongoing struggle to eliminate armed subversion from within, and it also seemed to be bringing inflation under control.[29]

Most important, although a number of American officials expressed growing apprehension about the North's military superiority over the South and although by June 1950 intelligence reports indicated a gradual concentration of North Korean tanks and troops along the 38th parallel, the consensus remained that North Korea would not invade South Korea. As for the possibility that the Soviets would support a North Korean attack on South Korea, that was generally regarded as unlikely. As late as June 19, John Foster Dulles, a prominent Republican spokesman on foreign policy, told President Rhee that it was the opinion of the best-informed minds in Washington that Moscow did not for the present wish to become involved in a shooting war.[30]

In contrast to conditions in Korea, the situation elsewhere seemed critical. Mao's success in China encouraged the tide of nationalist revolution throughout Asia, including Indochina and Indonesia, as well as an insurrectionary movement in the Philippines. In Indochina, a war that the French had been waging against Communist-led Vietminh guerrillas fighting for independence from France had turned against the French, and the administration was convinced that if the French colony fell to the Communists, the rest of Southeast Asia would be imperiled. In February 1950, therefore, the United States made its first commitment in Indochina by recognizing the nominally independent states of Laos, Cambodia, and Vietnam and by initiating plans to support them with economic and technical assistance. In May the administration formally extended military assistance to the French in Indochina.[31]

But from the White House's perspective, danger existed throughout the world. At any moment the Soviet Union might strike against Berlin, Iran, Greece, Turkey, or a number of other trouble spots, any of which could imperil the free world and bring on a new war. Indeed, the Cold War had entered its most perilous phase in 1950. In April the National Security Council sent to President Truman a report, NSC–68, which became the United States' field manual for waging the Cold War. "The assault on free institutions is worldwide," the report said, "and in the context of the present polarization of power a defeat of free institutions anywhere is a defeat everywhere." In order to meet the threat of Soviet aggression, the United States would have to increase its defense spending substantially. Although NSC–68 offered no specific figures, it stated that as rich as America was, it could afford to spend up to twenty percent of its Gross National Product (GNP) for military purposes instead of its current level of about five percent. In 1950 that would have been about $50 billion.[32]

It was not, therefore, that leaders in Washington were ignorant of Korea (although most Americans were) or that they did not regard an attack by North Korea on South Korea as a serious threat to American interests in the world. In the equation of the Cold War as it had developed by 1950, any Communist gain anywhere was a serious setback everywhere. Nor did administration officials fail to anticipate the possibility—even probability—of a Soviet-directed military initiative somewhere. It was simply that the administration expected that if a war came, it would not come in Korea. Indeed, Washington had received reports in the spring of 1950 of a Communist military thrust in Asia, but it anticipated that the probable target would be Indochina or Formosa.[33]

Yet on Sunday, June 25 (Korean time), 1950, North Korea invaded South Korea, and the United States responded almost immediately. During the next five days, as the situation in Korea continued to deteriorate rapidly, the White House increased the stakes involved in the invasion. Step by step, it broadened America's commitment in the conflict while bringing the invasion before the United Nations and turning its own military involvement into an international police action. What took place during these five days is fairly clear. Why North Korea invaded South Korea in the first place and why the United States reacted as it did are not as simple to explain.

The size of the forces that the North Koreans sent across the border was formidable and distinguished the attack from the numerous border crossings and skirmishes that had become common by the summer of 1950. Nearly 110,000 soldiers, more than 1,400 artillery pieces, and 126 tanks were committed to the invasion. Once word was received in Washington that a full-scale invasion was indeed underway, key officials from the Departments of State and Defense gathered at the State Department. Secretary of State Acheson also conferred with President Truman, who was at his home in Independence, Missouri. Preliminary steps were then taken to call for a special session of the UN Security Council. The next day the President gave his final approval for an emergency meeting at the United Nations and, after receiving additional news of the worsening situation in Korea, flew back to Washington.[34]

The Security Council met on Sunday afternoon, June 25 (New York time), and approved an American-sponsored resolution calling for the cessation of hostilities and a withdrawal of North Korean forces behind the 38th parallel. That same evening President Truman, having returned to Washington, met at Blair House with members of his cabinet, the Joint Chiefs of Staff, and other senior officials to map out America's response to North Korea's attack. At the meeting Truman approved recommendations by the Departments of State and Defense ordering General MacArthur in Tokyo to send supplies and a survey team to Korea and United States air and naval forces to prevent the North Korean army from interfering with the evacuation of American dependents from the Seoul-Inchon area. Put off for the moment was a third recommendation to send the Seventh Fleet to the Formosa Strait in order to prevent an attack on or from Formosa. In thus deciding to employ American military forces to maintain the Seoul-Inchon area, the President acted without reference to the United Nations. Implicit in his decision was the possibility of combat with North Korea. The decision also established a precedent for the later use of American ground forces.[35]

The fighting soon outpaced these preliminary steps. By the third day of hostilities the defenses of Seoul had nearly fallen and a general evacuation was ordered. Because of the rapidly deteriorating situation, Truman called a second Blair House meeting in which he agreed to lift all restrictions on air and naval operations in South Korea but not to permit attacks north of the 38th parallel. The President also consented to place the Seventh Fleet in the Formosa Strait. Of greater importance for the future, he agreed as well to accelerate aid to Indochina and the Philippines, where the government was fighting the Hukbalahap, a Communist-led guerrilla organization, and to increase American military forces in the Philippines.[36]

The next day, Tuesday, June 27, the Security Council placed its imprimatur on America's action in Korea by adopting an American-sponsored resolution calling for military sanctions against the invaders of the ROK. Even as this was happening, however, North Korean forces captured Seoul. During the next two days the military situation worsened even more. On June 29, Truman authorized military targets on North Korea and the use of American troops to secure the area around Pusan. The next day, on the recommendation of General MacArthur, the President approved the sending of a regimental combat team to Korea. Finally, following another meeting with his advisers at Blair House, Truman authorized MacArthur to engage whatever Army forces were available to him, subject only to Japan's security.[37]

Why, then, had North Korea invaded South Korea on June 25, and why did the Truman administration decide on military action in a part of the world that it had just a few months earlier dismissed as having no military or strategic importance? What were the political pressures that Truman was under and what influences did they have on his final decision to commit ground forces to Korea? Did he have other choices, and why, during the days of decision, was each action that he took less than what was needed but his basic determination of what was necessary went unchallenged? Finally, why was the fateful decision regarding Formosa and Indochina made so quickly and with so little debate?

The reasons for North Korea's invasion are not entirely clear, but they seem to have to do both with the Cold War struggle between the United States and the Soviet Union as well as with internal Korean politics north and south of the 38th parallel. In the spring of 1950, Stalin had approved a plan by Kim Il-sung to reunite Korea and had agreed to supply North Korea with military supplies and equipment. But apparently Stalin acted reluctantly and only after repeated overtures from the North Korean leader, who promised that the war would be won in three days. The Soviet leader did not want to be placed in the same embarrassing position as he had been a year earlier when he had to apologize for not providing adequate military backing to the Chinese Communists in their successful revolution. He also did not believe the United States would intervene militarily against the North Koreans. At the same

IV. CWIHP
Weatherby)

time, though, a war in Korea might divert America's interest and resources away from the strategically more important European theater and offset American efforts at reestablishing Germany and Japan as major economic and political powers.[38] The United States could even become bogged down in war in Korea, and the hostility that this was bound to create in Beijing would force the Chinese to be more dependent on Moscow, something Stalin preferred.[39]

In April, during a stop in Beijing on his way home from meeting with Stalin, Kim Il-sung also apparently won Mao Zedong's tacit approval for an invasion but, again, without any great enthusiasm on the part of the Chinese leader. Mao may have discussed an invasion with Kim as early as the end of 1949, and Beijing had certainly cooperated with Pyongyang for more than a year in repatriating Korean troops who had fought in the Chinese civil war. Not only was the Chinese leader angered by America's policy of supporting Chiang Kai-shek, he shared Stalin's view that America's policy of turning Japan once more into a major Asian power posed a potential threat to China not unlike that before World War II.

At the same time, though, the Chinese leader had to devote most of his attention to domestic problems, including China's economic reconstruction after the civil war, mopping-up operations against remnants of Chiang Kai-shek's forces still on the mainland, and gaining control over Formosa and Tibet. He was also still interested in maintaining communications with the United States. He hoped to take Formosa unopposed by Washington, which had indicated that the island was also not included in America's defense perimeter, and he understood that an invasion of Formosa after the Korean War began was more likely to draw some kind of military response from the United States.[40]

Yet Kim Il-sung was not simply the puppet of the Soviet Union (much less of the Chinese), as leaders in Washington liked to believe. Although the Soviet Union maintained close supervision over developments in North Korea and Kim undoubtedly owed his power and position to Soviet support, he had learned that he could not—nor need not—rely totally on Soviet good will; that one of the reasons the Soviets had backed him in the first place was his ability to organize cadres on the local and regional levels; that the Chinese, who were competing against Moscow for influence in Pyongyang and whom he preferred over the Soviets, gave him room for political maneuvering; and that his political survival in North Korea, where he still faced considerable political opposition, rested on his claim as the champion of Korean unification.[41]

But there seem to have been other reasons as well why Kim ordered the invasion of South Korea. He could anticipate continued military support from Moscow. The border incidents in which both sides had been involved since the spring of 1949 and Rhee's own martial pronouncements may have persuaded him of a long-term threat from South Korea, which would be eliminated only by a preemptive strike southward. The growing anti-Rhee sentiment in the South, as made evident by the results of the 1950 elections, seemed to auger well for a successful invasion from the North. Finally, Secretary of State Acheson's speech to the National Press Club in January may have led Kim to expect that the United States would not intervene in the struggle, although there is now considerable historical debate and controversy over this issue.[42]

The reasons behind the American response to the attack are also complex, although in the final analysis, they can be reduced to one fundamental consideration. In the first place, bringing the invasion to the United Nations appeared the only reasonable course of action. The United States had earlier acted within the framework of the United Nations, and taking the matter to the Security Council was a way of serving notice to the world as to how seriously the United States viewed the fighting in Korea. It was also a way of achieving a collective response to the invasion, which seemed preferable to unilateral American action.

Yet almost from the time they first received news of the invasion, American officials both in South Korea and in Washington responded in a way that made a unilateral American response likely. Most important, they perceived the North Korean move across the border as a Soviet-sponsored and Soviet-controlled attack meant to test American resolve to resist Communist expansion that would have serious consequences throughout the Far East and Southeast Asia. As a State Department intelligence estimate put it, the elimination of South Korea would influence both Soviet and Chinese moves in Indochina, Formosa, Malaysia, and Burma.[43]

In this regard, North Korea's invasion of South Korea came at a time when the United States was already undertaking a major shift in its far eastern policy as a result of the loss of China to the Communists. Anticipating the Communist victory in China, Washington had decided by 1949 to resurrect Japan as a major power in East

Asia, which would protect and promote the interests of the United States throughout the region. A politically stable and economically reconstructed Japan would play a central role in America's Pacific defense perimeter, as Secretary Acheson had outlined before the National Press Club in January. It would also provide markets and be an engine of economic growth and accompanying political stability for the very nations of Southeast Asia it had sought to incorporate into its World War II "Greater East Asia Co-Prosperity Sphere." Conversely, the Asian hinterland would provide the raw materials, markets, and resources necessary for Japan's own economic growth and stability.

From a geopolitical standpoint alone, therefore, it was necessary to prevent communist domination of Korea, whose vital port of Pusan was separated from Japan by only about 100 miles. But Secretary of State Acheson also regarded South Korea as a "breadbasket" for Japan, which, before World War II, had imported about thirty percent of its food supply (mainly rice) from Korea and which, on the eve of the Korean War, still needed to import large quantities of rice as well as other food supplies and raw materials. In addition, the secretary expected Korea to become a major market for Japan as the Japanese went through the process of reindustrialization. In short, control of Korea by the Communists posed as much a threat to Japan and America's other Asian interests as domination of Korea by an unfriendly power threatened the Soviet Union's Asian interests.[44]

In addition, a very real concern existed in Washington that the failure of the United States to take any action in Korea would cause significant damage to American prestige in Europe and the Middle East. Very much on the minds of America's leaders, including President Truman and Secretary of State Acheson, was the need to avoid another case of appeasement along the lines of the ill-fated and notorious Munich Conference of 1938, which they believed had nurtured Adolf Hitler's ambitions at world dominance.[45]

Domestic considerations also weighed heavily on the Truman administration's decision to intervene in Korea. As the historian Stephen Pelz has remarked, Truman "was vulnerable to serious charges from his domestic critics if he did not intervene." If Korea fell to the Communists so soon after the fall of China, this might very well lead to a congressional investigation into the military reasons for the fall. Such an investigation would show that the administration had left the United States badly weakened militarily. A cutback in conventional forces as a result of budget restrictions, the lack of an adequate atomic deterrent to a Soviet attack in Europe or elsewhere, and inadequate war planning would be some of the charges made by administration critics and confirmed by a congressional investigation. The insufficiency of America's military aid to South Korea would be another charge.[46]

Truman's own insecurity in foreign affairs; his frequent detachment and often episodic involvement in decision-making; his tendency to rely heavily on others he admired, such as Secretary of State Dean Acheson, for advice; his own strong anti-communism; and his inclination to react emotionally, spontaneously (and sometimes unwisely) against perceived injustices and personal affronts, all of which would become more apparent and instrumental as the war continued in Korea, must also be factored into any explanation of why the White House responded as it did to the North Korean invasion. For decision-making does not always follow in the orderly, rational, and deliberative manner that post-crisis analyses sometimes suggest. And there can be no doubt that Truman, who was ill-informed about Korea and caught completely off-guard by the North Korean attack, quickly came under great pressure to respond militarily.[47]

Similarly, Truman had to contend with the general climate of fear and crisis that gripped the United States in the spring and early summer of 1950. At the time that North Korea invaded South Korea, the United States seemed to many Americans imperiled by the threat of Communism both at home and abroad. Events of the previous year hardly augured well for the future. First there had been the news in September 1949 that the Soviet Union had successfully tested an atomic bomb several years ahead of schedule. A month later Americans had learned that China had been "lost" to the Communists. The following January, Alger Hiss, a former State Department official who in testimony before a congressional committee had denied charges that he had been a Communist in the 1930s, was found guilty of perjury. At about the same time, Klaus Fuchs, a high-level atomic scientist, confessed in England to giving atomic secrets to the Soviet Union. And in February, Senator Joseph McCarthy of Wisconsin announced before a group of Republican women in Wheeling, West Virginia, that he had a list of 205 officials of the State Department who were members of, or loyal to, the Communist Party.[48]

Taken together, these developments suggested to many Americans that the tide of the Cold War was running in favor of the Communists. More than that, they seemed to support charges of conspiracy even within Washington itself. Americans felt particularly betrayed by the "fall" of China, a country with which, it was widely believed, the United States had always had a special relationship. It mattered little that Chiang Kai-shek had been thoroughly corrupt or that his regime lacked popular support. For a large number of Americans, China could have been saved from communism had the administration been more resolute and forthcoming in its support of Chiang. A China lobby closely associated with the right wing of the Republican Party railed against the administration's Far East policy, attributing the Communist victory in China to the traitorous actions of diplomatic officials employed by Roosevelt and Truman.[49]

Much of the bipartisanship that had characterized American foreign policy in recent years and been responsible for approval of the Truman Doctrine and the Marshall Plan vanished amid partisan wrangling over the China issue and the priority the administration gave to affairs in Europe. The China lobby increased its political strength in Washington, and Senator McCarthy became headline news as he continued to make charges of internal subversion and espionage. A new word, "McCarthyism," was introduced into the language to describe unsupported accusations of disloyalty and demagoguery. But for many Americans McCarthy's accusations offered convincing explanations of why China had been lost to the Communists and why the Soviet Union had developed a nuclear capability so fast.[50]

The conspiratorial mentality that existed in America in 1950, however, was not limited to the anti-Communist hysteria and antics of Joseph McCarthy and those beholden to him. It was widespread and growing, and it intruded itself most forcibly in the national debate over the administration's far eastern policy. It was thus imperative for Truman to intervene in Korea, for the loss of that country so soon after the Communist victory in China would almost certainly have added to the storm of protest over the administration's Asian policy, raised additional accusations of internal subversion (which

happened anyway), and, at the very least, furthered the already existing charges that the President was "soft" on communism.[51]

In other words, the credibility of the administration's foreign
policy was at issue in the Korean war, both abroad and at home,
both among America's allies and its adversaries. In such a situation
of crisis as seemed to face the United States in the summer of 1950,
the President had to act forthrightly and unequivocally. Anything
less would be an indication of weakness on his part, which the enemies of the United States and the foes of the administration could
use to their benefits. Once Truman and his closest advisers accepted
these basic assumptions—as they did almost immediately after receiving news of the fighting in Korea—there really seemed no
course open to them other than the one they followed.

In fairness to Truman, he did not actually commit ground forces
to the defense of Korea until the fifth day of fighting, after Seoul
had fallen. Even then their function was limited to protecting military facilities in Pusan and helping supply ROK forces at the front.
The administration's whole purpose, in fact, was to try to contain
the war in Korea and, above all, to avoid a military showdown with
the Soviet Union and China. Thus, on the third day of fighting,
while Truman lifted restrictions on air and naval operations in
South Korea, he prohibited attacks north of the 38th parallel in
order to minimize the possibility of direct Soviet or Chinese intervention and to avoid letting the fighting turn into a general war
elsewhere. And on the fifth day, although he authorized strikes
against military targets in North Korea, he ordered that special care
be taken to ensure the operations in North Korea were in fact limited to military targets and stayed well clear of the Manchurian and
Soviet frontiers.[52]

At the same time, the United States could not allow Korea to
fall to the Communists by default. The stakes were too high and the
consequences too grave. As the military situation continued to deteriorate, therefore, the options that were open to the administration
seemed to come down to one, until, finally, on the sixth day of fighting, Truman released ground forces stationed in Japan for combat
use in Korea. But even then he anticipated that America's military
mission would be limited in scope and duration.[53]

One option that might have been pursued more discreetly was
direct negotiations with the Soviet Union. In order to avoid a confrontation with Moscow and to probe its position, Secretary of State

Acheson asked the Soviets to disclaim responsibility for the attack and to press the North Koreans to withdraw their forces north of the 38th parallel. But before Moscow could respond to this note, Acheson made it public. By thus denying the Soviets an opportunity to save face, he effectively undermined any small chance that might have existed that Moscow would cooperate with Washington to end the war. Instead, the Soviets responded on June 29 by accusing South Korea of provoking the hostilities and warning that it regarded foreign interference "in the internal affairs of Korea" unwarranted. With the United States holding the Soviet Union ultimately responsible for the war and with Moscow thus accusing the United States of aggression against North Korea (and China), the likelihood of a meaningful dialogue between the two powers seemed negligible, and no effort was made to preserve it.[54]

As for Truman's decisions to increase aid to Indochina and the Philippines and to send the Seventh Fleet into the Formosa Strait, they followed logically from Washington's perception of the Korean War as only the initial thrust of a much larger Communist offensive in the Far East. Washington had already emphasized the strategic importance it attached to Indochina by its commitment of military and economic assistance to the French. As for Formosa, its loss would have serious foreign and domestic repercussions, particularly in terms of endangering the security of Japan and unleashing a tremendous barrage of political flak at home. The neutralization of Formosa would also prevent an extension of the Asian war, something which the administration was anxious to avoid.

Washington's decision to intervene in Korea, then, was made deliberately and in consideration of a Soviet response either in Korea or elsewhere. Its action in expanding aid to Indochina and the Philippines and neutralizing Formosa was also in large measure a product of this perception of a worldwide Communist threat. It is true that the course it followed, particularly its commitment of combat forces to Korea, was made easier by the lack of military action or even preparation for a military attack by Moscow or Beijing, either in Korea or some other danger spot. But irrespective of other considerations, the Truman administration felt it had no alternative except to prevent South Korea from falling to the Communists. In simplest terms, American credibility in the world and its own credibility at home were at issue.

Throughout most of the period after World War II, the United States had attempted a policy of disengagement from Korea and all the rest of the Asian mainland. But the imperatives of the Cold War, the conviction that the world was in peril, that the tide of events was not going well for the United States, and that in the global confrontation with the Soviet Union America had to support any country and any regime threatened by communism, led the United States by 1950 into military involvement in a part of the world few Americans knew anything about and in a country that only a short time earlier had been deemed to be outside America's defense perimeter.

Notes

1. For this and the next six paragraphs consult especially John Lewis Gaddis, *The United States and the Origins of the Cold War, 1941–1947* (New York, 1972); Walter LaFeber, *America, Russia and the Cold War* (6th edition, New York, 1993), 1–29; Stephen E. Ambrose, *Rise to Globalism: American Foreign Policy Since 1938* (7th edition, New York, 1993), 102–135; Warren I. Cohen, *America in the Age of Soviet Power: The Cambridge History of American Foreign Relations*, IV (4 vols., New York, 1993), 3–20.

2. Soo Sung Cho, *Korea in World Politics, 1940–1950: An Evaluation of American Responsibility* (Berkeley, CA, 1967), 13–15.

3. William Whitney Stueck, Jr., *The Road to Confrontation; American Policy Toward China and Korea, 1947–1950* (Chapel Hill, NC, 1981), 19–21.

4. Bruce Cumings, *The Origins of the Korean War*, Vol. I: *Liberation and the Emergence of Separate Regimes, 1945–1947* (Princeton, NJ, 1981), 117–122.

5. *Ibid.*, 20; Mark Paul, "Diplomacy Delayed: The Atomic Bomb and the Division of Korea, 1945," in Bruce Cumings (ed.), *Child of Conflict: The Korean-American Relationship, 1943–1953* (Seattle, 1983), 88–91.

6. Gregory Henderson, *Korea: The Politics of the Vortex* (Cambridge, MA, 1968), 1–9 and 72–112; Michael Edson Robinson, *Cultural Nationalism in Colonial Korea, 1920–1925* (Seattle, WA, 1988), esp. 3–13.

7. Cumings, *The Origins of the Korean War*, I, 68–91.

8. *Ibid.*, 91–100.

9. Bruce Cumings, *The Origins of the Korean War, Vol. II: The Roaring of the Cataract, 1947–1950* (Princeton, NJ, 1990), 225–228; Robert T. Oliver, *Syngman Rhee: The Man Behind the Myth* (New York, 1954), 1–231; Joungwon A. Kim, *Divided Korea: The Politics of Development* (Cambridge, MA, 1975), 34–39; Edward Grant Meade, *American Military Government in Korea* (New York, 1951), 58; Lisle A. Rose, *Roots of Tragedy: The United States and the Struggle for Asia, 1945–1953* (Westport, CN, 1976), 34–36; Henderson, *Korea: The Politics of the Vortex*, 125; Cumings, *The Origins of the Korean War*, I, 22–33.

10. Kathryn Weathersby, "Soviet Aims in Korea and the Origins of the Korean War, 1945–1950: New Evidence from Russian Archives," *Cold War International History Project Working Paper No. 8* (Washington, DC: Woodrow Wilson International Center for Scholars, 1993), 5–16; Richard Whelan, *Drawing the Line: The Korean War, 1950–1953* (Boston, 1990), 16–18 and 29–31; Max Beloff, *Soviet Policy in the Far East, 1944–1951* (London, 1953), 156; Cumings, *The Origins of the Korean War,* II, 325–331. See also Kim, *Divided Korea,* 86–101; Dae-Sook Suh, *The Korean Communist Movement, 1918–1948* (Princeton, NJ, 1967), 253–395.

11. Kim, *Divided Korea,* 60–62; Cumings, *The Origins of the Korean War,* II, 217–227.

12. LaFeber, *America, Russia, and the Cold War,* 35–39; Thomas G. Paterson, *On Every Front: The Making of the Cold War* (New York, 1979), 52–54.

13. *Foreign Relations of the United States, 1946,* VIII, 706–709. Hereafter cited as *FR* with date and volume numbers; Robert H. Ferrell (ed.), *Off the Record: The Private Papers of Harry S. Truman* (New York, 1980), 80; James I. Matray, "Cold War of a Sort: The International Origins of the Korean Conflict," in Kim Chull Baum and James I. Matray (eds.), *Korea and the Cold War: Division, Destruction, and Disarmament* (Claremont, CA, 1993), 51–52; Cumings, *The Origins of the Korean War,* II, 223–227.

14. *FR,* 1946, VIII, 692–699; Henderson, *Korea: The Politics of the Vortex,* 131–134; Kenneth R. Mauck, "The Formation of American Foreign Policy in Korea, 1945–1953" (unpublished Ph.D. dissertation, University of Oklahoma, 1978), 90–102.

15. Stueck, Jr., *The Road to Confrontation,* 27; Cumings, *The Origins of the Korean War,* II, 252–262; Okonogi Masao, "The Domestic Roots of the Korean War," in Yonusuke Nagai and Akira Iriye (eds.), *The Origins of the Cold War in Asia* (New York, 1970), 308.

16. Stephen Pelz, "U.S. Decisions on Korean Policy, 1943–1950: Some Hypotheses," in Cumings (ed.), *Child of Conflict,* 110; *FR,* 1947, VI, 817–818 and 832–833; Stueck, Jr., *The Road to Confrontation,* 86–88; Cumings, *The Origins of the Korean War,* II, 59–61.

17. FR, 1947, VI, 625–628, 675–676, 738–741, 776, 790, 817–818, and 832–833. See also Leland M. Goodrich, *Korea: A Study of U.S. Policy in the United Nations* (New York, 1956), 28–29.

18. *FR,* 1947, VI, 776, 790, 817–818, and 832–833.

19. Masao, "The Domestic Roots of the Korean War," 309; Cumings, *The Origins of the Korean War,* II, 65–68.

20. *FR,* 1948, VI, 1093–1095, 1101–1113, and 1164–1169; Cho, *Korea in World Politics,* 184–197; Stueck, Jr., *The Road to Confrontation,* 96–98; Kim, *Divided Korea,* 196–207; Cumings, *The Origins of the Korean War,* II, 69–78.

21. John Merrill, "Internal Warfare in Korea, 1948–1950: The Local Setting of the Korean War," in Cumings (ed.), *Child of Conflict,* 142–145; Cumings, *The Origins of the Korean War,* II, 251–285.

22. *FR*, 1948, VI, 1325–1327.

23. Pelz, "U.S. Decisions on Korean Policy," 114–115; John Lewis Gaddis, "Korea in American Politics, Strategy, and Diplomacy, 1949–1950," in Nagai and Iriye (eds.), *The Origins of the Cold War in Asia*, 284; Cumings, *The Origins of the Korean War*, II, 379–381.

24. *FR*, 1949, VII, 40–41. See also Kim Chull Baum, "U.S. Policy on the Eve of the Korean War: Abandonment or Safeguard?" in Baum and Matray (eds.), *Korea and the Cold War*, 63–93.

25. Gaddis, "Korea in American Politics, Strategy, and Diplomacy, 1949–1950," 283; Cumings, *The Origins of the Korean War*, II, 382–383.

26. *FR*, 1949, VII, 1003–1005, 1010, 1014, 1041–1043, and 1063; *ibid.*, 1950, VII, 6–11 and 26–29.

27. Dean Acheson, *Present at the Creation: My Years in the State Department* (New York, 1969), 691; Cumings, *The Origins of the Korean War*, II, 420–423 and 428–430.

28. *FR*, 1950, VII, 40–41.

29. Merrill, "Internal Warfare in Korea, 1948–1950," 156; Cumings, *The Origins of the Korean War*, II, 285–290; Kim, *Divided Korea*, 115–129.

30. Memorandum of Conversation with President Rhee, June 19, 1950, Box 4262, Records of the Department of State, RG 59, 795.00/6–1950; *FR*, 1950, VII, 109–112; Stueck, Jr., *The Road to Confrontation*, 164–165; Glenn D. Paige, *The Korean Decision* (New York, 1968), 75.

31. George C. Herring, *America's Longest War: The United States and Vietnam, 1950–1975* (2nd edition, New York, 1986), 9–13.

32. *FR*, 1950, I, 237–292. See also LaFeber, *America, Russia, and the Cold War*, 97–100.

33. *FR*, 1950, VII, 95–96.

34. *Ibid.*, 125; Paige, *The Korean Decision*, 81–124.

35. Mauck, "The Formation of American Foreign Policy in Korea," 192; Paige, *The Korean Decision*, 125–141.

36. *FR*, 1950, VII, 178–183; Roy Appleman, *South to the Naktong, North to the Yalu* (Washington, DC, 1961), 31.

37. *FR*, 1950, VII, 428–453; Paige, *The Korean Decision*, 145–270.

38. On this point see below, 24–25. See also Whelan, *Drawing the Line*, xv.

39. Weathersby, "Soviet Aims in Korea and the Origins of the Korean War, 1945–1950," 24–27; William Stueck, Jr., "The Soviet Union and the Origins of the Korean War," in Baum and Matray (eds.), *Korea and the Cold War*, 116–120; Kim Hajoon, "Trends in Korean War Studies: A Review of the Literature," in *ibid.*, 28–29; John Merrill, "The Origins of the Korean War: Unanswered Questions," in *ibid.*, 106; Robert R. Simmons, *The Strained Alliance: Peking, Pyongyang, Moscow and the Politics of the Korean Civil War* (New York, 1975), 102–130; Strobe Talbott (ed.), *Khrushchev Remembers* (Boston, 1970), 367–368.

40. Michael H. Hunt, "Beijing and the Korean Crisis, June 1950–June 1951,"

Political Science Quarterly, 107 (Fall, 1992), 457; Anthony Farrar-Hockley, "The China Factor in the Korean War," in James Cotton and Ian Neary (eds.), *The Korean War in History* (Atlantic Highlands, NJ, 1989), 4–6; Hak Joon Kim, "China's Non-Involvement in the Origins of the Korean War: A Reassessment of the Traditionalist and Revisionist Literature," in *ibid.,* 11–29; Jonathan D. Pollack, "The Korean War and Sino-American Relations," in Harry Harding and Yuan Ming (eds.), *Sino-American Relations, 1945–1955: A Joint Reassessment of a Critical Decade* (Wilmington DE, 1989), 214; Hakjoon, "Trends in Korean War Studies," 24–25; Bruce Hao Yufan and Zhai Zhihai, "China's Decision to Enter the Korean War: History Revisited," *The China Quarterly,* 121 (March, 1990), 99–100; Cumings, *The Origins of the Korean War,* II, 361–364; He Dei, "The Evolution of the CCP's Policy towards the United States: 1944–1949," unpublished paper in author's possession.

41. Merrill, "The Origins of the Korean War: Unanswered Questions," 101–103; Weathersby, "Soviet Aims in Korea and the Origins of the Korean War, 1945–1950," 22–23; Cumings, *The Origins of the Korean War,* II, 291–234 and 331–349.

42. Cumings, *The Origins of the Korean War,* II, 388–407 and 426–427; Merrill, "Internal Warfare in Korea," 150–153. See also Robert R. Simmons, "The Korean Civil War," in Frank Baldwin (ed.), *Without Parallel: The American-Korean Relationship Since 1945* (New York, 1973), 146–147.

43. *FR,* 1950, VII, 148–155.

44. Ronald McClothlen, "Acheson, Economics, and the American Commitment in Korea, 1947–1959," *Pacific Historical Review,* 58 (February 1989), 23–53; Whelan, *Drawing the Line,* 75–88; Callum A. MacDonald, *Korea: The War Before Vietnam* (London, 1986), 9 and 18–19; Cumings, *The Origins of the Korean War,* II, 57–58, 157–158, and 168–182.

45. Harry S. Truman, *Years of Trial and Hope: Memoirs, 1946–1952* (New York, 1965), 377–386; Acheson, *Present at the Creation,* 405; David Rees, *Korea: The Limited War* (New York, 1964), 31.

46. Pelz, "U.S. Decisions on Korean Policy," 112–127.

47. D. Clayton James, *Refighting the Last War: Command and Crisis in Korea, 1950–1953* (New York, 1993), 14–15; Rosemary Foot, *The Wrong War: American Policy and the Dimensions of the Korean Conflict, 1950–1953* (Ithaca, NY, 1985), 29–31; Hunt, "Beijing and the Korean Crisis," 473.

48. Ambrose, *Rise to Globalism,* 184–188; LaFeber, *America, Russia, and the Cold War,* 89–97; Thomas C. Reeves, *The Life and Times of Joe McCarthy* (New York, 1982), 198–233.

49. David R. Kepley, *The Collapse of the Middle Way: Senate Republicans and the Bipartisan Foreign Policy, 1948–1952* (Westport, CT, 1988), 37–51.

50. *Ibid.,* 37–84; Reeves, *The Life and Times of Joe McCarthy,* 283; *Commonweal,* 51 (April 7, 1950), 675; *New Republic,* 122 (April 10, 1950), 4; *ibid.* (April 17, 1950), 3–4; *ibid.* (June 26, 1950), 10–12.

51. Lawrence S. Wittner, *Cold War America: From Hiroshima to Watergate* (New York, 1974), 89.
52. *FR*, 1950, VII, 178–183.
53. *Ibid.*, 248–253; Paige, *The Korean Decision*, 145–270.
54. Stueck, Jr., *The Road to Confrontation*, 192. See also Gaddis Smith, *Dean Acheson* (New York, 1972), 190.

CHAPTER TWO

War and the Climate of Crisis and Conspiracy

The sense of despair and crisis in the United States during the first half of 1950 was further exacerbated during the first few months of the Korean war as North Korean troops moved relentlessly southward, meeting small pockets of resistance. On the one hand, the war heightened, not diminished, the anti-Communist hysteria in America. On the other hand, the Truman administration, perceiving the war as part of a global struggle whose principal actors were the United States and the Soviet Union, expanded its scope to include not merely the containment of Soviet aggression, but the rollback of Communist forces from territory they had occupied prior to the outbreak of hostilities.

Similarly, Washington broadened the United States' commitments worldwide. Not only did the administration accelerate aid to Indochina, offer assistance to the Philippine government fighting the Hukbalahap insurrection, and neutralize Formosa, it used the opportunity afforded by the war to promote numerous measures in Europe that earlier were regarded as improbable because of American and European opposition. These included the arming of West Germany and its integration firmly into the western alliance, the commitment of American troops to the North Atlantic Treaty Organization (NATO), and the establishment of a unified command structure for NATO under General Dwight D. Eisenhower.

The conflict had important domestic consequences as well. First, the power of the executive branch over the conduct of foreign policy was reinforced in a battle between the White House and the chief military officer in Korea, General Douglas MacArthur. Second, important decisions had to be made regarding the war's effects on the domestic economy and on executive-congressional relations. Finally, by seeming to confirm many of NSC–68's assumptions about the bipolarity of world power and the determination of the Soviet Union to achieve world domination, the outbreak of hostilities in Korea made the implementation of its spending recommendations among the nation's highest priorities. By mid-July Truman's military budget requests had grown to approximately $30 billion. By December they would approach the $50 billion level.

The UN resolution of June 27 providing for military sanctions against North Korea requested member states to assist the Republic of Korea (ROK). Eventually sixteen nations, including the United States, provided armed forces. Another UN resolution of July 7 by the Security Council established a unified command under the UN flag and delegated the authority for the command to the United States. President Truman appointed General MacArthur as the Supreme United Nations Commander, and the United Nations Command (UNC) became the official title of the force.

For all of July and part of August the military situation in South Korea for UN forces remained bleak. Not only were North Korean troops able to capture Seoul within four days after their invasion of South Korea, they destroyed more than half of the ROK army. An American task force, which arrived from Japan on July 1, 1950, consisted of only two understrengthed rifle companies. Although more troops arrived by the second week in July, the best they were able to do was carry out an orderly retreat to a ninety-mile perimeter around Pusan at the southeastern end of the peninsula.[1]

From the very first days of the war, President Truman gave consideration to the possible use of tactical nuclear weapons if the Soviet Union should enter the conflict. At the first Blair House meeting on June 25, he asked Air Force Chief of Staff Hoyt S. Vandenberg about the feasibility of "taking out" Soviet bases near the Korean border. When Vandenberg responded that it was possible but would require atomic bombs, the president ordered preparations for a nuclear strike should the Soviets enter the war. As a clear indication of America's resolve not to be driven from the Korean peninsula, Truman also approved on July 11 the deployment of nuclear-configured B–29 bombers to Britain. But to avoid being unduly provocative while at the same time mollifying the British, who were concerned about the likely Soviet response, he allowed the deployment to be described in Washington and London as part of a "normal rotation."[2]

Three weeks later, Truman approved the sending of ten more nuclear-configured B–29s to Guam. By this time a military defeat of the UNC remained a real possibility. Furthermore, the Central Intelligence Agency (CIA) was reporting the buildup of Chinese Communist forces for an invasion of Formosa even as the commander of the U.S. Seventh Fleet, which had been sent into the Formosa straits immediately after the outbreak of the Korean conflict, was informing Washington that he could not fight in Korea and protect Formosa at the same time. The White House apparently intended the deployment of the B–29s to Guam as another statement of America's determination not to be driven out of Korea and as a warning to the People's Republic of China (PRC) not to attempt an invasion of Formosa. Truman may also have approved the deployment of the planes as a way of blunting Republican attacks on his administration's Korean policies.[3]

Yet the fact remains that at the time North Korea invaded South Korea on June 25, not a single American plane capable of delivering atomic bombs was located outside the continental United States. In the first weeks of the war, moreover, American and ROK forces were simply too ill equipped to stop the North Koreans. The first American troops had nothing better against North Korean heavily armored T–34 tanks than howitzers and bazookas of World War II vintage, which, for the most part, were incapable of penetrating the T–34's armor. The Sherman and Patton tanks, which might have stood up against the T–34s, were still in the factory in the United States. Under these circumstances the job of holding off the Communist tanks devolved largely on the Air Force, and here also problems existed. Although America's control of the air eventually proved decisive in stopping the enemy advance, the Air Force at first relied on its World War II tactic of strategic bombing, striking beyond the area of ground fighting and hitting such enemy installations as factories, warehouses, oil refineries, and communication facilities with non-nuclear B–29 medium bombers.[4]

The net result was, as one observer commented, that American ground troops in Korea were "fighting a World War III army with World War II weapons," and for much of the time with very little of the kind of air support they really needed. Only toward the middle and later parts of August did the situation around Pusan improve. By the end of August the number of ground troops had increased to about 180,000, including 92,000 ROK personnel, as opposed to about 133,000 North Koreans, many of whom were ill-trained conscripts. Tanks and vehicles had also begun to arrive in substantial numbers, so that by the end of the month U.S. troops had about 500 Pershing and Sherman tanks against the hundred or so T–34s that the enemy was estimated still to have in operating order. Control of the air over Korea had also been largely accomplished, and the UN Air Force was engaged in both tactical and strategic operations, providing close air cover for UN forces on the ground and hitting at targets well inside North Korea.

As a result, UN forces were able to beat back a major offensive that the enemy opened on the last day of August. Short of fuel, ammunition, and food, forced to rely on local conscripts to carry supplies, and the target of close air support by American planes, the North Koreans quickly spent themselves. By September 7 the offensive was over, and the Communists had suffered their first major defeat of the war. Soon UN forces would launch their own counteroffensive.[5]

It had been a trying and difficult eleven weeks for many Americans, however, and one of the ramifications of the war was to intensify the anti-Communist campaign of McCarthy and other Republicans, who in an election year used the fighting as an ideal topic for campaign oratory against the administration. McCarthy's first remarks on Korea came only a week after the war began. In a television interview on July 2, he charged that "American boys [were] dying in Korea" because "a group of untouchables in the State Department" had sabotaged the aid program Congress had voted for South Korea. In a Senate speech a few days later and on numerous occasions thereafter, he made similar charges and spoke of "highly placed Red Counselors" who were "far more deadly than Red machine gunners in Korea."[6]

Just as charges of an internal conspiracy had offered a ready explanation to many Americans of why China had fallen to the Communists in 1949, so the same accusations now seemed to explain why, in McCarthy's words, American boys were dying in Korea. Americans responded not only by attacking the alleged Communists in government but by seeking to eliminate the Communist threat wherever it was thought to exist. A veritable witch hunt took place in many parts of the United States as suspected Communists were ferreted out of employment and exposed to public damnation. A number of municipalities went even further. In Detroit, for example, the Common Council forbade sidewalk news vendors to sell "subversive literature" and gave the commissioner of police the responsibility for determining what was subversive. In Birmingham, Alabama, Police Commissioner "Bull" Connor, who would gain notoriety in the 1960s for unleashing vicious dogs and using fire hoses against civil rights demonstrators, pushed a new ordinance through the city commission banishing Communists from Birmingham. And in Columbus, Ohio, police juvenile officers warned teenage clubs to beware of "Communist agitators" and to be suspicious of any new member of a group whose background was "not an open book."[7]

Republicans in Congress sought to capitalize on this swell of anti-Communist emotion. The Republican Party Policy Committee made passage of the McCarran Internal Security Bill one of its highest priorities. This legislation required all Communist organizations to register with the government and to publish their records. Americans were also subject to prosecution on grounds as vague as "fomenting revolution," and Communists were barred from working in defense plants. So strong was the public demand for anti-Communist and antisubversive legislation that for purposes of self-preservation, even a number of Democrats noted for their libertarianism and commitment to free speech and free expression felt compelled to vote for the McCarran bill. As one of these lawmakers, Herbert Lehman of New York, explained, "the fever of fear was on my colleagues." With such bipartisan support, the legislation was passed in September by lopsided votes in both the House and the Senate, and later it was approved again, this time over the President's veto.[8]

By September both parties had begun to map out campaign strategy for the 1950 elections, and the Korean war figured prominently in the Republican plans to unseat the Democrats. In a fifty-six-page news release, "Background to Korea," Republicans blamed the administration for "its failure in 1945 to recognize the true aims and methods of the rulers of Soviet Russia," which they called "the major tragedy of our time." Democrats responded by accusing such Republican notables as Senator Robert Taft of Ohio of isolationism and by maintaining that the nation would have been much worse off if the Republicans had had their way on military and foreign policy issues since the end of World War II.[9]

Nevertheless, the Republican charges against the administration of internal subversion and the exposed position of its Far Eastern policy, first with respect to China and now in Korea, weighed heavily in the formulation of its foreign policy in the summer of 1950. In the first place, the administration rejected initial peace efforts by England and India while it reviewed plans to cross the 38th parallel and carry the war into North Korea once the tide of battle turned. At the same time, it expanded the scope of the war by using the conflict as a fulcrum to achieve policy objectives elsewhere, particularly in Europe. Korea thus became a "war for both Asia and Europe," in the words of the historian Walter LaFeber.[10] By broadening the aims and purpose of the conflict in this way, the administration was less vulnerable to domestic criticism from the "primitives," as Secretary of State Acheson called the right wing of the Republican Party, and presumably was in a stronger position to deal with the Communists over Korea.[11]

The British and Indian peace initiatives began early in July, soon after President Truman committed combat troops to Korea, when the British ambassador to Moscow, Sir David Kelly, met with Soviet Foreign Minister Andrei Gromyko. After assuring Kelly that the Soviet Union wanted a peaceful settlement to the war, Gromyko asked the British ambassador for specific proposals to end the conflict. At about the same time, the Indian government attempted to act as an informal mediator by making separate overtures to Moscow, Washington, and Beijing, which involved recognition of the PRC by the United States in return for ending the war.[12]

The United States showed mild interest in the British attempt at mediation but strongly disdained the Indian effort. In simplest terms, the administration was unwilling to link the China question—which, in addition to the matter of the PRC's admission into the United Nations, involved the problem of whether Formosa should be returned to the Beijing government—to a settlement of the Korean war. Acheson made it clear to both the Indians and the British, who also thought that the PRC should be seated on the UN Security Council and that its claim to Formosa was valid, that a resolution of the China question would not be the price paid by the United States for a settlement of the Korean question.[13]

One can legitimately ask whether the United States should have been more forthcoming in its response to the British and Indian peace initiatives. Certainly there would have been advantages in doing so. At the very least, by responding more positively to their efforts, Washington might have shifted more of the responsibility for the war's continuation onto the Communists and strengthened ties with India, a nation it hoped would play an important role in offsetting Communist China's influence in Asia. By linking the problem of Korea (which most concerned the Soviets) with the China question (which most interested the Beijing government), the administration might also have revealed important differences between the Soviet Union and the PRC that could later be used to America's advantage.[14]

Considering the prevailing political climate in the United States, however, any effort by the administration to resolve the China question as part of a bargain to end the Korean war almost certainly would have been wrought with the most serious political consequences. Acheson's "primitives" would have been up in arms against the administration. Charges of conspiracy and internal subversion would have proliferated, and demands for Acheson's resignation would have soared. Undoubtedly the administration would have been able to ride out this storm of anguish and anger, just as it was doing with respect to the fall of China, but its task in this regard would have been much more difficult. Most important, it would have confused the American public and weakened support for the administration's crash program of increased military spending. As it was, public opinion in the United States almost universally supported Washington's rejection of the Indian peace initiative, which most news commentators regarded as appeasement in its most despicable form.[15]

Indeed, neither much of the American public nor the administration was in the mood to negotiate with the Communists in the summer of 1950. A number of Americans openly talked of a preventive war, or preemptive nuclear strike, against the Soviet Union, and within the administration serious consideration was already being given to the possibility of carrying the war to North Korea at some future date. Although talk of a preventive nuclear war against the Soviet Union had been heard during almost every crisis since the Cold War began, there does seem to have been an unusual increase in public sentiment for such a war following the outbreak of hostilities in Korea. Instead of deterring such talk, knowledge that the Soviet Union had developed its own nuclear capability appears to have had just the opposite effect, the rationale being that the United States had better take out the Russians while it still enjoyed nuclear superiority. The sentiment for a preventive war was quite pervasive. In Washington and "everywhere else in the country, too, you can hear lots of 'preventive war talk'," one news writer thus reported toward the end of August. "When a man knows he has a good chance to be A-bombed," *Time* commented a month later, "nothing can stop him from considering whether there isn't something he can do to prevent it. That is why talk of 'preventive war' by the U.S. against U.S.S.R. stays on the tongues of the American people." Even within the administration, there was enough of that kind of talk for President Truman to order an official stop to it.[16]

Of far greater significance, however, was the consideration the administration gave to the question of what to do after the tide of battle had turned in Korea. Ultimately this boiled down to the issue of whether to contain Communist expansion by driving the North Koreans back above the 38th parallel or to seize the chance to roll back Soviet aggression (the North Koreans being regarded as agents of Moscow) by carrying the war into North Korea itself. In fact, by the time the decision was made in September to send UN forces across the 38th parallel, the administration had engaged in an extensive dialogue over a period of several months, weighing all the public ramifications of such an action. It concluded that the opportunities of taking the initiative in the Cold War outweighed the dangers of escalating the conflict into a yet larger war, possibly even into a nuclear confrontation with the Soviet Union.[17]

Concern as to what the Soviet Union would do if the UN forces moved north of the 38th parallel was central to the entire debate over Korea. Opponents of moving across the 38th parallel argued that it would increase the chances both of Soviet intervention in Korea and of global war. In contrast, advocates of crossing into North Korea admitted the risks involved but held that the danger of doing nothing was even greater. At the Pentagon, Defense Department planners had grown increasingly confident by the beginning of August that the Soviet Union would not intervene in North Korea if UN forces moved beyond the 38th parallel. They believed that Moscow's "uncompleted strategic position in the Far East" was likely to keep the Kremlin leaders from risking a general war over Korea but that, in any case, not to advance beyond the 38th parallel would result in the same military instability as before the outbreak of hostilities in June. It would also require a huge outlay of funds to reconstruct and secure South Korea. For these reasons the Defense Department felt the UNC should try to defeat North Korean forces north and south of the 38th parallel.[18]

In contrast to the Defense Department, the State Department was divided between those like George Kennan, who headed its Policy Planning Staff (PPS) and favored a return to the *status quo ante bellum*, and John Allison, who headed its Office of Northeast Asian Affairs and wanted to roll back Communism beyond the 38th parallel. Only after considerable bickering did the two sides finally agree to a document that left open the possibility of crossing into North Korea but postponed a final decision on the matter "until military and political developments provide additional information."[19]

As late as September 15, when UN forces began their counteroffensive, the White House had still not made any final decision on crossing the 38th parallel. The administration's most recent position, incorporated into a policy paper prepared by the National Security Council (NSC–81/1), amounted to a web of ambiguities strung along a fog of uncertainties. Nevertheless, the paper concluded that the United Nations' purpose in Korea was to bring about "the complete independence and unity" of that country and that if this could be accomplished "without substantially increasing the risk of general war with the Soviet Union or Communist China, it would be in [the United States'] interest to advocate the pressing of the United Nations actions to the conclusion." Such a position, while by no means a firm commitment, made a decision by the President to move north of the 38th parallel that much more likely.[20]

If the United States was moving toward broadening the war in Korea by shifting from the containment to the rollback of Communist aggression, it was taking additional steps that further expanded American commitments worldwide. Having responded to the initial outbreak of hostilities in Korea by increasing aid to Indochina and the Philippines and neutralizing Formosa, the administration moved, in the critical summer months that followed, to increase its commitment to the defense of western Europe. Indeed, after the initial shock of hostilities and throughout the remainder of the summer, Americans engaged in a wide-ranging debate as to where the country's foreign policy priorities should lie. The discussion did not always fit the neat prescription of earlier years, which pitted right-wing Republicans and other "isolationists," who argued that the administration was doing too much in Europe and too little in Asia, against "internationalists" of both the Democratic and Republican parties, who maintained that the nation's first priority had to be in Europe. Even respected internationalist journals like the *New Republic,* which always emphasized that America's main interests were in close ties with a strong and united Europe, now began to stress the need for a foreign policy that struck a better balance between Asia and Europe.[21]

Other internationalists, however, believed the war in Korea revealed just how vulnerable western Europe was to Soviet aggression from the east and how important it was to knit Europe into a tighter military, political, and economic fabric. Although the establishment of NATO in 1949 had been an important step in that direction, the alliance remained organizationally weak and quite incapable of repelling a serious challenge from the Soviet Union. Only $52 million of $1.3 billion in military assistance from the United States for America's NATO allies had been obligated, little had been done in the way of military planning, and only twelve divisions were at NATO's disposal in Europe. Still to be tackled, moreover, was the thorny question of Germany's role in the defense of Europe, which most political leaders were loath even to bring up so soon after the defeat of the Nazis.[22]

Would the Korean war deflect the United States from its European responsibilities? This was a common question asked in Europe as well as in the United States. But such a concern proved needless. Instead, the outbreak of hostilities underscored for the administration the imperative of a united and strong Europe able not only to resist an attack from the east, but to resolve common political and economic problems. Instead of vague promises of mutual assistance in case of attack, therefore, the United States offered the west European nations firm guarantees of military support and began to turn NATO into a military pact able to defend Europe against assault from the east. In doing so, it sought to achieve other political and economic objectives, including the full integration of West Germany into the western concert.[23]

No one felt more strongly about strengthening the NATO alliance and bringing Germany into it as a full member than did Dean Acheson, who worked tirelessly to bridge the ocean between the United States and Europe. Born into comfort, educated at Groton, Yale, and Harvard Law School, and combining public service with a successful law practice, Acheson embodied the Eastern elite against which so many right-wing conservatives directed their political attacks. Meticulous in appearance with a bushy moustache upturned at the ends, Acheson carried himself with the haughty demeanor of a British aristocrat with whom he was often compared. In fact, he believed the United States had to play a central role in forging a new Atlantic alliance to replace the Pax Brittanica that had brought peace, prosperity, and order to the nineteenth century. His whole foreign policy was predicated on close ties with the major capitals of Europe, and both as undersecretary of state from 1945 to 1947 and then as secretary of state after 1949 he operated with that principle in mind.[24]

More than ever the Korean conflict convinced Acheson of the need to strengthen NATO. As he later remarked about the summer of 1950, "it was time to consider our plans for European defense in the light of Korea." That immediately raised the question of the rearming of Western Germany. Although the secretary of state had told Congress as late as 1949, during hearings over the ratification of NATO, that under no circumstances would Germany be included in the NATO alliance, the outbreak of hostilities in Korea caused him to change his mind. "The idea that Germany's place in the defense of Europe would be worked out by a process of evolution was outmoded," he now said. Indeed, as far as he was concerned, the two major requirements for making NATO work were the inclusion of Germany in Europe's defense arrangements and the acceptance by America's European partners of more of the burden for their own defense. Congress shared a similar position. In House and Senate hearings legislators demanded to know what the allies' contribution of troops and funds for their common defense would be. They also insisted that Germany be included in the rearming of Europe.[25]

Here was the rub. Would the European allies accept Germany into NATO and would they be willing to bear more of the costs of defending themselves? The outlook was far from clear. The Korean war created a new mood in western Europe. Britain began a partial mobilization of its reserves, and France undertook to raise fifteen divisions with American aid. Yet by August 1950 fear of a Russian invasion and concern about American neglect of Europe had diminished considerably. At the same time, the terrific costs of rearmament dulled the enthusiasm for a massive European defense effort, and, among most French, Dutch, and Belgian politicians at least, there remained strong opposition to the establishment of a German army. Indeed, the economic and emotional costs of such a defense program reignited neutralist tendencies throughout Europe.[26]

The French proved implacable in their opposition to German rearmament, and the British went along with the Americans largely because they did not believe the French would accept the plan. Without French support and with only the lukewarm backing of the British, the American proposal floundered and then fizzled. In December, NATO approved the concept of a united command but accepted German participation only in principle.[27]

Nonetheless, the United States had taken several important incentives in response to the Korean war that extended America's commitment to Europe and strengthened the NATO alliance. In the first place, in cooperation with its European partners, Washington established a unified command structure for NATO. Although this would not happen officially until December, President Truman asked General Eisenhower in October to accept the appointment as supreme commander of NATO. Second, European rearmament, which had scarcely begun at the start of the Korean war, was well underway by the fall, and Truman had pledged to send four American divisions to Europe. Third, the United States endorsed the principle of a German army as part of NATO's military force.[28]

The commitments made by Washington in Europe and Asia, as well as the costs of the Korean war itself, meant an enormous increase in the nation's military budget. By confirming NSC–68's analysis of Communist aggression, the war also seemed to corroborate its estimate of the funds necessary to contain the Soviet threat. Until the outbreak of the conflict the administration had taken no action on NSC–68's recommendations. In fact, so much opposition existed in Congress to any major spending increases that President Truman had refused to allow publication of the report. Even after hostilities began in Korea, moreover, the Council of Economic Advisers assumed the fighting would be localized and concluded that no standby economic controls were necessary. But all this changed within a matter of a few weeks. As Secretary Acheson put it, the dispatch of American troops to Korea "removed the recommendations of NSC–68 from the realm of theory and made them immediate budget issues." On July 19 President Truman delivered a report to Congress in which he asked for a substantial increase in military and defense spending, including an expanded program of military assistance for America's allies. He also requested a package of economic controls that included the allocation of essential raw materials, limits on consumer credit, and certain production incentives.[29]

Over the next six months, Congress responded by passing a series of appropriation and supplemental appropriation bills, so that by the beginning of January the nation's military and defense spending approximated the recommendations of NSC–68. In addition, Congress approved the Defense Production Act (DPA) in September, which gave the White House almost everything it asked for in the way of economic controls. The DPA was a sweeping piece of legislation that vastly increased the power of the executive branch as it sought to mobilize the economy for wartime purposes. Not only did it grant the President various requisition and allocation powers for defense purposes, including a standby program of wages and price controls, it even permitted the President in certain circumstances to allow business arrangements deemed beneficial to the war effort to be exempt from the antitrust laws.[30]

Another of the indirect consequences of the war was to reinforce the power of the executive at the expense of the House and Senate. This came through the President's failure to consult with Congress on war-related matters and through an incident involving the President's authority as commander-in-chief. The issue of consultation with Congress came up very early in the war. On June 28 Senator Taft told Truman that while he supported the President's actions with respect to Korea, there was "no legal authority" for the steps he had taken. Two days later—on the same day, in fact, that Truman consented to the sending of a combat force to Korea—Republican Senator Kenneth Wherry of Nebraska, the minority leader, asked the President at a Blair House meeting if he was going to advise Congress before he sent ground troops into Korea. When Truman responded that some ground troops had already been ordered into Korea, Wherry replied that Congress should be consulted before the President made such moves. Although Truman said he was faced with an emergency situation and that there was no time for a lot of talk, Wherry persisted and on several more occasions during the meeting repeated his belief that Congress should be consulted before any large-scale actions were taken again. Senator H. Alexander Smith of New Jersey also recommended that Truman request a joint resolution of Congress to approve his actions. The president replied that if any large-scale moves were to take place, he would tell Congress about them.[31]

Clearly Truman did not think a congressional resolution was necessary since most of Congress already supported his actions. But an even more important reason why he decided not to go to Congress for its approval was the fact that he did not think at first that the conflict in Korea would lead to a world war, and he did not want to increase the stakes in Korea or unnecessarily alarm the American public or world opinion by asking for a declaration of war or anything like that. As Truman's biographer, Robert J. Donovan, has remarked, the President "seems not to have had a sense of a major war's blossoming in Korea, although he was ready to go 'all out,' if necessary to squelch the Communist invasion." And by the time it had become clear that Korea was a full-blown war, it was probably too late to get the kind of resolution unanimously approved by Congress that Truman would have wanted.[32]

In the long run, it would probably not have made that much difference had the President taken Congress more into his confidence. Later criticism of the war had little to do with Truman's failure to consult Congress but was a result of a limited war in which the United States failed to achieve a quick victory. At the same time, though, it is hard to see what political harm it could have caused. Indeed, stealing the thunder of the opposition by going to Congress for its approval might have been of some immediate benefit to the administration. A joint resolution of approval in July would have made it all the more difficult for Truman's opponents later to criticize the intervention.[33]

Of much greater concern to the White House, however, than the constitutional issue of informing Congress before taking military action in Korea was another, related, constitutional matter having to do with the role of the President as commander-in-chief of the armed forces. In what proved to be a portent of the administration's greatest domestic crisis, the President clashed with General MacArthur over a major policy question regarding the future of Formosa. Appointed by President Truman on July 8 as commander of the UN forces in Korea, MacArthur was also commander-in-chief, Far East, and supreme commander, allied powers, Japan. Of heroic stature and great forcefulness, MacArthur was also deeply egotistical and vainglorious. Brilliant, austere, possessed of the gift of total recall, he "could never see another sun . . . in the heavens," as Eisenhower later said of him. He was also a person of deep conviction and moral certitude, whose absolute views, arrogance, and personal rectitude made his vision sometimes narrow and parochial and incapable of fathoming the larger picture into which his own command had to be fitted. But so great was his personal fame, so overwhelming was his character, so eloquent was his rhetoric, that his views on military and nonmilitary matters alike were listened to with reverential respect by a broad cross-section of the American public.[34]

Essentially, MacArthur was one of those who believed in 1950 that the United States had shown too great an interest in European affairs and not enough in the Far East, whose "billions of inhabitants," he once said, "will determine the course of history for the next ten thousand years." More specifically, he believed in the summer of 1950 that the United States had the obligation to preserve Formosa and its leader, Chiang Kai-shek, against possible attack by Communist China. In fact, he seems to have been as much, or more, concerned with restoring Chiang to the mainland than with developments in Korea. At the end of July he visited Formosa allegedly to assess the military situation there. Returning to his headquarters in Tokyo, he ordered three squadrons of jet fighters to Formosa without the knowledge of the Pentagon. He also issued a statement in which he remarked that plans had been formulated for the effective coordination of Chinese and American forces in case of an attack on the island. Shortly thereafter Chiang issued his own statement to the effect that his meeting with MacArthur had laid the basis for the joint defense of Formosa and "Sino-American military cooperation."[35]

Chiang's announcement caused tremendous consternation in Washington, whose policy was as much to avoid an expansion of the conflict in Asia by keeping Chiang from launching an attack against the mainland as it was to prevent an attack from being launched against him. After MacArthur issued a caustic statement in which he charged that the purpose of his trip had been "maliciously misrepresented to the public by those who invariably in the past have propagandized a policy of defeatism and appeasement in the Pacific," the administration issued a new directive to the general that he was not to authorize any attack from Formosa against the mainland. MacArthur wrote back that he understood the Presidential decision of June 27 "to protect the Communist mainland."[36]

This was the situation at the end of August when MacArthur sent a lengthy message to the Veterans of Foreign Wars in which he wrote about the "misconceptions currently being voiced concerning the relationship of Formosa to our strategic potential in the Pacific" and predicted dire consequences defensively if Formosa fell into hostile hands. To pursue any course other than defending Formosa, he said "would be to turn over the fruits of our Pacific victory to a potential enemy. It would shift any future battle over 5,000 miles eastward to the coast of the American continent, our own home coast."[37]

Truman was appalled when he learned of MacArthur's remarks the next day. Modest where MacArthur was grandiloquent, folksy where MacArthur was ceremonious, Truman could nevertheless be as crafty as any political leader. After meeting with the Joint Chiefs of Staff, members of his cabinet, and White House aides, he told Defense Secretary Louis Johnson that he "decisively repudiated" the statement MacArthur had made, that it directly contradicted the nation's foreign policy, and that he wished MacArthur's statement canceled. A short while later, he ordered that the general withdraw his statement in writing, and when the Defense Department appeared to procrastinate, he called Johnson on the phone and virtually dictated the content of the message sent to the general. MacArthur complied with the directive at once. Later Truman stated that he "gave serious thought" to replacing MacArthur as military field commander in the Far East with General Omar Bradley but decided against such a step because it "would have been difficult to avoid the appearance of a demotion and [he] had no desire to hurt MacArthur personally." Undoubtedly Truman was also aware of the unpopularity of such a move and the backlash against the administration it would have generated.[38]

The first few months of the war, then, had been critical ones for the United States in a number of respects. Most important, of course, UN forces had been able to stabilize the war, successfully defend a perimeter around Pusan, and even make preparations for a counterattack, which would take place very shortly. Beyond that, the administration had given consideration to the use of nuclear weapons to prevent defeat in Korea, and it had deployed nuclear-configured B-29 bombers to Britain and Guam. It had also taken under advisement the possibility of crossing the 38th parallel when the tide of battle should turn, and it had framed the issue in such a way that made an affirmative decision about crossing into North Korea more than likely. Third, it had expanded America's commitments in Europe as well as in Asia. Having committed itself to containing communism everywhere, the administration sought, nevertheless, to bolster the defenses of western Europe, the part of the world that still meant the most to the United States. To meet the expenses of its new commitments as well as the cost of the war itself, the administration had asked for—and would receive before the year was out—almost a quadrupling of funding for defense purposes much along the lines set down by NSC–68. Finally, it had dealt with certain issues of a constitutional nature that also had long-term political implications. In all these respects the administration had acted out of a sense of urgency complicated by a domestic climate of crisis and conspiracy.

Notes

1. James F. Schnabel, *Policy and Direction: The First Year* (Washington, DC, 1972), 81–114; Edgar O'Ballance, *Korea: 1950–1953* (London, 1969), 36–40.
2. Roger Dingman, "Atomic Diplomacy During the Korean War," *International Security*, 13 (Winter, 1988–89), 50–60.
3. *Ibid.*, 60–64.
4. Richard Whelan, *Drawing the Line: The Korean War, 1950–1953* (Boston, 1970), 173–178; Schnabel, *Policy and Direction,* 81–114; O'Ballance, *Korea,* 36–40.
5. O'Ballance, *Korea,* 40–44; David Rees, *Korea: The Limited War* (New York, 1964), 41–54; Max Hastings, *The Korean War* (New York, 1987), 76–98; *New Republic,* 123 (July 24, 1950), 11–13.
6. Thomas C. Reeves, *The Life and Times of Joe McCarthy* (New York, 1982), 305–314 and 328–329.
7. *Time,* 56 (July 31, 1950), 13.
8. *New Republic,* 123 (July 17, 1950), 8; Reeves, *The Life and Times of Joe McCarthy,* 311 and 329–330; Robert C. Griffith, *The Politics of Fear* (Lexington, KY, 1970), 117–122.
9. *Commonweal,* 52 (July 21, 1950), 355–356; *Nation,* 171 (September 12, 1950), 199–200; *New Republic,* 123 (August 28, 1950), 5; *ibid.* (September 11, 1950), 7; David R. Kepley, *The Collapse of the Middle Way: Senate Republicans and the Bipartisan Foreign Policy, 1948–1952* (Westport, CT, 1988), 92–96.
10. Walter LaFeber, *America, Russia, and the Cold War* (6th edition, New York, 1993), 101–127.

11. *Nation*, 171 (August 26, 1950), 181.

12. Clement Attlee, *Twilight of Empire: Memoirs of Prime Minister Clement Attlee* (New York, 1962), 230–231; *FR*, 1950, VII, 327–328, 331–332, 337–379, 340–343, 355–360, and 365–367; Dean Acheson, *Present at the Creation: My Years at the State Department* (New York, 1969), 418–420.

13. Acheson, *Present at the Creation*, 418–420; *FR*, 1950, VII, 312–313, 315–316, 327–328, 347–351, 359–360, 395–399, and 426–427; Acheson to American Embassy, London, July 10, 1950, Box 4262, Records of the Department of State, RG 59, 795.00/7–1050; William Whitney Stueck, Jr., *The Road to Confrontation: American Policy Toward China and Korea, 1947–1950* (Chapel Hill, NC, 1981), 198–201.

14. Stueck, Jr., *The Road to Confrontation*, 200–202.

15. Daily Opinion Summary, Department of State, July 21, 1950, Box 71, George M. Elsey Papers, Harry S. Truman Library (Independence, Missouri); *Nation*, 171 (July 22, 1950), 72–73.

16. *New Republic*, 122 (August 21, 1950), 3; *Time*, 56 (September 18, 1950), 30.

17. *FR*, 1950, VII, 272, 386–387, and 393; Rosemary Foot, *The Wrong War: American Policy and the Dimensions of the Korean Conflict, 1950–1953* (Ithaca, NY, 1985), 71; Kenneth R. Mauck, "The Formation of American Foreign Policy in Korea, 1945–1953" (unpublished Ph.D. dissertation, University of Oklahoma, 1978), 214–225; Charles E. Bohlen, *Witness to History* (New York, 1973), 292–294.

18. *FR*, 1950, VII, 346, 393–395, 449–454, 458–461, 483–485, and 502–510; Whelan, *Drawing the Line*, 192–199.

19. *Ibid.*, 393–395, 449–454, and 458–461; Stueck, *Road to Confrontation*, 203–204.

20. *FR*, 1950, VII, 712–721.

21. *New Republic*, 123 (August 7, 1950), 14–16.

22. *Commonweal*, 52 (July 28, 1950), 380–381; *ibid.*, (August 4, 1950), 410–411; Robert McGeehan, *The German Rearmament Question: American Diplomacy and European Defense After World War II* (Urbana, IL, 1971), 4–20; Lawrence S. Kaplan, *The United States and NATO: The Formative Years* (Lexington, KY, 1984), 8–9; Lawrence S. Kaplan, "The Korean War and U.S. Foreign Relations: The Case of NATO," in Francis H. Heller (ed.), *The Korean War: A 25-Year Perspective* (Lawrence, KS, 1977), 46–52; Walter LaFeber, "NATO and the Korean War: A Context," *Diplomatic History*, 13 (Fall, 1989), 461–477.

23. *Commonweal*, 52 (July 28, 1950), 380–381; Gaddis Smith, *Dean Acheson* (New York, 1972), 25–51 and 59–78.

24. Smith, *Dean Acheson*, 25–51 and 59–78; Daniel Yergin, *Shattered Peace: The Origins of the Cold War* (New York, 1990), 276–279.

25. Acheson, *Present at the Creation*, 435–437; Harry S. Truman, *Years of Trial and Hope: Memoirs* (New York, 1965), 290–292; McGeehan, *The German*

Rearmament Question, 25–39; Kaplan, "The Korean War and U.S. Foreign Relations," 51–53.

26. Kaplan, "The Korean War and U.S. Foreign Relations," 53–54.

27. Acheson, *Present at the Creation,* 437–440; Truman, *Years of Trial and Hope,* 291–292; McGeehan, *The German Rearmanent Question,* 49–93.

28. Kaplan, "The Korean War and U.S. Foreign Relations," 56–60; Stephen E. Ambrose, *Eisenhower: Soldier, General of the Army, President-Elect* (New York, 1983), 495–497.

29. Acheson, *Present at the Creation,* 414–415; "Special Message to the Congress Reporting on the Situation in Korea," July 19, 1950, *Public Papers of the Presidents: Harry S. Truman,* 1950 (Washington, DC, 1965), 527–537.

30. Chester J. Pach, Jr., *Arming the Free World: The Origins of the United States Military Assistance Program* (Chapel Hill, NC, 1991), 231; "The Defense Production Act of 1950," *Senate Reports,* 81st Congress, 2d Session (report no. 2250), 1–8, 11–12, and 52–53; "Defense Production Act of 1950," *House Reports,* 81st Congress, 2d Session (report no. 2759), 1–4, 13, 22–23.

31. "Unsigned Memorandum" [June 30, 1950?], Box 71, Elsey Papers; Kepley, *The Collapse of the Middle Way,* 89–90; Arthur M. Schlesinger, Jr., *The Imperial Presidency* (Boston, 1970), 130–135; Acheson, *Present at the Creation,* 410 and 413.

32. Robert J. Donovan, *Tumultuous Years: The Presidency of Harry Truman, 1949–53* (New York, 1982), 219–224; Kepley, *The Collapse of the Middle Way,* 90.

33. Acheson, *Present at the Creation,* 414–415.

34. D. Clayton James, *Refighting the Last War: Command and Crisis in Korea, 1950–1953,* (New York, 1993), 29–40; Ambrose, *Eisenhower: Soldier, General of the Army, President-Elect,* 93–94.

35. Michael Schaller, "Douglas MacArthur: The China Issue, Policy Conflict, and the Korean War," in Kim Chull Baum and James I. Matray (eds.), *Korea and the Cold War: Division, Destruction, and Disarmament* (Claremont, CA, 1993), 177–179; John W. Spanier, *The Truman-MacArthur Controversy and Korean War* (Cambridge, MA, 1959), 67–71; Hastings, *The Korean War,* 65–67.

36. Spanier, *The Truman-MacArthur Controversy,* 72–73.

37. Quoted in *ibid.,* 74.

38. "Memorandum for the Files," August 26, 1950, Box 62, Elsey Papers; Truman, *Years of Trial and Hope, 1946–1952,* 405–406; "From the President Personal for General MacArthur," Box 15, Selected Records Relating to the Korean War, Harry S. Truman Library (Independence, Missouri).

CHAPTER THREE

The UN Offensive and Chinese Intervention

On September 15, 1950, UN forces conducted a successful amphibious landing at Inchon, about twenty miles from Seoul and about 180 miles behind the North Korean lines at the Pusan perimeter. The next day the Eighth Army began a cautious offensive against the perimeter. A day later UN forces recaptured the Kimpo Airfield outside of Seoul. By September 19, enemy forces at Pusan had begun to collapse, and by September 28, Seoul was recaptured and UN forces were in full pursuit of North Korean armies fleeing behind the 38th parallel. Immediately the Truman administration was faced with the crucial decision of whether to move beyond the 38th parallel and to seek to reunite Korea by military forces. Weighing the alternatives, the administration decided that so long as there was no evidence of a major Soviet or Chinese intervention in the war, the UN forces (which were composed largely of American and ROK troops) should pursue the North Koreans beyond the 38th parallel. So began the period of the UN offensive, which by October led General MacArthur to predict that American troops would be home by Christmas, but which ultimately resulted in the intervention by the Chinese Communists on a massive scale.

General MacArthur had conceived of an amphibious operation against the enemy during the first week of battle, even before the first clash of American and North Korean troops. Since his first counteroffensive against the Japanese in New Guinea in 1943, he had specialized in the amphibious end run. He believed an attack against the enemy's rear on Korea's west coast would cut North Korea's supply lines and means of communication and open the way for a pincer operation, with UN forces striking the North Koreans along both their front and their rear. Although he considered several landing sites, he settled on Inchon as the best place to strike.[1]

Most of the military's high command disagreed with Mac-Arthur, believing, in fact, that he could not have selected a worse place for an amphibious operation. The tides at Inchon were the second highest in the world, averaging twenty-nine feet between low and high tides. The tides also moved rapidly, and a boat could become mired in the mud in a matter of only a few minutes. Moreover, Inchon was protected from the ocean by a high seawall, and invading troops would come ashore into a city with a population of 250,000 where each building could be used as a bunker by enemy troops.[2]

MacArthur responded to his critics by emphasizing the element of surprise, which would come about precisely because of the unlikelihood of an invasion against Inchon. On July 23 the general cabled Washington: "Operation planned mid-September is amphibious landing of a two-division corps in rear of enemy forces in conjunction with attack from south by Eighth Army. I am firmly convinced that early and strong effort behind his front will sever his main line of communication and enable us to deliver a crushing blow."[3]

The Joint Chiefs of Staff (JCS) hesitated, and toward the end of August General J. Lawton Collins, Army chief of staff, and Admiral Forrest Sherman, chief of naval operations, visited Tokyo, where they tried to dissuade MacArthur from his plan. Sherman and Collins proposed that instead of attacking Inchon, MacArthur aim for the west coast port of Kunsan, which was much farther south and presented few of Inchon's physical obstacles. Again stressing the element of surprise in his plan, MacArthur replied that an attack on Kunsan would be largely ineffective and indecisive. It would not envelop the enemy or destroy his supply lines or distribution center.[4]

MacArthur persuaded the Joint Chiefs on August 29 to approve his planned attack at Inchon. But this did not settle the matter entirely, for as the day planned for the invasion (September 15) drew closer, the Joint Chiefs of Staff began to have second thoughts and sent a message to MacArthur asking him again to evaluate the feasibility and chances of success of the projected operation. There was no question in his mind on either score, MacArthur wrote back.

SEPTEMBER TO NOVEMBER, 1950

U.S.S.R.

Vladivostok

C H I N A

(MANCHURIA)

– – – U.N. advances
Controlled by U.N.
Controlled by Communists

Tumen R.

Yalu R.

Chosan

Hyesanjin

Sinuiju

Pyongyang ★

November 24, 1950

Chongjin

October 26, 1950

Iwon

Hungnam

Wonsan

N O R T H
K O R E A

Tongchon

October 7, 1950

SEA OF
JAPAN

38th parallel

Ongjin

Inchon

Chunchon

Seoul

S O U T H
K O R E A

September 26, 1950

YELLOW
SEA

Inchon landing
Sept 15, 1950

Taejon

Pohang

Kunsan

Mokpo

Sunchon

Pusan

September 26, 1950

JAPAN

0   300

Miles

Canceling the Inchon landing would "commit us to a war of indefinite duration, of gradual attrition and doubtful results." Reluctant to challenge a field commander so vigorous in defense of his strategy and so widely esteemed in political and military circles, the Joint Chiefs gave their final consent to the Inchon invasion after obtaining President Truman's approval for the landing.[5]

As previously planned, the attack began early in the morning of September 15 when American Marines landed on the island of Wolmi, which protected Inchon Harbor. Meeting little resistance, they secured the island in about two hours, with only one man killed. They remained on the island while the tide ebbed and flowed, but in the late afternoon UN forces were able to strike at Inchon itself. The operation was as successful as MacArthur had predicted. The North Koreans were overextended and stretched thin. There were only about 2,000 North Korean troops in the Inchon area to defend against a combined UN force of 70,000 personnel, and while they offered some resistance, they were, for the most part, easily routed.

Although there was considerable mopping up to be done, by midnight Inchon had been taken. The next morning X Corps, consisting of the First Marine Division and the Army's Seventh Infantry Division and commanded by Major General Edward M. Almond, headed east toward Kimpo Airfield and Seoul. Although the troops met stiff resistance, they took Seoul by September 28, and the next day Syngman Rhee moved his government back to the capital city. By this time also, the Eighth Army under the command of General Walton H. Walker had broken through the Pusan perimeter and linked up with elements of X Corps advancing from the northwest. North Korean resistance had collapsed, and North Korean forces were in total disarray.[6]

The rapid and overwhelming success of UN forces following the invasion made MacArthur into even more of a national hero than before and ensured his lasting military fame. Admiral William F. Halsey telegraphed the UN commander to say, "The Inchon landing is the most masterly and audacious strategic stroke in all history." The successful landing also boosted morale at home, colored political discourse, and led opinion makers to speculate on the course the administration should follow in the coming weeks and months.[7]

Of particular note was the fact that the UN offensive took place just about the same time that Truman fired Defense Secretary Louis Johnson, who had brought relations between the Pentagon and State Department to their lowest ebb and was known to support Chiang Kai-shek and his Nationalist forces in the civil war in China. Truman named George Marshall to replace Johnson. Truman's appointment of the former secretary of state and Army chief of staff outraged the China lobby, which was sharply critical of the administration for not providing more aid to Chiang. As Truman's representative to China from 1945 to 1947 and then as secretary of state from 1947 to 1949, Marshall was considered one of the architects of the policy that had led to the loss of China to the Communists. Senator William Jenner even attacked Marshall personally, suggesting that he was "eager to play the role of a front man, for traitors." Senator Robert Taft added that Marshall's appointment was a "reaffirmation of the tragic policy of the administration in encouraging Chinese communism which brought on the Korean war."[8]

Nevertheless, Marshall's appointment was generally a popular one both in Washington and in most west European capitals. The new secretary of defense was widely respected for his judiciousness, broad-mindedness, and reasonableness. This was particularly important to those concerned by the loose talk of a preemptive nuclear strike against the Soviet Union. Also, Marshall was expected to work closely with Acheson in formulating and carrying out defense policy, and his appointment was seen by many as indicating American sensitivity both to European interests and to the rising tide of nationalism in Asia. On September 20 the Senate approved Marshall's nomination by a vote of 57 to 11.[9]

By this time the national mood had already begun to change from one of despair and even desperation to one of optimism. "With the Marines just outside Seoul and General Marshall already in the Pentagon," political columnist Richard Rovere reported from Washington, "many of the dark anticipations of a month ago are giving way to something approaching hope, and even confidence, here." Already, too, a national debate over the future conduct and direction of American foreign policy had begun that would continue well into October. On one level, previous demands were renewed for the resignation of Secretary of State Acheson, who was held responsible for the fall of China to the Communists because of his neglect of Asia and his emphasis on Europe.[10]

On another level, Washington observers considered the problem of what policy to follow in Korea (and Asia) after the North Koreans had been driven back above the 38th parallel. The most immediate question was whether to carry the war into North Korea in order to roll back Communist expansion and bring about Korean unification. Although there was a variety of opinions on these issues, the majority sentiment was to expand the war by crossing into

North Korea. Some concern was expressed that the Soviet Union or China might intervene if UN forces moved above the 38th parallel, but *Life* expressed the general sentiment of most journalists when it commented that "the danger of Chinese or Soviet intervention if the North Korean Communists are pressed close to the Manchurian border is, in our curbstone opinion, negligible."[11]

The Joint Chiefs of Staff, who likewise felt the chances of Soviet or Chinese intervention were small, called the 38th parallel "a geographical artificiality violating the natural integrity of a singularly homogenous nation" and "the eastern outpost of the iron curtain." Crossing the 38th parallel would provide "the US and the free world with first opportunity to displace part of the Soviet orbit . . . short of all-out war . . . disturb the 'strategic complex' which the Soviets were building in the Far East, and turn "a free and strong Korea [into] an outlet for Manchuria's resource." In Congress Republicans made it clear that they would regard a decision *not* to carry the war above the 38th parallel as an act of appeasement. Representative Hugh D. Scott, Jr., of Pennsylvania went so far as to accuse the State Department of planning "to subvert our military victory by calling a halt at the 38th parallel."[12]

It is hard to imagine that these winds of war did not weigh heavily on the White House's decision to expand the war into North Korea, particularly with congressional elections just about six weeks away. By this time, though, President Truman had already decided to allow MacArthur's forces to cross into North Korea. On September 27 Marshall presented him with a draft directive for MacArthur prepared by the Joint Chiefs of Staff and based on NSC–81/1. Agreed to by both the defense secretary and Secretary of State Acheson, the directive instructed MacArthur to move beyond the 38th parallel if necessary to destroy North Korean armed forces, provided that there was no intervention or threat of intervention by major Soviet or Chinese forces. As a matter of policy, no non-Korean ground forces were to be used in the northeast provinces of Korea bordering the Soviet Union or in the area along the Manchurian border. In case of Soviet military intervention MacArthur was to assume the defense, report to Washington, and make no move to aggravate the situation. In case of Chinese intervention MacArthur was to continue military action as long as it offered a reasonable chance of successful resistance.[13]

Truman approved the directive to MacArthur on the same day he received it. Two days later Marshall sent the UN commander a personal "eyes-only" message telling him that he should "feel unhampered tactically and strategically to proceed north of the 38th Parallel." On October 7 the UN General Assembly gave its consent to this policy. In effect, the purpose of the war had been fundamentally altered. Hitherto the war aim had been to repel aggression. Now it was to produce a unified Korea that was also clearly intended to be non-Communist.[14]

The administration continued to be concerned, however, about Soviet and Chinese intentions should the United States cross the 38th parallel. On this issue intelligence reports were constantly changing. For example, on September 20 the American ambassador to India, Loy Henderson, reported that a conversation had taken place between the Indian ambassador to Beijing, M. Panikkar, and the Chinese foreign minister, Zhou Enlai, the gist of which was that China had no intention of entering the Korean conflict short of a world war. On October 2, however, the Chinese warned the United States through Pannikar that they would not permit the American forces to cross the 38th parallel without taking some retaliatory measures (they said nothing about the Republic of Korea forces crossing the parallel).[15]

Most recent scholarship indicates that the People's Republic of China had pursued a cautious policy following the outbreak of hostilities in Korea in June 1950 and, as late as October, was still extremely reluctant to enter the war. Even after the United States sent 30,000 troops to Korea in July, Chinese leaders regarded as unlikely the possibility that the United States might widen the war by threatening its interests in Northeast China. As a precaution against an American attack and as a warning to Washington of the risks involved in a war with China, the Beijing government transferred 90,000 of its best troops to the region. But it believed that the United States lacked the military strength to counter the Soviet Union's preponderant military power in Europe, much less to engage in a war with China. It also placed great faith in the deterrent effect of the Sino-Soviet Treaty that it had signed with Moscow in February 1950.

General MacArthur's two-day visit to Formosa at the end of July and the buildup of UN forces over the summer caused Chinese

NOVEMBER, 1950 TO JANUARY, 1951

U.S.S.R.
Vladivostok

C H I N A
(MANCHURIA)

Tumen R.

Chongjin

Chinese Intervention
November, 1950

Hyesanjin

Yalu R.   Chosan

Iwon

Sinuiju   N O R T H
K O R E A   Hungnam

SEA OF
JAPAN

Pyongyang ★   Wonsan

U.N. evacuations
Dec. 5-15, 1950

Tongchon

38th parallel

Ongjin   Jan 24,
1951

Seoul ★

⬚ Controlled by U.N.
— Communist advances
⬚ Controlled by
  Communists

S O U T H
Taejon K O R E A

YELLOW   Kunsan   Pohang

SEA

Mokpo   Sunchon   Pusan

JAPAN

0   300
Miles

leaders to reassess the situation in Korea. Even before the Inchon invasion, they began to fear that the United States might seek to unify the Korean peninsula under UN auspices, something totally unacceptable to them. By August, they had begun to prepare for military intervention; on August 18, Chinese commanders were ordered to complete their preparations by September 30. The success of the Inchon invasion in September followed by the advance of UN forces toward the 38th parallel made the situation seem even more perilous. Furthermore, China came under considerable pressure from Moscow and from Kim Il-sung to come to North Korea's aid.

Nevertheless, Chinese leaders remained torn over the sacrifices China would have to make and the chances of victory in a war with the United States. There is even some evidence that Chairman Mao, who finally decided in October—after UN forces had crossed into North Korea—that war with the United States was inevitable and that China had to intervene in Korea regardless of the risks and costs involved, was reluctant to enter the conflict. He did so mainly because he concluded that China could not allow a UN presence along its border with Korea that could turn into an invasion of Manchuria, especially since the presence of the U.S. Seventh Fleet in the Formosa Straits and the visit of General MacArthur to Formosa the previous July suggested an alliance between Washington and Chiang Kai-shek's government on Formosa aimed at its destruction.[16]

Viewed in this context, Panikkar's warning to the United States about the dangers of crossing into North Korea represented a desperate effort on China's part to avoid a military commitment in Korea that it did not want and was extremely reluctant to undertake and over whose outcome there was divided counsel and much uncertainty. Unfortunately for the United States, neither this warning nor others received by the administration kept it from giving MacArthur the go-ahead to advance beyond the 38th parallel. White House officials placed little faith in the credibility of Ambassador Panikkar, whom President Truman regarded as little more than an agent of Chinese propaganda. Even if Pannikar's information could be trusted, however, the President believed that China's warning was probably only "a bald attempt to blackmail the United Nations," which was considering the resolution authorizing UN forces to cross the 38th parallel, by threatening to send troops into Korea should that happen.[17]

More important, the administration shared a curiously bifurcated image of China, which, on the one hand, held the Beijing government as little more than an agent provocateur of Moscow and, on the other, as an independent regime pursuing its own interests quite apart from those of the Soviet Union. Coexisting with this second image of the People's Republic of China was the conviction that Beijing's motivation was more nationalist than Communist; that the negotiations over the 1950 Sino-Soviet Treaty had revealed sharp differences between Beijing and Moscow, especially over the continuing Soviet presence in Manchuria; and that the traditional friendship between the United States and China could be resumed once the affair in Korea was settled. This led the White House and State Department officials to the additional assumption that if the United States made clear to China's leaders that America harbored no ill will or aggressive designs against them, China would not intervene should UN forces advance above the 38th parallel.[18]

Despite the continuing reports it received about Soviet or Chinese intervention, therefore, the administration concluded that neither Moscow nor Beijing was likely to send troops into Korea, that the time for intervention would have come much earlier (well before UN forces reached the 38th parallel), and that Moscow and Beijing were anxious to avoid hostilities with the United States. Accordingly, on the day after the United Nations passed its resolution authorizing UN forces to pursue the enemy beyond the 38th parallel, the first American troops began crossing the parallel. (South Korean forces had already crossed the line on October 1, and General MacArthur had called on North Korea to surrender to UN forces.) The UN troops met relatively little resistance from the North Koreans, and on October 10 South Korean forces captured Wonsan on North Korea's east coast before MacArthur could carry out a plan he had devised for another amphibious landing at the port. Nine days later the capital of Pyongyang fell to the UN troops. By this time the first Chinese troops—the People's Volunteers—had secretly entered Korea from Manchuria.[19]

The advance into North Korea by American troops represented a political decision to bring about the unification of Korea through military means. As such it was based on faulty intelligence to the effect that neither the Soviet Union nor Communist China would intervene militarily to save North Korea. Even after UN forces crossed into North Korea, the Central Intelligence Agency (CIA) determined that Chinese or Soviet intervention was highly unlikely.[20]

But if there remained any doubts on this score, the Wake Island conference of October 15 between President Truman and General MacArthur served to dispel them. Although Truman later stated in his memoirs that he made his 18,000-mile trip to this coral waystation half-way between San Francisco and Japan because he had never met MacArthur and thought that they should get better acquainted, he seems to have gone to Wake Island mainly for political reasons. In an election year when the Republicans were blaming the Korean war on the White House's weak and vacillating Far East policy, Truman wanted to regain the political spotlight by meeting with America's foremost national hero, even though he considered him disloyal and referred to him in his diary as "Mr. Prima Donna." He also wanted to make clear to MacArthur that Korea and the entire Far East were only part of America's larger global responsibilities and that statements like the general's August message to the Veterans of Foreign Wars were inappropriate because they falsely implied that Communist China could be overcome by force.[21]

At the Wake Island meeting, MacArthur told the president that formal resistance in Korea would end by Thanksgiving, that he hoped to withdraw the Eighth Army by Christmas, and that there was little need to fear Soviet or Communist Chinese intervention. When Assistant Secretary of State Dean Rusk, who accompanied Truman on his trip, mentioned to the general that the Chinese had threatened privately to enter the Korean war if UN forces crossed the 38th parallel, MacArthur replied that he did not understand fully why the Chinese made such a statement and that they were probably greatly embarrassed by the predicament in which they now found themselves.[22]

Both Truman and MacArthur left the Wake Island conference confident they had made their respective positions clear to the other. Truman was satisfied that he had established a more cordial and harmonious relation with his field commander. MacArthur even apologized for his Veterans of Foreign Wars message of August, and as Truman stated on his return to the United States, he had "never had a more satisfactory conference" since becoming President. For his part, MacArthur returned to Tokyo with a sense of greater freedom than when he had left. The general had good reason to feel this way. MacArthur's personal sense of infallibility and invincibility was contagious, and he left the President and members of Truman's party fully expecting an early end to the Korean war.[23]

Illusion prevailed over reality. As Hanson Baldwin of the *New York Times* reported, Chinese troops were already beginning to mass along the Chinese frontier. Baldwin estimated that there were about 250,000 troops near the Korean frontier and 200,000 more elsewhere in Manchuria. Yet until the time the Chinese Communists entered the fighting in Korea and the first Chinese prisoners were taken on October 26, the United States lacked a meaningful contingency plan with respect to Chinese intervention. The presumption at the Pentagon was that the United States could deal militarily with any Chinese military intervention and that if China entered the war, the United States would be justified in attacking Chinese territory. But the specifics of an American response were never fully spelled out. The American position was contained in a vaguely worded October 9 directive from the Joint Chiefs of Staff to MacArthur, which was intended as an amplification of their earlier September 27 directive. "Hereafter in the event of the open or covert employment anywhere in Korea of major Chinese units, without prior announcement," the Joint Chiefs of Staff instructed MacArthur, "you should continue the action as long as, in your judgment, action by forces now under your control offers a reasonable chance of success." MacArthur was also to "obtain authorization from Washington prior to taking any military action against objectives in Chinese territory."[24]

The Truman administration continued to believe that as long as it made clear to Beijing that the United States harbored no offensive intentions against China, the Chinese would not intervene militarily in Korea. For this purpose the administration kept up a major diplomatic effort at the United Nations and elsewhere even after passage of the October 7 resolution authorizing UN troops to enter North Korea. Despite new warnings from Beijing that it would not tolerate an American advance toward its borders, the administration held firm to this position. While not dismissing these threats out of hand, Washington remained convinced that the most favorable moment for Chinese (and Soviet) intervention had passed and that if intervention did occur, it would be limited in scope and be nominally covert instead of overt.[25]

Indeed, in the United States the overwhelming assumption through at least October was that the war in Korea would be over in a matter of weeks or, at the most, a few months. On this basis Democratic political fortunes improved markedly. Although opponents of the administration remained defiant and the administration's principal antagonist, Senator Joseph McCarthy of Wisconsin, received more invitations to speak than all the other senators combined, political analysts reported that Democratic chances in the upcoming congressional elections remained in the upswing.[26]

Now that victory in Korea seemed ensured, Americans even tried to draw larger lessons from the war. For a number of these persons, the most important lesson to be learned from Korea was the need to be more responsive to the economic requirements and political wishes of the world's underdeveloped areas, particularly in Asia. A few commentators even made the point that since the Korean war had been fought under the aegis of the United Nations, the manner in which the United Nations responded to the reconstruction needs of Korea would determine its future effectiveness among Third World nations. Yet Americans were also reminded that Korea was not the only trouble spot in Asia and that in the future the United States would need to be extremely leery of supporting undemocratic regimes or propping up colonial enterprises, such as the Bao Dai government in Vietnam. So, too, the Rhee government in South Korea came under strong criticism for being repressive, unpopular, and unrepresentative of all Koreans. A fundamental point was even raised over whether Rhee's administration was to be tossed overboard as preparations were made to establish a government of national unification.[27]

By the beginning of November, all intelligence estimates agreed that Chinese forces had entered North Korea. But there was still disagreement over the size and purpose of the invasion, and as late as November 4, General MacArthur expressed his doubts to the Joint Chiefs that the Communists intended in any direct way to intervene militarily in Korea. Not until November 6 did a sense of the magnitude of the Chinese invasion begin to set in. By then, there could be no doubt along the front lines that the Chinese had crossed the Yalu River into North Korea in large numbers. In response, MacArthur ordered a bombing mission to take out a key bridge across the Yalu River from Sinuiju (Korea) to Antung (Manchuria).[28]

The Defense Department learned of MacArthur's orders only by chance and less than four hours before they were to be carried out. Deputy Secretary of Defense Robert Lovett informed Secretary of State Acheson and Assistant Secretary of State Dean Rusk of the planned operation. Acheson then telephoned President Truman in Kansas City, recommending that the mission be scrubbed until the reasons for it were more clearly known. The British informed Washington that they would withdraw their forces from the UNC if the United States pushed China into an all-out war. Soon thereafter the

Joint Chiefs of Staff, acting on the President's instructions, ordered MacArthur to postpone all bombing of targets within five miles of the Manchurian border.[29]

MacArthur was irate. In contrast to his report just two days earlier, he now wrote the Pentagon that materiel and personnel were "pouring across all bridges over the Yalu from Manchuria." The only way to stop this reinforcement of the enemy, he said, was "the destruction of these bridges and the subjection of all installations in the north area supporting the enemy" to American bombing. "Under the gravest protest that I can make," he told the Joint Chiefs, "I am suspending this strike and carrying out your instructions. . . . I trust that the matter be immediately brought to the attention of the President as I believe your instructions may well result in a calamity of major proportion for which I cannot accept the responsibility without his personal and dir[ect] understanding of the sit[uation]."[30]

In urging presidential approval of the Joint Chiefs' orders, MacArthur's response bordered on insubordination. Nevertheless, the Joint Chiefs of Staff felt they had little choice except to defer to their commander in the Far East. To a considerable measure they were responsible for their own dilemma. In the past, when the general had challenged accepted administration policy, they had voiced no objection. Only two weeks earlier, MacArthur had ordered troops to advance in some places to within thirty-five miles of the Manchurian border, ignoring Washington's acknowledged policy of using South Korean troops to pacify the northern part of Korea. But the Joint Chiefs made no protest. On October 24 the general ordered American troops to march to the Yalu River. Once again the Joint Chiefs failed to countermand the order.[31]

The fact was that the situation in Korea, as seen from Washington, was thoroughly confused. First there had been the standing instructions to MacArthur since the end of September to feel unhampered in proceeding north of the 38th parallel. Second was the broad latitude that the general took in carrying out those instructions. Third was the need to redefine policy now that the Chinese Communists had entered the war. On this matter the administration was indecisive and vacillating. "We all agree that if the Chinese Communists come into Korea, we get out," General Omar Bradley, the chairman of the Joint Chiefs of Staff, had said on October 23 during a meeting of the American and British chiefs of staff. But matters were not as simple as that. To cede Korea to the Communists was to undermine the United States' whole position in the Far East. In this respect the administration's analysis of Chinese foreign policy abruptly changed; instead of nationalism being the motivating factor behind China's policy, now it was communism, and the Chinese were once more seen as puppets of Moscow. Under these circumstances it behooved the Joint Chiefs of Staff (and the rest of the administration) to give MacArthur the necessary authority to beat back the Chinese and to bring the Korean war to a successful conclusion.[32]

Consequently, on November 6, the same day that they received MacArthur's blistering communication, the Joint Chiefs of Staff reversed themselves and authorized MacArthur to hit targets at Sinuiju and the Korean side of the Yalu bridges, "provided that at the time of the receipt of this message you still find such action essential to [the safety] of your forces." However, the general was to take extreme care to avoid violating Manchurian territory and airspace and to report promptly hostile action from Manchuria.[33]

By this time news of the Chinese invasion had filtered out from the White House, the State Department, and the Pentagon. Chinese forces had already penetrated up to seventy miles south of the Yalu River, and there were reports of four Republic of Korea armies being "chopped up piecemeal" by the Red armies. Almost certainly news of the Chinese invasion hurt Democrats at the polls on November 7. Throughout the campaign, charges had been pinned against the administration of "communism, confusion, and corruption." The latest news from Korea seemed to confirm at least the first two of those charges and to undermine the optimism about the war apparent just a few days earlier. As a result of the elections, the Republicans picked up four Senate and twenty-eight House seats.[34]

Almost as abruptly as they had entered the war in Korea, however, the Chinese cut off their attack. There then followed a three-week lull in the fighting. In effect, the United States was given an opportunity to redefine its policy and strategy with respect to Korea. During this time, the administration did reconsider its directives to MacArthur. On November 8 the Joint Chiefs of Staff informed MacArthur that his objective of destroying North Korean armed forces might "have to be reexamined in the light of the Chinese intervention." What most troubled administration officials was the possibility that Chinese involvement in Korea was merely a prelude to a larger global war involving the Soviet Union, without whose encouragement, they believed, the Chinese would never have intervened.[35]

Nevertheless, nothing was done to limit MacArthur's advance to the Yalu River. "[I]t would be fatal," MacArthur told the Joint Chiefs in response to their November 8 message, "to weaken the fundamental and basic policy of the United States to destroy all resisting armed forces in Korea and bring that country into a unified and free nation." To give up any portion of North Korea to the aggression of the Chinese Communists, he added, "would be the greatest defeat of the free world in recent times." Faced with such a grim analysis of American options in Korea, the Joint Chiefs of Staff, along with other members of the National Security Council, reaffirmed on November 9 the discretionary power they had given to MacArthur in September and October. The CIA even concluded that while the commitment of Chinese Communist forces, with Soviet assistance, indicated that Moscow was willing to risk a general war in Korea, it "was not probable" that UN attacks south of the Yalu would alone trigger such action.[36]

Following the National Security Council meeting of November 9, the administration tried again to reassure China that it had no hostile aims against that country. In the United Nations the United States co-sponsored a Security Council resolution stating that it was "the policy of the United Nations to hold the Chinese frontier inviolate and fully to protect legitimate Chinese and Korean interests in the frontier zone." Less than a week later President Truman remarked that the United States had no designs on China's border or any desire to expand the war. But with the Chinese having apparently withdrawn from the war and with MacArthur's discretionary power reaffirmed, there was nothing to prevent the Far East commander from resuming his drive northward, which he did toward the end of the month.[37]

A sense of despair hung over policy makers in Washington and among America's European allies as MacArthur made plans to resume the offensive. Few if any within the administration wanted to expand the war into a global confrontation involving the Soviet Union as well as Communist China. They realized that the entry of Chinese troops into the fighting could change the whole complexion of the war, and there was growing uncertainty as to what the Beijing government (and Moscow) might do if UN forces should advance to the Yalu. Also, the war diverted attention from the difficult task of rebuilding Europe and preventing the spread of communism on that continent. Yet the war had become a test of wills between the Communist and non-Communist worlds. America's standing in the Far East and its commitment to democratic forces everywhere were on the line.[38]

In an effort to reassure America's allies and especially England, which was particularly anxious to bring about a quick diplomatic solution to the war, that it, too, wanted to contain the war and bring about an early end to hostilities, the administration rejected a proposal supported by the Joint Chiefs of Staff that would have allowed American planes to pursue enemy aircraft across the Manchurian border. A number of administration officials, including Secretary of State Acheson, also supported a British plan to create a buffer zone on each side of the Yalu River. But as already noted, the National Security Council, at its November 9 meeting, took no action on the proposal, merely restating the discretionary power it had already given MacArthur.[39]

The lull in the fighting, which continued until the last weeks in November, found the British still trying to gain American backing for the concept of a demilitarized zone between Manchuria and Korea.[40] But on November 24 MacArthur launched his "final offensive," which he promised would have American troops home by Christmas. The first two days of the offensive went well enough. The attack was planned so that the Eighth Army would strike on a broad front northward in the west and center, while in the east X Corps, which had been transported by ship from Inchon to Wonsan as part of MacArthur's plan for an amphibious invasion of North Korea's east coast, would move in a northwest direction to cut off the enemy's supply lines. Between the two forces lay the high mountainous spine that cut vertically across the Korean peninsula. This meant a gap of as much as fifty air miles between the Eighth Army and X Corps. But MacArthur believed sufficient communication could be maintained between the two forces so as not to jeopardize them, and because of the impenetrable mountains responsible for the gap, it never afforded the Chinese a significant tactical advantage.[41]

Almost without opposition the Eighth Army advanced up to eight miles in the far west, while elements of X Corps to the east advanced northward toward the Yalu River. But then the Chinese struck in force along both fronts. In what the military historian Roy E. Appleman has called "one of the worst defeats an American Army has ever suffered," the Chinese changed the complexion of the war almost overnight. The Second Infantry Division was cut to pieces, losing all its guns and most of its transport and suffering 80 percent casualties. The ROK II Corps also came under heavy fire in the area of Tokchon on the Taedong River. Efforts by Turkish and British forces to relieve the South Korean troops were blocked by repeated Chinese ambushes and concentrated Chinese fire. Moving at first at night but then during the daytime, attacking in overwhelming numbers, yelling and blowing bugles and loud whistles, the Chinese terrified the UN forces and inflicted heavy casualties even as they took enormous losses themselves. In the east, the 1st Marine Division was trapped at the Chosin Reservoir north of the town of Hagaru-ri. In the west, plans to hold the North Korean capital of Pyongyang were abandoned, and in what Appleman believes was one of the war's great mistakes, General Walton Walker, the commander of the Eighth Army, ordered a hasty retreat of his forces south of the 38th parallel instead of defending along the narrow waist of Korea that stretched roughly from Wonsan on the east to Pyongyang on the west.[42]

President Truman reacted to this sudden turn of events by convening a special meeting of the National Security Council at the White House on November 28. The session was as somber as any that one could recall. Secretary Acheson remarked that the Chinese attack had moved the United States very much closer to a general war. Everyone at the White House was troubled and angered by the fact that MacArthur had badly misjudged the capacity and willingness of China to invade Korea.[43] As a result of the meeting, the administration all but abandoned its objective of bringing about the political reunification of Korea through military means. Instead, the National Security Council agreed that the White House should not allow itself to be pulled into any war with China and that no new directive should be given to MacArthur in addition to the one of the previous September that he continue fighting the Chinese Communists as long as feasible. Maintaining that the Soviet Union had always been behind every move of aggression, Acheson argued that the United States had to realize that it faced the Russians around the world. America's great objective in Korea, he concluded, must be to hold an area, terminate the fighting, turn over some region to the

Republic of Korea, and get out so that it could go ahead with building up its own strength and that of Europe.[44]

Europe or Asia? This perennial question of Cold War diplomacy and American politics was thrashed out anew as Americans and Europeans sought to evaluate the short- and long-term consequences of the Chinese intervention and the subsequent UN military disaster. At home and abroad the collapse of MacArthur's offensive produced serious diplomatic and political problems. "There is no doubt that confidence in General Douglas MacArthur, even on Capitol Hill, has been shaken badly as a result of the events of the last few days," wrote James Reston of the *New York Times* on November 30. "Similarly, there is no doubt that the United States leadership in the Western world has been damaged by President Truman's acceptance of the bold MacArthur offensive."[45]

In the United States MacArthur was assailed mostly for the lack of good intelligence behind his Thanksgiving offensive, which was widely attributed to his reliance on his own intelligence organizations rather than on regular intelligence services, and for poor military planning. Several of his sharpest critics pointed to the gap between the Eighth Army and X Corps, which they erroneously claimed the Chinese had infiltrated. Others argued that the Chinese offensive might have been contained if MacArthur had concentrated his forces instead of spreading them thinly over a 350-mile front. They would have been on even stronger ground had they also criticized the UN commander for failing to establish a unified command over the two UN forces, which would have resulted in a more coordinated military effort; as it was, the two commands operated virtually independently of each other.[46]

In Europe MacArthur was regarded more as a symbol of what was wrong in American foreign policy. Europeans remained terribly afraid that the Korean war might balloon into a worldwide confrontation between East and West, most of which would be fought on their continent. They also nursed other grievances, mainly having to do with Washington's failure to consult them often enough.

The rumblings of discontent in Europe reached a crescendo on November 30, when President Truman raised the possibility of using nuclear weapons in Korea. The Joint Chiefs of Staff had been studying this very question since at least November 20, even before MacArthur's Thanksgiving offensive and the Chinese counteroffensive. On November 28, the Joint Chiefs asked the Joint Strategic Survey Committee for recommendations concerning the use of the atomic bomb against the Soviet Union should it intervene in Korea and against China since it already had intervened. On November 30, Far East Air Force Commander G.E. Stratemeyer warned the Strategic Air Command (SAC) "to be prepared to dispatch without delay medium bomb groups to the Far East." "This augmentation," he also said, "should include atomic capabilities."[47]

Although the Joint Chiefs had not reached any final decision on the employment of atomic weapons, at his regular press conference on November 30—the same day that Stratemeyer sent his warning to SAC—Truman stated that the United States would use every weapon at its disposal to meet the military situation in Korea. When a reporter asked the President whether that would include the atomic bomb, he responded, "That includes every weapon we have." When asked again whether he meant that there was active consideration about using the atomic bomb, Truman replied that there had "always been active consideration of its use." He even remarked that the military commander in the field would decide whether to employ nuclear weapons. Western Europe was shocked and outraged by the President's statement. Newspapers in Stockholm, Rome, and Vienna joined others in London and Paris in condemning it. England's Prime Minister Clement Attlee was virtually forced to go to Washington in protest, so great was the public reaction against the President's press conference.[48]

By the time that Attlee arrived in Washington, the administration felt it had to offer some plan for extricating UN forces from Korea without appearing to be run out of the country by the Communists. The possibility of UN troops being driven off the peninsula with a large loss of life was real. In Tokyo General MacArthur began preparations for a possible evacuation by sea of American troops in North Korea, while in Washington Secretary of State Acheson proposed to General Bradley the possibility of a cease-fire—probably along the 38th parallel—which could form the basis for negotiations to end the conflict. Otherwise Acheson feared the Korean conflict might escalate into a larger conflict with China, in which case he was afraid that many of America's allies would desert the United States and deal directly with the Soviet Union in a bid to end hostilities.[49]

In his talks with President Truman, conducted during the first two weeks in December, Attlee made the argument that the United

Nations' position in Korea was so weak and precarious that the United States had no choice but to negotiate with China. Attlee also conveyed to Truman Europe's feeling that MacArthur was "running the show" in Korea and that the other partnership countries were generally being ignored. The British even proposed some sort of committee to direct the war.[50]

As a result of these negotiations, the British prime minister was able to straighten out some of the misgivings that had developed between the United States and its European allies over Korea. But Attlee returned to London with far less than he had hoped to achieve. In the final communique of the summit conference, Truman stressed his hope that world conditions would never require the use of the atomic bomb, and he promised to keep the British leader informed at all times if developments warranted a change. Attlee was thus able to take back with him assurances from Truman that he did not anticipate using nuclear weapons in Korea. But this was not the partnership Attlee had sought. Furthermore, atomic diplomacy was discarded not only because of the adverse effect it had on America's allies but also because the Pentagon, having reviewed the issue of using nuclear weapons in Korea, concluded in December that they should only be used for defensive purposes rather than for deterrence or coercion; atomic weapons, they also pointed out, would have little tactical value against relatively small enemy units carrying most of their supplies on their backs. In other words, the United States still retained the option to use nuclear weapons without consulting its allies. Also, on the question of Washington's relations with Beijing, the Americans and British remained far apart; the United States would not bargain recognition, Formosa, or a seat at the United Nations for a cease-fire in Korea. As far as the administration was concerned, there could be no thought of appeasement, which would amount to rewarding aggression.[51]

Certainly this was the policy the United States pursued at the United Nations, where efforts were already under way to bring about a negotiated settlement to the war. The People's Republic of China (PRC) was represented at the United Nations for the first time, having been previously invited to send a delegation in order to discuss the Formosa question. Even under allied coaxing, the American delegation refused to budge from its position that an acceptable cease-fire would have to precede negotiations on any other Far Eastern question. For their part the Chinese insisted that their claim to Formosa and a seat at the United Nations had to be part of any cease-fire proposal, and after returning to Beijing, they declared on December 21 that all actions taken by the United Nations without Chinese participation were illegal.[52]

By this time, the 1st Marine Division had been able to break out of its trap at the Chosin Reservoir and to make it to the coast at Hungnam, where it was evacuated to Pusan. The story of these 10,000 Marines is both painful and heroic at the same time. Facing as many as 60,000 Chinese troops and enduring brutal winds fed by subzero temperatures in a wasteland of ice and snow during the harshest winter of the Korean war, they were able to fight their way relentlessly to safety. By the time the division made it to safety, more than 700 Marines had been killed and another 3,500 wounded. Almost everyone else suffered some form and degree of frostbite. General Oliver P. Smith, the divisional commander, reflected the valor of those who managed to escape from the Chinese grip when he remarked to his forces, "Retreat hell! We're only attacking in another direction." The military historian of the Korean war, Roy Appleman, has rightly described the Marine escape from the Chosin Reservoir as "one of the great military operations of United States history—many would say in world military history."[53]

By mid-December other UN forces had also made it to a defensive line approximating the 38th parallel, and the White House had made the decision to stay in Korea as long as possible. It also took steps to prepare for the fighting that lay ahead. Making full use of the Defense Production Act, the administration sought additional legislation to put the economy on a wartime footing. On December 15 Truman announced plans to increase defense production, to expand the armed forces, and to establish wage and price controls. On December 16, he declared a state of national emergency, for which he sought bipartisan support, and set up the Office of Defense Mobilization to direct and coordinate the government's mobilization effort.[54]

Even as the administration was lobbying Congress and appealing to the American people, however, it continued to debate the next steps it should pursue under the changed circumstances of the war. Ironically, the State Department now gave higher priority to continuing the fighting than did the Pentagon. Both the Department of State and the Department of Defense were in agreement as to a cease-fire if it could be worked out with the enemy. But in the interim the State Department was for continuing the war at least at its present level, whereas the Defense Department wanted to wind it down and perhaps withdraw entirely from Korea. State Department officials believed that American prestige in the world would suffer a severe blow if the United States was driven from Korea, whereas the Defense Department and Joint Chiefs of Staff were more concerned with saving enough troops from Korea to defend Japan. But even in the case of the State Department, there was now no contemplation of absolute victory; that had disappeared with the Chinese invasion a month earlier.[55]

In Japan, General MacArthur held a different view. He asked the Joint Chiefs of Staff for all four of the National Guard divisions now in the United States in order to reinforce his position in Japan. On December 22, the Joint Chiefs of Staff informed MacArthur that no additional divisions would be sent to the Far East until the administration had decided on future courses of action. Less than a week later Marshall approved a Joint Chiefs' memorandum for MacArthur along much the same lines except that, in order to satisfy the State Department, language was included to emphasize the great political advantage of resisting in Korea as long as possible and inflicting maximum damage upon the enemy. The decision to evacuate Korea, the Joint Chiefs stressed to MacArthur, "should not be based on political grounds; rather it should be based on our best military judgment as to whether or how long it is possible to maintain combat forces in Korea."[56]

One can thus understand MacArthur's chagrin at the confusion of military and political considerations that went into his operational orders in Korea. The State Department wanted a stronger military effort in Korea than did the Defense Department, and MacArthur was to maintain maximum military pressure, but no additional forces were to be assigned to him. He was not to win the war in any conventional sense, but neither was he to allow the enemy to claim victory in Korea. MacArthur's response was to ask for additional troops and to request that he be allowed to blockade China, to destroy China's industrial capacity to wage war, and to employ Chinese Nationalist troops in Korea and for diversionary action against the Chinese mainland.

At the Pentagon there was considerable support for approving the general's requests. Even General Bradley, the chairman of the Joint Chiefs of Staff, thought that some of the restrictions imposed on MacArthur should be lifted, and on January 9, 1951, the Joint Chiefs told MacArthur that the retaliatory measures he recommended would be "given serious consideration." But the Joint Chiefs then went on to inform MacArthur that most of his recommendations would not be adopted any time soon. For example, a blockade of the Chinese coast, if undertaken, would have to await a stabilization of the American position in Korea or an evacuation of Korea. Indeed, expansion of the war was conditioned on, and subordinate to, providing for the safety of UN forces and maintaining the support of America's allies. Instead of being given authority to carry out retaliatory measures against China, therefore, MacArthur was instructed once more to defend against the enemy on successive positions, "inflicting maximum damage subject to primary consideration of the safety of your troops and your basic mission of protecting Japan."[57]

An irate MacArthur considered his latest orders a "booby trap" that offered two contradictory alternatives—successful resistance at some point in Korea would be desirable, but Korea was not the place to fight a major war. Responding again to the Joint Chiefs of Staff, the general told them, in effect, that they could not have it both ways; that present policy as determined by the Joint Chiefs and approved by the President was not feasible. In his memoirs, Truman described himself as "deeply disturbed" by MacArthur's communication. Secretary of State Acheson was even more upset. "[N]othing further was needed," he later wrote, "to convince me that the General was incurably recalcitrant and basically disloyal to the purposes of his Commander-in-Chief."[58]

Yet MacArthur had not been given clear instructions. On the one hand, he was told that the world prestige of the United States and the United Nations was at stake in Korea. It was essential that he hold the line there as long as possible. On the other, he was told that it was necessary for America's security interests to preserve his troops for use in Japan and elsewhere. To complicate matters even more, Truman emphasized to the Joint Chiefs and members of his administration that he was "unwilling to abandon the South Koreans to be murdered."[59]

On January 12 the Joint Chiefs of Staff gave MacArthur new instructions approved by the President that were hardly an improvement over earlier orders except that they were accompanied by a series of actions that the UN Command might take against China should it be forced to withdraw from Korea. Although the list included three recommendations suggested by General MacArthur in his December 30 message, only one, removal of restrictions on Nationalist forces, was adopted without qualification. The others, a naval blockade and bombardment of Chinese territory, appeared only as contingent possibilities. It cannot be emphasized too strongly that these were proposals only, not directives. But it is not too difficult to understand how MacArthur, given his world view and sense of priorities, could interpret them as policy parameters within which he could still operate, even at this late date, to achieve a UN victory in Korea.[60]

Events of the previous two months, however, had changed the complexion of the war in a way that MacArthur could not understand. By the end of December and beginning of January the administration had firmly committed itself to a cease-fire and, for all practical purposes, had abandoned any thought of unifying Korea. Yet it was not the Chinese intervention alone that had led to this decision. The crosscurrents of public opinion and political pressures at home and abroad were also crucial. Indeed, as UN forces had retreated southward in December, Americans were divided over foreign policy in a way they had not been since Pearl Harbor.

Almost all segments of American public opinion were shocked and disheartened by the tide of battle as winter approached in Korea. For those who believed that President Truman and Secretary of State Acheson had courted disaster in Asia by their misdirected attention toward Europe, the retreat of UN forces toward the 38th parallel confirmed their worst fears. Opponents of General MacArthur were also accused of villifying him, and MacArthur's highly publicized views on the Communist threat were cited as gospel by those who would give him carte blanche to turn back the Red tide in Asia. *Life* even conducted a mock interview with the general to explain his views on Korea. "General MacArthur is not infallible—far from it," said *Life*. "But his estimate of the actual situation in Korea, and his attitude toward the Communist aggressors, are in healthy contrast to the sick and fearful atmosphere of London, Washington and Lake Success [temporary headquarters of the United Nations]." Such political pressure made it virtually impossible for the United States to be "internationalist" in Europe and "isolationist" in Asia.[61]

In fact, influential voices were being heard in the United States from those who would follow an isolationist policy in both Asia and Europe. The view that the United States should make itself strong at home, largely ignore Europe, and be prepared to stand alone against foreign threats was most clearly articulated at the end of December in a speech by former President Herbert Hoover in which he said that the United States should strive for hemispheric and economic self-sufficiency, turning the Western Hemisphere into the "Gibraltar of Civilization," protected only by a cordon of ocean bases in the Pacific—Formosa, the Philippines, and Japan—and perhaps by England in the Atlantic.[62]

Dismissed by some as the mutterings of a failed leader rapidly growing senile, Hoover's remarks were, nevertheless, widely disseminated and received enormous press coverage—some critical, most favorable. Commenting on the reponse to the speech, *Nation* referred to "a widespread revival of blind isolationism," while *Commonweal* pointed to a "new surge of isolationism." Contributing to this growing isolationism was the speculation, which many Americans shared with Europeans, that the world was closer to a global conflict than at any time since 1945.

Not since the first days of the Korean conflict, in fact, did so many Americans believe that World War III was imminent. Americans talked of being "A-bombed" and made civil defense preparations in case of war. Booklets were distributed on what to do if a nuclear attack took place. Bomb shelters were set up. Plans for evacuating city populations—and for feeding, clothing, and sheltering them—were started. Talk of "preventive war" was heard again, and sentiment grew for using nuclear weapons against the Communists. The national commanders of the American Legion, Veterans of Foreign Wars, Disabled American Veterans, and Amvets wrote President Truman a joint letter urging him to give General MacArthur full authority to bomb Chinese bases in Manchuria, and Republican Presidential aspirant Harold Stassen called on the United Nations to demand that the Chinese agree to a cease-fire in Korea and to "A-bomb" targets in China if they refused.[63]

All this discourse was part of what *Life* labeled a "great debate on foreign policy that tugged at the nation's mind and soul." Stemming from America's involvement in Korea, the issues involved had built gradually over the summer and fall and had been joined in the November elections. But the current round of debate stemmed from remarks made soon afterward by Senator Robert Taft of Ohio, who asked, "Is Europe our first line of defense? Is it defendable at all?" and called for a thorough review of the Truman foreign policy. Widespread dismay at the latest war news from Korea after the Chinese invasion, the harping criticisms by America's allies, particularly on the China question, and their procrastination in rearming caused many Americans to ask similar questions and make similar demands. As a result, by the time Hoover delivered his "Gibraltar" address, he was assured a receptive audience.[64]

A new dimension was added to this dialogue when an earlier issue involving the constitutional powers of the President over foreign policy was raised once more by Republican opponents of the administration. This time, however, the doubts expressed had to do not with the President's conduct of the war in Korea but with his authority to send American troops to Europe without congressional approval. On both constitutional and strategic grounds, Republicans in Congress, led by Senator Taft, challenged the White House on this issue and threatened to paralyze its conduct of foreign policy. A highly partisan politician who sought to make political capital out of the Red Scare, Taft honestly believed that China had been lost to the Communists by the stupidity and treasonable actions of the State Department. He also objected to the European orientation of Democrats on foreign policy, and he was convinced that North Korea's invasion of South Korea could have been prevented had the United States not withdrawn its troops in 1949 and given ample warning that it would repulse any invasion from above the 38th parallel.[65]

No less important than these other issues to Taft, however, was his commitment to defending what he considered the constitutional prerogatives of Congress in formulating and executing foreign policy. Although he had supported Truman's original decision to send American military forces to South Korea after the North Korean invasion, he also had serious reservations about the President's authority to do so without first consulting Congress. As the war continued, Taft became increasingly protective of Congress's place in formulating foreign policy. On January 5 he took the Senate floor to deliver a 10,000-word harangue against the administration in which he charged that Truman had "simply usurped authority—in violation of the laws and the Constitution—when he sent troops to Korea to carry out the resolution of the United Nation, in an undeclared war."[66]

In making his remarks, the Ohio senator was actually more concerned about the administration's plan to send additional American forces to Europe than he was about the war in Korea. Taft and other Republicans were opposed to any large contingent of American soldiers going to Europe, much less without prior approval of Congress. Although the administration had decided in September to send more troops as part of a NATO army, Taft did not learn of this plan until November, and he took a strong stand against it. "The President had no power to agree to send American troops to fight in Europe," he argued in the Senate.[67]

Taft's speech kept alive the foreign policy debate. Supporters of a strong NATO army and backers of Truman's policy in Korea came to the administration's defense. Even *Life*, which was generally critical of the president, took issue with Taft. Certain "fundamentals" of foreign policy must always be kept in mind, the popular weekly stated. "One of these fundamentals is the duty and power of the President to act for the U.S. in foreign affairs."[68]

In the weeks that followed, the issue of the president's constitutional right to send armed forces outside the United States bounced back and forth between the White House and Congress. The White House claimed that Taft's position was contradicted even by the senator's own father, President and later Chief Justice William Howard Taft, an accusation the Ohio senator denied emphatically. In January, Taft gave his powerful backing to a resolution introduced by Kenneth Wherry of Nebraska, stating that it was the Senate's sense that no ground troops to be sent to Europe for use by the North Atlantic Treaty Organization without congressional authority.[69]

Almost immediately the Wherry Resolution became the focal point of the foreign policy debate. Weeks and then months were taken up discussing the merits of sending American troops to Europe and arguing the constitutional questions involved. Not until April, when the Wherry Resolution was finally defeated and a compromise reached authorizing the sending of four American divisions to Europe, were these matters finally resolved. Even then there was included among the many provisions of the legislation one that stated that no additional ground forces should be sent to Europe "without further Congressional approval."[70]

The entire debate over foreign policy, lasting from the end of 1950 into the spring of 1951, was watched closely in Europe and Canada. America's Western European allies were fearful of both the isolationist sentiment and talk of nuclear war that seemed to coexist in America. Many of them believed this reflected the capricious and unstable nature of the American character and the unreliability of American foreign policy. Apprehensive that the United States might retreat from its world responsibilities, just as it had after World War I, they remained even more afraid of a nuclear war between America and Russia in which, the Europeans believed, they would be its first victims. Seeking to resolve differences between East and West, they persisted in their protests against Washington's Chinese policy. Although they continued to support the American position at the United Nations, they frequently did so reluctantly. Furthermore, they criticized American smugness and challenged the argument that the United States was carrying most of the responsibility for containing Communist expansion in the Far East. Lastly, they worried about General MacArthur's influence on American foreign policy and were fearful that Chiang Kai-shek on Formosa might be unleashed to attack the China mainland. "The Europeans are just plain scared," said a Parisian journalist, "that if the U.S. sent Chiang Kai-shek into the fight, Russia would introduce its air force and we would have a world war."[71]

Because of their concern about a world war largely fought on their soil, the West European governments encouraged a dialogue between Moscow and Washington. They were greatly upset, therefore, at the administration's rejection of a proposal by the Soviets, who were plainly alarmed at the possibility of a rearmed West Germany, to hold Big Four talks involving the foreign ministers of Britain, France, the United States, and the Soviet Union on this and other Cold War issues. But European—and Canadian—displeasure became even more apparent when an open rift developed at the United Nations over an American resolution to brand China as an "aggressor nation" and to impose sanctions on it.[72] Every one of America's western allies objected to the American proposal, arguing that it would make negotiations with the Chinese even more difficult and might lead to Soviet involvement in the Korean war. Instead, they backed another attempt at arranging a cease-fire, this time to be followed by an international conference on the Far East issues, as Beijing had always demanded.[73]

Backed into an embarrassing corner by its own allies and anticipating that China might yet turn down another effort at peacemaking in the hope of gaining even greater concessions later, including prior admission to the United Nations and American withdrawal from Formosa, the United States agreed to a formula at the United Nations for ending the Korean war that included an immediate cease-fire (which the United States wanted), to be followed by a conference on Far Eastern problems (which Beijing wanted). As Secretary of State Acheson, who was responsible for this strategy, had hoped, the Chinese turned down the UN proposal, stating that it was still based on a cease-fire in Korea prior to negotiations on other essential questions, and the General Assembly responded by easily approving the American resolution labeling China an "aggressor nation" on February 1.[74]

Even so, Washington did not win at the United Nations without applying considerable pressure and without causing a wound within the Western coalition requiring significant diplomatic healing. America's allies were willing finally to vote for a resolution of condemnation because, like the United States, they believed the fact of Chinese aggression in Korea should not go totally ignored by the United Nations. Also, as the American proposal was presented to the United Nations, it provided for a cessation of hostilities without precluding further discussions with China if Beijing wanted them. The American resolution was a call to Beijing to desist from aggression, but it was also a promise of a peaceful settlement if it did. Western powers could live with that.[75]

Yet there can be no denying that America's Western allies had also been pushed and shoved into approving a resolution they did not fully support. And they resented that fact. Although the British voted for the American resolution, they remained strongly opposed to Washington's persistent hard line toward China. They also remained miffed at the administration's habit of ignoring allied advice. *The New Statesman and Nation* expressed this British feeling when it remarked on the UN debate on China, "The real issue of this week's events is whether the Western alliance is to be a pact of equals or the suzerainty of one over all the rest."[76]

In fairness to the administration, it was under intense domestic pressure to follow a hard line toward Beijing. Not only had White House critics attacked President Truman and Secretary of State Acheson when they had supported the last cease-fire proposal at the United Nations, but on January 19 both the House and Senate approved by voice vote similar resolutions calling on the United Nations to declare China an aggressor in Korea. Under these circumstances it would have been risky business indeed for an already embattled administration to have defied Congress by following the dictates of diplomats at the United Nations wanting a modified version of the American resolution or no resolution at all. For this reason the White House was not being entirely disingenuous when it warned its NATO allies that their votes at the United Nations could determine the level of congressional aid they might receive in the future.[77]

Nevertheless, the American resolution of condemnation accomplished little except perhaps to appease some of the administration's harshest opponents. And even this had a price, for by its action at the United Nations and its position on such other matters as four-power talks with the Soviet Union, the administration also demoralized many of its strongest backers at home, including those who sought a peaceful end to the Korean war through a more flexible policy toward China, meaning a resolution of the China question.[78]

Even more serious, the administration, by its seemingly reckless, provocative, and intractable foreign policy, raised new doubts overseas about American leadership. Indeed, by late winter, a substantial number of Europeans—and Canadians—including many committed to a strong Atlantic alliance, were accusing Washington of insipid self-righteousness and challenging its claim that, almost alone, the United States was containing Communist aggression in the Far East. This did not mean, of course, that the Western coalition was about to be shattered or that the United States abandoned by its allies. But it did mean significant strain in the Atlantic alliance that made it even harder for Western heads of government to explain and defend their support for the United States.[79]

Lastly, by pushing through the resolution of condemnation at the United Nations while ignoring Beijing's counterproposals, the Truman administration effectively eliminated any chance for an early end to the Korean war. This was regrettable, for there were substantial reasons, both in terms of the gains already achieved and the military dangers ahead, why Beijing might have been anxious to find a solution to the Korean war acceptable to the West. After all, less than eighteen months had passed since the People's Republic of China had been established, and it still had to contend with pockets of resistance to its authority. Its invasion of Tibet, begun in October, was running into trouble. It had gone to war with obsolete military equipment, and the possibility that the United States would use the bomb against her could not be ignored. At the same time, the war had already begun to stabilize by the end of January. China's superiority in manpower was being matched by UN superiority in fire and air power. China's supply lines were overextended. Lacking transport, China was forced to rely on about 300,000 conscripts to carry some 500 tons of supplies daily to meet the bare minimum of its forces in Korea. Even then, they were forced to move only at night, for UN air attacks were having a crippling effect in North Korea, freely bombing and strafing every visible target. It is for these reasons that military historian Appleman believes the Chinese invasion might have been contained much earlier (by the third week of the invasion) and much farther north (at the narrow waist of Korea running from Wonsan westward through Pyongyang) had Eighth Army Commander William Walker not ordered a retreat all the way to Seoul and the Imjin and Han River lines.[80]

The administration remained convinced, however, that Korea was a test of America's will to resist Communist aggression, that to make concessions to Beijing in return for a cease-fire in Korea was a form of appeasement, which would invite further aggression, and that America's credence as a world leader was at issue in the Korean war. Not only that, the administration had to contend with domestic politics and with the realization that any concessions to the Chinese, apparent or real, would complicate and further inflame the political dialogue already under way in the United States and hamper even more its conduct of foreign policy.[81]

In a real sense, then, while the complexion of the Korean war had changed dramatically since the Chinese invasion in November, the basic issue before the administration had returned to what it had been at the time President Truman committed American military forces in June 1950. No longer did the White House envision the rollback of Communist expansion. Once more the central issue had become one of credibility, both American credibility in the world and the administration's credibility at home. There was an irony in all this. Just as concern with "saving face" had traditionally been an important consideration to the Chinese, it had become no less important to top administration officials in the United States.

Notes

1. James F. Schnabel, *Policy and Direction: The First Year, The United States Army in the Korean War* (Washington, DC, 1972), 111–114 and 139–140; D. Clayton James, *Refighting the Last War: Command and Crisis in Korea,*

1950–1953 (New York, 1993), 157–177; Richard Whelan, *Drawing the Line: The Korean War, 1950–1953* (Boston, 1990), 185–189; David Rees, *Korea: The Limited War* (New York, 1964), 78.

2. Schnabel, *Policy and Direction*, 146–149.
3. Quoted in Courtney Whitney, *MacArthur: His Rendezvous with History* (New York, 1955), 343–344 and 348–350. See also Douglas MacArthur, *Reminiscences* (New York, 1964), 348–351.
4. Schnabel, *Policy and Direction*, 149–150; James F. Schnabel and Robert J. Watson, *The History of the Joint Chiefs of Staff, III, The Korean War* (Wilmington, DE, 1979), 213.
5. MacArthur to Joint Chiefs of Staff, September 8, 1950. Box 15, Selected Records Relating to the Korean War; MacArthur *Reminiscences*, 351–352; Schnabel, *Policy and Direction*, 154; Joseph C. Goulden, *Korea: The Untold Story of the War* (New York, 1982), 198–199.
6. Schnabel, *Policy and Direction*, 173–177; Whelan, *Drawing the Line*, 190–191; Rees, *Korea: The Limited War*, 85–88.
7. Russell F. Weigley, *The American Way of War: A History of United States Military Strategy and Policy* (New York, 1973), 386–387.
8. Doris M. Condit, *The Test of War: 1950–1953* (Washington, DC, 1988), 31–39; James T. Patterson, *Mr. Republican: A Biography of Robert A. Taft* (Boston, 1972), 455; Whelan, *Drawing the Line*, 215; Ronald J. Caridi, *The Korean War and American Politics: The Republican Party as a Case Study* (Philadelphia, 1968), 65.
9. Caridi, *The Korean War and American Politics*, 65; *New Yorker*, 26 (September 30, 1950), 86–88; *Nation*, 171 (September 23, 1950), 263; *New Republic*, 123 (September 25, 1950), 3.
10. *Life*, 29 (September 25, 1950), 34; *New Yorker*, 26 (September 30, 1950), 86–93; *New Republic*, 123 (October 16, 1950), 3.
11. *New Republic*, 123 (September 25, 1950), 5–7; *New Yorker*, 26 (September 30, 1950), 86–93; *Life*, 29 (October 9, 1950), 38; *Nation*, 171 (September 23, 1950), 257; *Commonweal*, 52 (October 6, 1950), 621; *ibid.*, 53 (October 13, 1950), 3.
12. *FR*, 1950, VII, 503–508; Robert J. Donovan, *Tumultuous Years: The Presidency of Harry S. Truman, 1949–1953* (New York, 1982), 277. See also Shu Guang Zhang, *Deterrence and Strategic Culture: Chinese-American Confrontations, 1949–1950* (Ithaca, NY, 1992), 80.
13. Directive to the Commander of the United Nations Forces in Korea, September 27, 1950, attached to Marshall to Truman, September 27, 1950, Box 243, President's Secretary File, Truman Papers; *FR*, 1950, VII, 781–782 and 792–793; Schnabel, *Policy and Direction*, 179–181.
14. *FR*, 1950, 826; Dean Acheson, *Present at the Creation: My Years in the State Department* (New York, 1969), 453–555; Schnabel and Watson, *The History of the Joint Chiefs of Staff, III, The Korean War*, 213. For a different

view that argues that Truman's policy was always the political unification of Korea, see Whelan, *Drawing the Line*, 196–197.

15. *FR*, 1950, VII, 742, 765, 791, 795–796, and 851.
16. Jonathan D. Pollack, "The Korean War and Sino-American Relations," in Harry Harding and Yuan Ming (eds.), *Sino-American Relations, 1945–1955: A Joint Reassessment of a Critical Decade* (Wilmington, DE, 1989), 215–222; Russell Spurr, *Enter the Dragon: China's Undeclared War Against the U.S. in Korea, 1950–1951* (New York, 1988), 60–85; Zhang, *Deterrence and Strategic Culture*, 88–101; Sergei N. Goncharov, John W. Lewis, and Xue Litai, *Uncertain Partners: Stalin, Mao, and the Korean War* (Stanford, CA, 1993), 154–187; Yufan Hao and Zhai Zhihai, "China's Decision to Enter the Korean War: History Revisited," in James Cotton and Ian Neary (eds.), *The Korean War in History* (Atlantic Highlands, NJ, 1989), 141–165; Anthony Farrar-Hockley, "The China Factor in the Korean War," in *ibid.*, 6–9; Michael Hunt, "Beijing and the Korean Crisis, June 1950–June 1951," *Political Science Quarterly*, 107 (Fall, 1992), 459–470. See also Mineo Nakajima, "The Sino-Soviet Confrontation: Its Roots in the International Background of the Korean War," *The Australian Journal of Chinese Affairs*, no. 1 (January, 1979), 32–39.
17. Harry S. Truman, *Years of Trial and Hope: Memoirs* (New York, 1956), 462–463.
18. John Lewis Gaddis, "The American 'Wedge' Strategy, 1949–1950," in Harding and Ming (eds.), *Sino-American Relations, 1945–1955*, 157–165; Rosemary Foot, *The Wrong War: American Policy and the Dimensions of the Korean Conflict, 1950–1993* (Ithaca, NY, 1985), 46–49, 55, 81–83, and 87.
19. Foot, *The Wrong War*, 77–80; Whelan, *Drawing the Line*, 218–230; Rees, *Korea: The Limited War*, 111–112 and 123–128; Schnabel, *Policy and Direction*, 193–197, 202–210, and 215–232.
20. *FR*, 1950, VII, 933–938 and 980–991; Schnabel and Watson, *The History of the Joint Chiefs of Staff*, III, *The Korean War*, 258–259.
21. Truman, *Years of Trial and Hope*, 413–414; David McCullough, *Truman* (New York, 1992), 399–400; Caridi, *The Korean War and American Politics*, 77–78 and 93–94; John W. Spanier, *The Truman-MacArthur Controversy and the Korean War* (Cambridge, 1959), 104–113; Donovan, *The Tumultuous Years*, 284–285.
22. *FR*, 1950, VII, 948–962; Truman, *Years of Trial and Hope*, 416–418.
23. McCullough, *Truman*, 800–808; Truman, *Years of Trial and Hope*, 419–422; Whelan, *Drawing the Line*, 233–234; Stueck, Jr., *The Road to Confrontation*, 238–239; Spanier, *The Truman-MacArthur Controversy and the Korean War*, 114–228; *FR*, 1950, VII, 1025–1026.
24. Foot, *The Wrong War*, 82–84. *FR*, 1950, VII, 901–902, 915, and 921; Acheson, *Present at the Creation*, 451–452.

25. Allen S. Whitney, *China Crosses the Yalu: The Decision to Enter the Korean War* (Stanford, CA, 1960), 114–128; *FR*, 1950, VII, 944.

26. *Nation*, 171 (October 28, 1950), 385–388; *New Republic*, 123 (October 30, 1950), 7; *Time*, 56 (November 6, 1950), 19.

27. *Nation*, 171 (September 23, 1950), 257; *Atlantic Monthly*, 186 (September 1950), 4, 6, and 8; *New Yorker*, 26 (October 21, 1950), 23.

28. *FR*, 1950, VII, 1023–1026; Clubb to Dean Rusk, November 7, 1950, Box 4262, Records of the Department of State, RG 59, 795a.5/11-750. See also Foot, *The Wrong War*, 88–90.

29. Acheson, *Present at the Creation*, 463–464; Truman, *Years of Trial and Hope*, 426–427; Whelan, *Drawing the Line*, 246–247.

30. MacArthur to Joint Chiefs of Staff, November 6, 1950, Box 15, Selected Records Relating to the Korean War.

31. Schnabel and Watson, *The History of the Joint Chiefs of Staff*, III, 274–276; Whelan, *Drawing the Line*, 241–242.

32. *FR*, 1950, VII, 1078–1085 and 1101–1106.

33. *Ibid.*, 1075–1076.

34. Richard M. Fried, *Men Against McCarthy* (New York, 1976), 118–121; *New Republic*, 123 (November 20, 1950), 3; *Time*, 56 (November 13, 1950), 19; *ibid.* (November 20, 1950), 20–21.

35. *FR*, 1950, VII, 1097–1098, 1101–1106, and 1117–1122.

36. *Ibid.*, 1107–1108; Schnabel and Watson, *The History of the Joint Chiefs of Staff*, III, *The Korean War*, 304–305; Truman, *Years of Trial and Hope*, 432–433.

37. Schnabel, *Policy and Direction*, 248–259.

38. *Nation*, 171 (November 25, 1950), 474; *New Yorker*, 26 (December 9, 1950), 67.

39. *FR*, 1950, VII, 1145–1146 and 1205; Foot, *The Wrong War*, 91–93; Peter N. Farrar, "A Pause for Peace Negotiations: The British Buffer Zone Plan of November 1950," in Cotton and Neary (eds.), *The Korean War in History*, 66–69. See also Leon D. Epstein, *Britain—Uneasy Ally* (Chicago, 1954), 216–217.

40. Farrar, "A Pause for Peace Negotiations," 70–77; Peter Lowe, "The Frustrations of Alliance: Britain, the United States, and the Korean War, 1950–1951" in Cotton and Neary (eds.), *The Korean War in History*, 86.

41. Roy E. Appleman, *Disaster in Korea: The Chinese Confront MacArthur* (College Station, TX, 1989), 26–31.

42. Appleman, *Disaster in Korea*, xvi. This volume and two others by Appleman, *Escaping the Trap: The US Army X Corps in Northeast Korea, 1950* (College Station, TX, 1990) and *Ridgway Duels for Korea* (College Station, TX, 1990) provide the definitive military account of the war between the time of the Chinese invasion and the beginning of truce talks on July 10, 1951. But for the month following the invasion, see also Max

Hastings, *The Korean War* (New York, 1987), 128–146; T.H. Fehrenbach, *This Kind of War: Korea: A Study in Unpreparedness* (New York, 1964), 320–413; Schnabel, *Policy and Direction*, 274–283

43. National Security Council Meeting of November 28, 1950, Box 72, Elsey Papers. See also Cabinet Meeting of November 20, 1950, *ibid.*; Meeting of the President with Congressional leaders, December 1, 1950, Box 73, *ibid.*; FR, 1950, VII, 1242–1249.

44. *Ibid.*

45. *New York Times*, November 30, 1950.

46. Appleman, *Disaster in Korea*, 31–33.

47. Quoted in Bruce Cumings, *The Origins of the Korean War, Vol. II: The Roaring of the Cataract, 1947–1950* (Princeton, NJ, 1990), 748. See also Foot, *The Wrong War*, 116; and Roger Dingman, "Atomic Diplomacy During the Korean War," *International Security*, 13 (Winter, 1988–1989), 65–66.

48. *New Yorker*, 26 (December 9, 1950), 67–70; *ibid.* (December 16, 1950), 78–90; *New Republic*, 123 (December 11, 1950), 5; *Nation*, 171 (December 9, 1950), 520; *Time*, 56 (December 11, 1950), 17; The President's News Conference of November 30, 1950, *Public Papers of the Presidents of the United States: Harry S. Truman, 1950* (Washington, DC, 1965), 724–128; Acheson, *Present at the Creation*, 472; "Analysis of Public Comment Contained in Communications to the President Received December 4 to 8, 1950," Box 73, Elsey Papers; Cullum A. MacDonald, *Korea: The War Before Vietnam* (New York, 1986), 74–75.

49. FR, 1950, VII, 1276–1281, 1291–1296, 1308–1310, and 1323–1324. See also Schnabel and Watson, *The History of the Joint Chiefs of Staff*, III, 347–348 and 378; Acheson to Robert Lovett, December 3, 1950, Box 8, Selected Records Relating to the Korean War; *New Yorker*, 26 (December 23, 1950), 44–46.

50. FR, 1950, VII, 1361–1374, 1392–1408, 1449–1464, and 1468–1472; Lowe, "The Frustrations of Alliance," 86–89.

51. Cumings, *The Origins of the Korean War*, II, 748–749; Dingman, "Atomic Diplomacy during the Korean War," 66–67; Qiang Zhai, *The Dragon, the Lion, and the Eagle: Chinese/British/American Relations, 1949–1958* (Kent, OH, 1994), 84–85.

52. Loy Henderson to the Secretary of State, December 2, 1950; Warren Austin to the Secretary of State, December 4, 1950; UN General Assembly, January 2, 1951, Box 8, Selected Records Relating to the Korean War; FR, 1950, VII, 1359–1360, 1486–1488, 1509–1512, 1518–1520, 1540–1541, and 1549–1550; *Yearbook of the United Nations: 1950* (New York, 1951), 242–249.

53. Roy E. Appleman, *Escaping the Trap*, 203–318; Hastings, *The Korean War*, 147–164.

54. Memorandum for Mr. Murphy, December 7, 1950; Economic Mobilization Meeting, [December 11, 1950?]; Meeting of the President on the Economic Situation, December 11, 1952; Memorandum for the Chairman of the Joint Chiefs of Staff, December 13, 1950; Meeting of the President with Congressional Leaders, December 13, 1950, Box 73, Elsey Papers. See also *Public Papers of the Presidents of the United States: Harry S. Truman, 1950*, 741–745.

55. *FR*, 1950, VII, 1570–1576; *ibid.*, 1951, VII, 66–67.

56. *FR*, 1950, VII, 1588–1590 and 1625–1626.

57. *Ibid.*, 1630–1633; *ibid.*, 1951, VII, 41–43; Foot, *The Wrong War*, 118–120.

58. Truman, *Years of Trial and Hope*, 492–493. See also Acheson, *Present at the Creation*, 515.

59. *FR*, 1951, VII, 68–70. See also Kenneth R. Mauck, "The Formation of American Foreign Policy in Korea, 1945–1953" (unpublished Ph.D. dissertation, University of Oklahoma, 1978), 312–313.

60. Schnabel and Watson, *The History of the Joint Chiefs of Staff*, III, 414–419.

61. *Life*, 29 (December 4, 1950), 42. See also *Commonweal*, 53 (December 29, 1950), 291; *Time*, 56 (December 18, 1950), 17; David S. McLellan, *Dean Acheson: The State Department Years* (New York, 1976), 301; McDonald, *Korea*, 79–81.

62. Joan Hoff Wilson, *Herbert Hoover: Forgotten Progressive* (Boston, 1975), 261–263; *Time*, 57 (January 1, 1951), 9; *Life*, 30 (January 1, 1951), 18.

63. *Nation*, 172 (January 6, 1951), 3; *Commonweal*, 53 (January 5, 1951), 315; *Time*, 56 (December 11, 1950), 17; *ibid.*, (December 18, 1950), 21; *ibid.*, 57 (January 15, 1951), 18–19; *Life*, 29 (December 18, 1950), 78; *Atlantic Monthly*, 187 (January, 1951), 12.

64. *Life*, 30 (January 8, 1951), 10–13. See also David R. Kepley, *The Collapse of the Middle Way: Senate Republicans and the Bipartisan Foreign Policy, 1948–1952* (Westport, CT, 1988), 101–116; Patterson, *Mr. Republican*, 477.

65. Patterson, *Mr. Republican*, 453 and 475–476. See also *Time*, 57 (January 15, 1951), 12; *Life*, 30 (January 15, 1951), 26.

66. *Ibid.*; McDonald, *Korea*, 79–80.

67. Patterson, *Mr. Republican*, 477; *New York Times*, January 6, 1951; *Congressional Quarterly Almanac*, VII (1951), 220–221.

68. *Life*, 30 (January 15, 1951), 24; *Nation*, 172 (January 13, 1951), 21; *ibid.* (January 20, 1951), 52.

69. "Power of the President to Send the Armed Forces Outside the United States," February 16, 1951, Box 33, Elsey Papers; Patterson, *Mr. Republican*, 480–481.

70. *Congressional Quarterly Almanac*, VII (1951), 223–232.

71. *New Republic*, 124 (January 8, 1951), 9; *New Yorker*, 26 (January 13, 1951), 46; *Atlantic Monthly*, 187 (February 1957), 6; *Commonweal*, 53 (March 2,

1951), 514–515. See also *Nation*, 172 (January 20, 1951), 57; *Life*, 30 (January 22, 1951), 32–33.

72. *Nation*, 172 (January 6, 1951), 6 and 8; *ibid.* (January 13, 1951), 26–27; *ibid.* (February 3, 1951), 99–100; Acheson, *Present at the Creation*, 551; Department of State, "For the Press," January 17, 1951, Box 8, Selected Records Relating to the Korean War; *FR*, 1951, VII, 7–9, 74–76, and 83–85; Dennis Stairs, *The Diplomacy of Constraint: Canada, the Korean War, and the United States* (Toronto, 1974), 160–161.

73. *FR*, 1951, VII, 9–12, 18–21, and 37–39; Acheson, *Present at the Creation*, 513; Stairs, *The Diplomacy of Constraint*, 160–161; McDonald, *Korea*, 81–82; *New Yorker*, 26 (January 27, 1951), 58. See also Unsigned Memorandum of Conversation, January 24, 1951, Box 66, Papers of Dean Acheson, Harry S. Truman Library (Independence, Missouri).

74. *FR*, 1951, VII, 44–47, 53–54, 64, and 91–92; *Time*, 57 (January 22, 1951), 13; *Nation*, 172 (January 27, 1951), 76–77; Stairs, *The Diplomacy of Constraint*, 168–169; McDonald, *Korea*, 82–83; *Yearbook of the United Nations: 1951*, 207–225.

75. UN General Assembly, "Provisional Summary Record of the Four Hundred and Twenty-Ninth Meeting," January 23, 1951; Acheson for Sebald, January 23, 1951; Statement of Warren R. Austin, January 27, 1951; "Memorandum of Conversation," January 27, 1951, Box 8, Selected Records Relating to the Korean War; *FR*, 1951 VII, 123–125 and 127–129; Stairs, *The Diplomacy of Constraint*, 168–172.

76. *New Yorker*, 26 (February 10, 1951), 83; *Nation*, 172 (February 3, 1951), 103–104. See also Lowe, "The Frustrations of Alliance," 89–93.

77. *Congressional Quarterly Almanac*, VII, 1951, 238; *Time*, 57 (January 29, 1951), 19; *Nation*, 172 (February 3, 1951), 102–103.

78. *New Yorker*, 26 (January 27, 1951), 70–78; *ibid.* (February 10, 1951), 85; *Nation*, 172 (February 17, 1951), 15. See also *New Republic*, 124 (January 1, 1951), 6; *Commonweal*, 53 (February 9, 1951), 431.

79. *Commonweal*, 53 (February 16, 1951), 463; *New Yorker*, 26 (February 10, 1951), 83; McDonald, *Korea*, 84–87.

80. Appleman, *Disaster in Korea*, 341–360. See also Hastings, *The Korean War*, 171; Adam Ulam, *Expansion and Coexistence: Soviet Foreign Policy* (New York, 1974), 530; Joseph Camilleri, *Chinese Foreign Policy: The Maoist Era and Its Aftermath* (Oxford, England, 1980), 38–39; Allen S. Whiting, *China Crosses the Yalu: The Decision to Enter the Korean War* (Stanford, CA, 1960), 165; *Time*, 172 (February 12, 1951), 25.

81. *Commonweal*, 53 (February 2, 1951), 411; Edgar O'Ballance, *Korea: 1950–1953* (London, 1969), 80–81 and 96–98.

CHAPTER FOUR

The Recall and the MacArthur Hearings

During the late winter and early spring of 1951, the immediate military crisis facing the UN Command (UNC) was overcome successfully when the Chinese offensive was halted south of Seoul and UN forces were able to launch a counteroffensive that took them above the 38th parallel once more. But in the United States a crisis of an entirely different, but equally dangerous, kind developed after General Douglas MacArthur directly challenged the constitutional authority of the President as commander-in-chief. Although President Truman, in one of the most courageous acts of the modern Presidency, reaffirmed his power by recalling MacArthur from active duty, the political fallout was a repudiation of his administration by the overwhelming majority of the American public.

China's logistical weakness was already evident when Matthew B. Ridgway assumed command of the Eighth Army at the end of December, succeeding Walton Walker, who had been killed in a freak traffic accident. However, it had become even more apparent in the next several weeks. Throughout this period Communist forces had remained on the offensive. Moving in close formations and striking in overwhelming numbers against the flanks and rears of UN troops, they recaptured Seoul on January 4 and then proceeded to take Osan to the south. Once Osan was evacuated, the road to Taejon became clogged with refugees fleeing southward, making the withdrawal of American forces difficult. In the east, the town of Wonju, an important railroad center, was attacked from three sides by North Koreans before being abandoned by UN forces twenty-four hours later. By the time the Communist offensive was halted on January 24, UN forces had withdrawn to defensive positions run along a line approximating the 37th parallel. The Eighth

Army had completed the longest retreat in American military history, more than three hundred miles.[1]

The Communist offensive, however, had been neither an unqualified victory for the Chinese nor an unmitigated disaster for the Americans. Because of such inherent difficulties as primitive communications and problems of supply, the Chinese were not always able to exploit their opportunities. Had they been able to do so, they might have been able to drive UN forces back to the Pusan perimeter or even out of Korea entirely. But they were forced to stop every five or six days to regroup and be resupplied, thereby allowing UN troops to withdraw rapidly but in orderly fashion. This had been the case before the Chinese had moved on Seoul, and it was the case after they had taken the capital city. During the retreat American planes had also engaged in close and effective air support, inflicting high casualties on the Chinese and easing some of the pressure on UN forces. As the Chinese advanced south after taking Seoul, moreover, they encountered stiff resistance and were subjected to some of the heaviest artillery firing of the war. Below Wonju the U.S. Second Division, aided by French and Dutch battalions, carried out the first counterattack since the fall of Seoul, briefly fighting their way into the town before withdrawing under small arms fire. Although a horseshoe salient just south of Wonju was subsequently given up in order to shorten and straighten the UN line, artillery and air protection prevented enemy interference with the withdrawal.[2]

Finally, on January 15, UN forces launched OPERATION THUNDERBOLT, a major counteroffensive that would last for the next three months and would, by February 10, result in the capture once again of Kimpo and Inchon and the neutralization of Seoul. Marching north, UN forces attacked the Chinese with tanks, heavy guns, napalm, and naval gunfire from ships offshore. Using coordinated artillery, infantry, armor, and air power, they left more than 4200 Chinese dead in just one phase of the advance while offering only 70 losses themselves. As UN troops below Seoul closed in on the Han River, *Time* reported that the fire from tanks and artillery "reached such a furious volume that some Chinese who surrendered had blood streaming from nose and ears because of concussion."[3]

Much of the credit for reversing the direction of the war belonged to Ridgway. A tough field commander who was known for his trademark of a single grenade and first-aid kit hooked to a web

JANUARY, 1951 TO JULY, 1953

U.S.S.R.

Vladivostok

C H I N A
(MANCHURIA)

Chongjin

Hyesanjin

Chosan

Iwon

Sinuiju

NORTH
KOREA

Hungnam

SEA OF
JAPAN

Pyongyang ★

Wonsan

Tongchon

Iron
Triangle

Armistice line
July 27, 1953

Truce talks Oct 10, 1951
to July 27, 1953

38th parallel

Panmunjom

Seoul ★

U.N. advances
Controlled by U.N.
Controlled by
Communists

Ridgway counter-offensive
Jan 25-April 21, 1951

YELLOW

Pohang

Kunsan

SOUTH
KOREA

SEA

Pusan

JAPAN

Mokpo

Sunchon

0

300

Miles

harness that he wore over his trench coat, he had led the 82nd Airborne Division during World War II. Brought to the Pentagon in 1949 as deputy chief of staff, he quickly earned a reputation as a hard-driving administrator, demanding precision from his staff and boiling into rage when someone gave an evasive answer. At the time he was ordered to Korea, he was regarded by many insiders at the Pentagon as a likely candidate for Army chief of staff.[4]

Privately, Ridgway, who had carefully studied the military situation in Korea, had become critical of MacArthur's offensive deployments in North Korea and the reluctance of the Joint Chiefs of Staff to question his orders. Upon arriving in Korea on December 26 after being briefed in Tokyo by MacArthur, who gave him total authority over the Eighth Army, Ridgway's purposes were to clean house, rebuild his forces, and inflict maximum casualties on the enemy. He was eminently successful in all these respects. On orders from the Pentagon, X Corps was merged into the Eighth Army, thereby unifying the command of all ground forces in Korea. Convinced the principal problem before his newly reorganized command was the low morale of his troops after an extended retreat, Ridgway sought to fire their enthusiasm and rekindle their spirits. To restore their confidence and fighting vigor he emphasized stern discipline, tough training, a sense of esprit de corps, and professional pride. Similarly, he adopted a "meat grinder" strategy of seeking out the enemy and striking at him again and again while making maximum use of tanks and fire power. By the time UN forces approached the Han River on about February 10, they had inflicted a grueling punishment on the enemy, whose toll of battle casualties since January 25 was estimated at more than 80,000.[5]

Meanwhile, troop morale under Ridgway's command had improved markedly. Indeed, a Pentagon team headed by General J. Lawton Collins, which had been sent to Korea in mid-January to assess the morale problem after MacArthur had described it as dismal, reported that conditions in Korea were, in fact, encouraging. "On the whole," Collins told the Joint Chiefs, "Eighth Army is now in position and prepared to punish severely any mass attack." Henceforth, the Joint Chiefs of Staff and President Truman increasingly bypassed MacArthur, choosing instead to deal directly with Ridgway.[6]

On February 11 the Communists launched a counterattack against the relatively weak center of the UN line that now stretched north of Hoengsong, forcing Ridgway to withdraw his troops once more to Wonju. Two days later the Chinese struck farther west, aiming at the vital crossroads town of Chipyong. The battle around Chipyong raged for three days, as the Chinese smashed against the UN forces with repeated human wave attacks. But UN forces responded with artillery salvos and aerial bombardment, and by week's end had defeated the counteroffensive at a cost to the Communists of an estimated 33,000 casualties.[7]

Seizing the initiative as the Chinese withdrew to defensive positions farther north, Ridgway launched a series of operations whose purpose was to destroy as many Chinese personnel as possible and to establish a strong defensive line in the vicinity of the 38th parallel. Although Seoul was reclaimed on March 24, the UN advance proved slow and difficult. Most of the Chinese forces were able to escape the several pincer movements aimed at trapping them and to retreat to safety. But by April 22, when the Chinese launched their great spring offensive, UN forces had established a new defensive line, LINE WYOMING, which again took them above the 38th parallel and which, in the center, reached almost to the "Iron Triangle," a heavily defended area encompassed by a triangle with Pyyonggang (not to be confused with the capital city of Pyongyang) at the northern angle, Chorwon at the left angle, and Kumhwa at the right angle.[8]

Considerable wrangling had preceded the decision allowing Ridgway to send his troops so far into North Korea. The State Department had been against the idea. Technically, UN forces still operated under the October 7, 1950 directive to establish "a unified, independent, and democratic Korea." But after the Chinese invasion and the retreat of UN forces in late November and December, few State Department officials considered that realistic. Nor, for that matter, did most top military leaders at the Pentagon. What caused difficulty, however, was the State Department's reluctance to define precise war aims without an assessment of America's military capabilities, which, in the opinion of the Joint Chiefs of Staff and the Defense Department, was a case of the tail wagging the dog.[9]

In general, the State Department's new—or, more accurately, reconstructed—aim in Korea was reasonably clear. It was to achieve a cease-fire agreement followed by UN negotiations leading to the restoration of the status quo before June 25, 1950. Enough military pressure should be applied against the enemy and enough casualties inflicted on him to bring the Communists to the negotiating table. UN forces might even be allowed to cross the 38th parallel in order to interrupt enemy offensive operations. Under no circumstances, however, should UN forces engage in a general offensive into North Korea without the clearance of America's coalition partners, something which the State Department realized was highly unlikely.[10]

In the opinion of the Joint Chiefs of Staff, the State Department's position was imprecise and amounted to determining future military decisions without stating the political objectives on which these decisions should be based. By prohibiting UN forces from moving above the 38th parallel in any major way, the State Department would also give the Communists impunity to regroup and rebuild in order to launch their own attack across the parallel. Until America's political objectives in Korea were more clearly defined, UN troops should not be limited in crossing into North Korea to provide for their own safety.[11]

Seeking to scale down the war in Korea or to withdraw entirely, the Pentagon thus advocated policies that, in fact, could escalate the fighting considerably. The State Department, anxious to maintain military pressure against the Communists, nevertheless proposed limits on military action that might endanger American forces. Implicit in this conundrum of paradoxes and cross-purposes were some fundamental problems having to do with fighting a limited war in a nuclear age, particularly when the enemy could find sanctuary adjacent to the principal theater of military operations. First, any military planning had to take into account the ever-present danger of global escalation and nuclear war. In the case of Korea, the State Department's fear that a deep penetration of North Korea would increase the danger of a larger conflict, possibly involving the Soviet Union, was complicated by its concern that such a drive might fragment allied unity. But that only underscored the need for integrating political considerations into military planning.

Second, the Korean war suggested very strongly that any major policy decisions involving military power could not be made in a political vacuum. Rather, they had to reflect the military's basic concern for the safety of its forces and its awareness of such domestic constraints as public opinion and budget restrictions. Indeed, the Korean war even indicated that while the military needed to be more sensitive to the political implications of military planning, it could no longer function in its historic role as a mere executor of foreign policy. Instead, it had to be more articulate in explaining to civilian authorities the limitations inherent in the nation's military capabilities.

These larger issues involved in defining the proper relationship between political objectives and military means and the role of the military in the decision-making process were largely ignored. Instead, the Pentagon and State Department patched over their fundamental differences with a series of inadequate compromises. There was thus to be no forceful attempt to unify Korea. Military and political objectives were to be distinguished. The right of the theater commander to operate across the 38th parallel was recognized within limits. A prospective wider war, including operations against China, as had been urged by General MacArthur in January, was ruled out. In other words, the 38th parallel was not to be an artificial barrier to essential military operations, but any military action that might unnecessarily widen or extend the war was to be avoided.[12]

Although UN forces began to hold against and then turn back the Chinese penetration of South Korea, it was recognized in the United States that the Chinese still had immense reserves of manpower, and real uncertainty remained as to what the Chinese might do in Korea in the next few weeks. In Washington reports circulated that they and the North Koreans were massing for another major push south. There were also unsubstantiated rumors of a heavy concentration of Soviet airplanes in Manchuria. The conviction that Korea was just one battleground of an ongoing struggle against Communist aggression, which could explode at any time into a nuclear war with the Soviet Union, continued to be shared by many Americans. In California there was even a run on bomb shelters ranging from a wood-covered dirt hole to elaborate $5500 shelters complete with telephones, water, radios, and inside and outside Geiger counters.[13]

Among America's allies doubts and skepticism continued to be expressed as to the maturity, consistency, and wisdom of American foreign policy. Europeans criticized both Washington's reluctance to engage in a serious dialogue with Moscow over German rearmament and the general "sterility" of American anti-Communism. Distrust of General MacArthur and others in the United States who would escalate the Korean war into a larger conflict against China itself remained widespread. The China question stayed a sore point, particularly in England, where "Peace with China" councils began to spring up all over the country. In England a serious split developed within the ranks of the ruling Labor Party as Prime Minister Attlee was attacked by more radical Laborites for adhering too closely to the dictates of Washington and for allowing Great Britain to be "dragged into a war with China by the Americans." Partly to mollify the opposition within his own party, Attlee had to reassure them that in no way would he support the recrossing of the 38th parallel without full consultation at the United Nations.[14]

In other words, although the tide of battle appeared to be turning in favor of the United States once more, there remained considerable concern both in the United States and abroad about future prospects in Korea, and fear of a nuclear confrontation between the United States and the Soviet Union stayed very much alive. Yet some of the despair and sense of crisis that had been evident within the United States since the end of November began to be replaced by February with renewed optimism about the war's outcome. For one thing, the success against the Chinese in Korea was widely regarded as having a beneficial effect throughout Asia. By throwing back the last two Communist offensives, UN forces, a number of military experts believed, had saved not only South Korea from the Communists but probably Indochina and perhaps the rest of Southeast Asia as well. They maintained that the Chinese had taken such a dreadful mauling in Korea that they had been rendered incapable of undertaking any further aggression for some time. Also lifting the spirits of Washington was the fact that the war moblization effort, which had gotten off to a bad start, had finally been cranked up. Between June 1950 and the spring of 1951, the Army grew from about 600,000 to 1.1 million personnel, the Air Force grew from forty-eight groups to about seventy, naval manpower increased 60 percent, and the number of combat ships ready for service increased by 50 percent.[15]

In Europe, too, the outlook appeared far more promising than it had even a few months earlier. Notwithstanding the concerns that Europeans continued to express about American policy and despite the fact that NATO's military strength remained negligible, the alliance seemed to be firmer politically than ever before. Although the China question still rankled many quarters, the issue of German rearmament, which had threatened to tear NATO apart, had been adroitly set aside, and General Eisenhower's eleven-nation tour of Europe as a salesman of collective security had been a thundering success. Important defections from the Communist parties in France and Italy also raised democratic morale.[16]

The prevailing mood of optimism in the United States and among America's European allies penetrated the White House as well, convincing Truman to undertake a major peace initiative. The rationale for a negotiated settlement was fairly simple. Because most of South Korea had been liberated from the Communists and UN forces had inflicted heavy casualties on the Chinese, it would be in the interests of both sides to end hostilities. But the United States was also under heavy pressure at the United Nations, where Secretary General Trygve Lie urged Washington to make a diplomatic approach directly to the North Koreans, bypassing China and the Soviet Union.[17]

Both the State Department and the Defense Department approved of the idea of a peace initiative, although they felt the President should appeal directly to the Chinese. The State Department drafted a message by which Truman would announce that the UNC was ready to enter into arrangements for a cease-fire. The statement offered no concessions to the Chinese, but it held out the possibility of subsequent negotiations on broader issues affecting the Far East. The Joint Chiefs of Staff then informed General MacArthur on March 20 of the planned announcement, telling him, in effect, to maintain contact with the enemy for the next few weeks but not to undertake a major offensive above the 38th parallel.[18]

MacArthur was irate. Although he had participated only marginally in planning the recent advance by the Eighth Army, he took much of the public credit for it. On March 7 he predicted a military stalemate in Korea unless he could strike at the enemy's war-making potential. A week later he defied a Presidential order prohibiting unauthorized statements to the press by giving one to the United Press in which he criticized stopping the Eighth Army's advance at the 38th parallel or short "of accomplishment of our mission in the unification of Korea."[19]

MacArthur did not stop here, however. Determined to undermine the President's proposed peace initiative, the general issued a statement on March 24 so contrary to the administration's purpose that Truman believed it would have only confused the world if he had gone ahead with his peace offer. In his statement, MacArthur portrayed China as an overrated military power on the brink of de-

struction should it continue its war in Korea. Only the United Nations' decision to limit its conflict with China to Korea had kept
China from being annihilated. Should the United Nations expand
its military operations to China's coastal areas and interior bases, it
would "doom Red China to the risk of imminent military collapse."
This being the case, "there should be no insuperable difficulty arriving at decisions on the Korean problem if the issues are resolved on
their own merits, without being burdened by extraneous matters
not directly related to Korea, such as Formosa and China's seat at
the United Nations." As commander of UN forces in Korea, Mac-
Arthur stood ready to meet the commander-in-chief of the enemy's
forces in order to consider carrying out the political objectives of the
United Nations in Korea without further bloodshed.[20]

In delivering this ultimatum to the Chinese, MacArthur had not
known the full content of the proposed Presidential message. Also
there was precedent for his offer to confer with the enemy; after the
successful Inchon invasion, the Department of State had even told
the Defense Department that a "cease-fire should be a purely military matter" worked out by "the Commanding General of the Unified Command [MacArthur]." Nevertheless, Truman was infuriated—and understandably so—at MacArthur's statement to the
Chinese to surrender on the battlefield or face total destruction. To
spread the war to China and risk a global war with the Soviet
Union, as implied by MacArthur's ultimatum, was totally contrary
to the thrust of the administration's policy of limiting the war to
Korea and negotiating its peaceful end. In addition, Truman was incensed by MacArthur's violation of the Presidential directive of December 6 to coordinate with Washington all public statements concerning Korea, by MacArthur's violation of the Presidential
directive of December 6 to coordinate with Washington all public
statements concerning Korea, by MacArthur's implicit criticism of
national policy, by the adverse reaction among America's allies that
his statement was bound to produce, and, above all, by Mac-
Arthur's tacit preemption of Presidential authority. "[O]nce again,"
Truman later wrote, "General MacArthur had openly defied the
policy of his Commander in Chief, the President of the United
States."[21]

MacArthur must have known how little chance there was that
China would simply lay down its arms and admit defeat, especially
when it still controlled more than half of the Korean peninsula. To

ask China to surrender under these circumstances was to ensure the rejection of any peace overture and the continuation of the war. Surely this was MacArthur's real purpose in issuing his statement. By prolonging the war, it seems clear, MacArthur hoped to create a situation of public frustration in the United States so great that the administration would have to increase its military effort against the Chinese, including liberating North Korea from Communist control.[22]

Less than twenty-four hours after he received the news of MacArthur's pronouncement, Truman summoned to the White House Deputy Secretary of Defense Robert Lovett, Assistant Secretary of State Rusk, and Secretary of State Acheson. Lovett was furious. The general must be removed and removed at once, he told Acheson. Acheson and Truman agreed. But there were problems. In the first place, Truman was afraid that firing MacArthur might upset negotiations then under way for a peace treaty with Japan. Second, he feared that recalling MacArthur would break up his multiplicity of commands and cause great logistical difficulties. Most important, the administration was perfectly aware of the tremendous popularity that MacArthur enjoyed in the United States and was sensitive to the political ramifications MacArthur's recall would cause. Indeed, Lovett warned Acheson that MacArthur's remarks were "probably the most popular public statement anyone has ever made." It offered peace and held out the hope of getting out of Korea. "If the president challenged it, he would be in the position at once of being on the side of sin."[23]

Instead of firing MacArthur or demanding his resignation, therefore, Truman merely reminded him of his December 6 directive against making public statements without first consulting Washington and ordered him to seek instructions from the Joint Chiefs in case the Communists sought an armistice. Still, there is little doubt that after March the President was on a collision course with the general that could only result in MacArthur's firing. Already, in fact, MacArthur had sent a telegram to the House minority leader, Republican Joseph Martin of Massachusetts, which would lead to MacArthur's removal from command and to the most serious domestic upheaval of the entire Truman administration.[24]

MacArthur wrote his telegram to Martin in response to a letter the minority leader had sent him asking him to comment "on a confidential basis or otherwise" on using Chinese Nationalist forces on

Formosa to attack the Chinese mainland. MacArthur's statement, which was sent on the same day he released his ultimatum to the Chinese, seemed to challenge existing national policy. "It seems strangely difficult for some to realize that here in Asia is where the Communist conspirators have elected to make their play for global conquest," the general told Martin. In Asia, we fight Europe's war. Lose the war in Asia, Europe is doomed. "[W]in it, and Europe would most probably avoid war and yet preserve freedom. As you pointed out, we must win. There is no substitute for victory." In other words, the administration was wrong to fight a limited war in Korea for fear of weakening American strength in Europe. Unless the White House resisted Communist aggression in Korea with adequate military power, both Europe and Asia would fall to the Communists.[25]

Because MacArthur had not indicated that he wanted his remarks kept confidential, Martin decided to read them on the floor of the House. As soon as Truman read what MacArthur had said, he scheduled a White House meeting for the next day with Defense Secretary Marshall, Secretary of State Acheson, General Omar Bradley, and Ambassador Averell Harriman. What made MacArthur's remarks particularly worrisome to the administration was that they came at a time when intelligence reports indicated a buildup of Chinese and Soviet troops in Manchuria and the redeployment of Soviet submarines northeast of Japan. The President was so concerned that this might be the prelude to a new offensive to drive UN forces out of North Korea, coordinated with a Soviet effort to cut off the supply lines between Japan and Korea, that he ordered the deployment of nine atomic bombs to Guam and the transfer of their control from the Atomic Energy Commission (AEC) to the Air Force. Truman intended the deployment of these weapons to the Far East mainly as a warning to China and the Soviet Union not to escalate the war in Korea. But the last thing he could allow was someone in command of the Far East capable of creating an incident leading to their use.[26]

At the White House meeting Harriman stated that MacArthur should have been dismissed two years earlier. Acheson also believed MacArthur should be fired, but he cautioned the President that the general's dismissal would trigger "the biggest fight of your administration." Marshall wanted more time before making a decision on what to do with MacArthur. Bradley too wanted to wait in order to consult first with the Joint Chiefs.[27]

The meeting at the White House was held on Friday. The President conferred again with his advisers the next day and with Acheson alone on Sunday morning. By this time a consensus had been reached among Truman's top aides that MacArthur should be recalled to the United States. On Monday, April 9, Marshall told the President that the Joint Chiefs unanimously recommended that MacArthur be relieved of all his commands. Truman then had the necessary orders drawn up. The President intended to notify MacArthur of his dismissal through Army Secretary Frank Pace, who was on an inspection tour of Korea. Pace was to fly to Tokyo to meet MacArthur. But because of a breakdown in communciations and out of concern that the Chicago *Tribune* was about to leak the story, Truman decided to break the news at a press conference called for 1 A.M. on April 11—before the general had received official word that he had been fired. To replace MacArthur, Truman named Ridgway. On the night of April 11 the President went on radio to explain the administration's Korean policy, including why it had become necessary to relieve MacArthur.[28]

Europeans overwhelmingly supported Truman. They had been dismayed by MacArthur's earlier ultimatum to the Chinese, which the Norwegian ambassador to the United States had referred to as the general's "pronounciomento" and which the pro-American London *Economist* regarded as a piece of unmitigated "mischief." When word was received, therefore, that Truman had fired MacArthur because the general had made still another defiant statement challenging the President's authority and posing the danger of a military escalation in Asia, they made clear their relief that they would not have to contend any longer with a megalomaniac like MacArthur.[29]

In the United States, however, the vast majority of Americans expressed outrage at the news that Truman had relieved MacArthur of his commands. In fact, the public furor caused by the firing of MacArthur stands out as one of the singular events in modern American political history. Although not entirely unexpected, the way in which the general was fired (MacArthur first learning of his dismissal secondhand) only added to the public outcry against a deeply unpopular President whose failures in China and "no-win" policy in Korea contrasted sharply with MacArthur's formula for victory in Asia.

No less important to many Americans than the policy issues separating MacArthur from Truman, however, were issues of character. If MacArthur stood as an authentic national hero whose probity, stature, bearing, and even elegance were legend, Truman seemed in so many ways to demean the office he served. Furthermore, the President's problems stemmed beyond the charges of corruption and scandal that tainted his administration or even beyond other domestic issues, such as his unpopular imposition of wage and price controls in January. They also involved matters of personal style and taste. In contrast to MacArthur, Truman was known to cuss and use salty language, to enjoy barnyard humor, to engage sometimes in heavy drinking, and to play poker with his political cronies. Even for a President, he was unusually combative and testy with the press, snapping at such respected journalists as Arthur Sulzberger, David Lawrence, Marquis Childs, and the Alsop brothers, whom he referred to as the "Sop sisters." His public antics, such as lambasting the Washington *Post's* music critic for his "lousy review" of his daughter Margaret's singing voice, sometimes made him look ridiculous. Alone, none of these matters made Truman unpopular. Together, they left an image of a President who remained little more than an ordinary machine politician from Jackson County, Missouri, serving by an act of fate in an office for which he was unfit and threatening by his firing of MacArthur to jeopardize the very security of the United States.[30]

Throughout the country, therefore, Americans lashed out at the President in a variety of ways. In Illinois the state legislature expressed its "unqualified confidence in General MacArthur and vigorously condemn[ed] the irresponsible and capricious action of the President in summarily discharging him from command." The legislatures of Michigan, California, and Florida passed similar resolutions. In San Gabriel, California, students hanged an effigy of Truman from a flagpole. Effigies of Truman were also hanged in the hills of Tennessee. Flags were lowered in protest in Oakland, California; Little Rock, Arkansas; Zanesville, Ohio; and Eastham, Massachusetts. Thousands of letters poured into the White House and to Congress demanding President Truman's resignation or impeachment.[31]

Talk of impeachment was not confined to the general public. On Capitol Hill the issue was raised at an emergency caucus of the House and Senate Republican leaders. Senator McCarthy said Truman's decision to dismiss MacArthur was fogged with "bourbon and benedictine" and that he should be fired. On the Senate floor Jenner of Indiana charged that the United States "was in the hands of a secret inner coterie which is directed by agents of the Soviet Union. Our only choice," he concluded, "is to impeach President Truman." Few took McCarthy and Jenner very seriously, and no organized effort was made to bring charges against the President. But the House and Senate invited MacArthur to address a joint meeting of Congress. Plans were also made for a full-scale investigation into the administration's Far East policy, including the reasons for MacArthur's recall.[32]

Familiar critics of MacArthur, like the Washington *Post*, the *Nation*, and the *New Republic*, did voice their support for the President. Most Democrats, and even a few Republicans, including the two Republican senators from Massachusetts, Leverett Saltonstall and Henry Cabot Lodge, Jr., also defended Truman. The President had no alternative, Saltonstall remarked, "but to take some affirmative action against General MacArthur." "To permit a continuous dispute," Lodge added, "is unthinkable."[33]

Nevertheless, when MacArthur returned to the United States on April 17, he met a hero's welcome unsurpassed in American history. Landing at San Francisco, he was greeted by a crowd so big that it took the general and his entourage two hours to travel the fourteen miles to his hotel. On the eighteenth he traveled to Washington to address the Congress. Arriving at National Airport shortly after midnight on the nineteenth, he was met by twelve thousand well-wishers, who broke through the police lines and made a shambles of the greeting ceremonies that had been planned for him.[34]

Twelve hours later MacArthur entered the House chamber, where he was widely and wildly cheered by the assembled senators and representatives as well as by the public in the galleries, which were filled to overcapacity. Eloquent, charismatic, unhurried, resonant of voice, sometimes austere but always in control, the deposed commander delivered a thirty-minute address that even his foes in the Senate and House admitted was a *tour de force*. Restating his major premises for a victory in Korea, the seventy-one-year-old general laid the basis for future controversy by declaring that these aims "have been fully shared by practically every military leader, including our own Joint Chiefs of Staff." More generally, he reiterated his conviction that foreign problems were "global and interlocked" and that neither Asia nor Europe could be considered separately. Under no condition, he warned again, must Formosa fall under Communist control, and those who would appease Red China he called "blind," adding that it was unlikely that the Soviet Union would enter the conflict in Korea if it was pressed more vigorously. Closing his remarks, he referred to a refrain about old soldiers never dying but just fading away. "And like the old soldier of that ballad," he concluded, "I now close my military career and just fade away—an old soldier who tried to do his duty as God gave him the light to see that duty. Good-bye."[35]

The reaction to the address, carried on national television, was sensational. MacArthur was applauded time and time again as he delivered his remarks. Afterward James Reston of the *New York Times* wrote that the general had heated political passions already near the boiling point and had divided "Washington more profoundly than it has ever been divided at any time since the start of the cold war." Following his speech, MacArthur received the key to the city of Washington and then led a motorcade down Pennsylvania Avenue as a quarter of a million people watched and as jet fighters and bombers flew overhead. The next day, in New York City, seven and a half million people (nearly twice the number that had watched General Eisenhower return from Europe in 1945) turned out to see and cheer the soldier-turned-statesman.[36]

Considering the emotion that MacArthur's return to the United States generated, the Democratic leadership on Capitol Hill had little choice but to agree to Republican plans to hold a full-scale investigation of the administration's Far East policy. The hearings, which were conducted by the Senate Armed Services and Senate Foreign Relations Committees and which lasted seven weeks, began on May 3. The first witness was General MacArthur, who answered questions for twenty-one hours during a three-day period. The general brought no prepared statement, saying that he had commented fully in addressing Congress. He then sat back to await the first questions by Richard Russell of Georgia, the chairman of the Armed Services Committee. Democrats on the Senate panel had prepared well for MacArthur's appearance, deciding ahead of time to handle the general with great deference but at the same time to pinpoint his views on foreign policy and military matters in order to make clear to the American public just how fuzzy and fraught with danger his position really was.[37]

The questions the Democrats prepared, therefore, touched on such matters as the implications and consequences of a bombardment of Manchuria, the effectiveness of a blockade of China, and the likely results of an invasion of the Chinese mainland by forces of Chiang Kai-shek, all of which MacArthur had advocated in his speech to Congress. What evidence did MacArthur have, for example, that the Soviet Union would not go to war if the United States should bomb Manchuria? Did he believe that the United States could hold its allies together while following his program? To what extent did MacArthur believe his policy of aerial bombardment of Manchuria should be carried out? Should it be mere tactical bombing of troops and supply concentrations? Or should it involve strategic bombing of Manchurian and Chinese cities? These and other similar questions comprised a substantial list, which the Democrats believed would pin down MacArthur politely but firmly to precise details.[38]

As in his speech to Congress, MacArthur remained supremely confident in his three days of testimony. In essence what he said was that victory, not prolonged indecision, must be the objective of war and that once the United States engaged in conflict in Korea, it had no choice but to do what was necessary to bring about victory. There was no substitute for victory. Although it was possible that his strategy might bring the Soviet Union into the war, that was highly unlikely, considering America's superior industrial and military power; in any case, the possibility of Soviet intervention had been discounted in America's original decision to fight in Korea. Furthermore, MacArthur concluded, his views were "fully shared" by the military commanders in the field and by the Joint Chiefs of Staff, as indicated by their recommendations of January 12.[39]

Articulate, voluble, courteous, and patient, MacArthur was in many ways a model witness as he portrayed himself as a humble theater commander merely trying to carry out his orders and instructions as he interpreted them even when he believed them dangerous and potentially disastrous. Quite effectively and with little difficulty he fielded the first group of questions asked of him. No, he did not believe it was in the Soviet's capacity to mass a major attack from the Asiatic continent. Yes, if he had been permitted to use his air power when the Chinese entered the war in November, he had not "the faintest doubt" they would have been thrown back. No, one could not draw an easy line all the time between the military and political sides of a foreign policy matter. Nevertheless, when locked in battle, there "should be no artifice under the name of politics, which should handicap [one's] own men, decrease their chances of winning, and increase their losses."[40]

Despite MacArthur's virtuoso performance, as the hearings continued into the afternoon of the first day and then into the second and third days, the questions became harder and more probing and MacArthur more testy. Perhaps the most damaging testimony for his case against the administration was his admission on a number of occasions that he was only a theater commander who was not qualified to comment on questions outside his field of command. Democratic Senator Brien McMahon of Connecticut pressed MacArthur particularly hard on this issue. What would happen, he asked the general, if his estimate of the world situation was wrong and if the United States was plunged into an all-out war? "That doesn't happen to be my responsibility, Senator," MacArthur replied. "My responsibilities were in the Pacific, and the Joint Chiefs of Staff and the various agencies of this Government are working day and night for an over-all solution to the global problem." That was exactly right, McMahon responded. The President must consider all matters on a global basis. "You as a theater commander by your own statement have not made that kind of study, and yet you advise us to push forward with a course of action that may involve us in that global conflict." MacArthur must have realized the mistake he made in casting himself in the role of "only a theater commander," because the next day he tried to make the point that a general knowledge of global problems was, of course, necessary by all theater commanders to coordinate the demands of their own theater with larger global problems. But the point about his limited knowledge of other areas had already been made part of the record.[41]

On another matter the general repeated a statement that clearly was not true. This was his assertion that the Joint Chiefs of Staff, in their memorandum of January 12, had agreed with the course of action he recommended to them, namely an economic and naval blockade of China, the end of restrictions on air reconnaissance of

China's coastal areas and of Manchuria, and the end of restrictions on the operations of the Chinese Nationalist forces against the Chinese Communists. As the next witness, Defense Secretary Marshall, pointed out, MacArthur's proposals were only four of sixteen options that were put forward when the military situation was bleak in Korea and the Joint Chiefs of Staff had to consider the possibility of an evacuation. Furthermore, as the military situation in Korea improved toward the middle of January, it became unnecessary to put into effect all the courses of action outlined in the Joint Chiefs' memorandum of January 12.[42]

Having disposed of the Joint Chiefs' memorandum, Marshall then touched on a number of other salient points. He especially criticized MacArthur's ultimatum of March 24 to the Communists. This action aborted negotiations at the diplomatic level, "thus losing whatever chance there may have been at that time to negotiate a settlement of the Korean conflict." In addition, Marshall stated that MacArthur would have the United States carry the war against the Communists beyond Korea and would take the risk of all-out war not only with Communist China but with the Soviet Union. "He would have us do this even at the expense of losing our allies and wrecking the coalition of free peoples throughout the world. He would have us do this even though the effect of such action might expose Western Europe to attack by millions of Soviet troops poised in Middle and Eastern Europe."[43]

The most forceful spokesman for the administration, however, was not Marshall, but General Omar Bradley, who followed the defense secretary to the witness stand. The Joint Chiefs of Staff had "global responsibilities," he said, and were "in a better position to assess the risks of a general war than a theater commander." The Soviet Union and not China was the United States' chief opponent. Getting further involved with Communist China would not guarantee a Korean victory, but could mean leaping from a smaller conflict "to a larger deadlock at greater expense." Indeed, Korea was just one phase of the battle to contain Communist expansion under Soviet leadership. The United States was not in a position to seek a showdown with the Soviet Union. MacArthur's plans would put the United States "in the wrong war, at the wrong place, at the wrong time and with the wrong enemy." In addition, the policy the government was following was recommended by the Joint Chiefs of Staff and, in Bradley's opinion, was the most prudent course for the

United States to follow in Korea, even though he could not guarantee that it would produce decisive results. Refusing to enlarge the fight to the point where America's global capacities were diminished was certainly not appeasement; rather it was a militarily sound course under the present circumstances. Like Marshall, Bradley also stressed the importance of maintaining America's friendly relations with its allies and noted the disadvantages that would follow the loss of their approval.[44]

By the time Bradley finished his testimony, it had become increasingly clear, even to the Republicans on the Senate panel, that MacArthur had stepped out of line and that Truman had acted within his authority in firing him. Each of the Joint Chiefs who then followed Bradley, moreover, reaffirmed, on strictly military grounds, his approval of the decision to fire MacArthur. Of the Chiefs, the most important testimony came from Air Force General Hoyt Vandenberg, who, better than anyone else, dispelled the notion that the Joint Chiefs of Staff had allowed personal animus rather than strictly professional considerations to color their views on MacArthur. Bombing Manchuria, Vandenberg stated, would have committed a "shoestring" air force and left the United States "naked" in other areas that needed protection without any guarantee of bringing about a decisive victory in Korea. Besides, MacArthur's proposal required twice as many strategic bombing groups than the United States possessed.[45]

The emotional climax of the hearings came on Friday, June 1, when Secretary of State Acheson took the witness stand. For nine days the senators bore in with questions for Acheson. On trial was not simply the firing of MacArthur but the administration's entire Far East policy. In response to the release by the Republicans of a 1949 classified document on Formosa, whose import was that the Department of State should emphasize Formosa's military incompetence in case it should fall to the Communists, Acheson delivered a three-hour statement that amounted to a diplomatic history of Sino-American relations from before World War II. The crux of his remarks consisted of the intricacies of Chinese politics and the complexities of discussions on China. If there was a central theme to Acheson's commentary, it was, as he later said, "the century-long disintegration of China's ancient institutions and ways of life from collision with the Western world." The United States, according to

Acheson, did not "lose" China; it was the corruption of the Chiang Kai-shek regime and its failure to broaden the government that accounted for that.[46]

By the last two days of Acheson's testimony, all sides had become so tired of the hearings that on June 18 they voted to hear only four more witnesses from a prospective list of more than a hundred. Three of these were high military officers who had served in the Far East. The fourth was retired General Patrick Hurley, who had been ambassador to China from 1944 to 1945. But they added little to what had already been said.[47]

The hearings over, the Senate panel decided to issue no final report. As Dean Acheson later explained, Chairman Russell believed that a majority report would invite a minority report, which would be divisive and serve no useful purpose. Russell chose instead to deal "with those gloriously broad generalities to which the wise and just could repair, thus turning the committee from unhappy differences to universal agreement." But eight of the twelve Republicans on the panel did issue a series of "conclusions" in which they took the administration to task on a number of accounts. They criticized the manner in which MacArthur had been relieved of his duties, the lack of plan for victory in Korea except as MacArthur advocated, and the fact that the White House had been more concerned with conciliating the other members of the United Nations than with advancing the security of the United States. They also attributed Chiang Kai-shek's defeat in China solely to the fact "that he did not receive sufficient support, both moral and material, from the United States." But on the central question of Truman's decision to relieve MacArthur, the Republicans remarked that the "removal of Gen. MacArthur was within the constitutional power of the President." On that note one of the most dramatic and politically important confrontations of the postwar era ended.[48]

Following the hearings, MacArthur traveled throughout the country, speaking out even more strongly against the administration than he had during his testimony before the Senate panel, but always to diminishing audiences. In June the general traveled to Texas for a four-day, six-city tour. In Houston, free shuttle service was provided to Rice Institute's new stadium where he was to speak. But when the general delivered his address, only about 20,000 of the stadium's 70,000 seats were filled. At the Cotton Bowl in Dallas, MacArthur attracted an equally small crowd of about 27,000. By the time he had finished his tour, in fact, fewer than 100,000 Texans had bothered to hear him speak. The general had simply become old news, and the American public had tired of the controversy surrounding his firing.[49]

As for Truman, a Gallup poll in June showed that only 24 percent of those polled now approved of his handling of the Presidency. Even many of those who had stood firmly behind Truman in his decision to fire MacArthur and who had generally supported his conduct of the war were now wondering aloud about his effectiveness as President. Partly this concern reflected their fear that the White House was trying to preempt the opposition by adopting a more inflexible anti-Communist position. Here they had mainly in mind the firm stand against UN membership for Communist China or discussion of the Formosa question that Secretaries Marshall and Acheson had taken in their testimony during the MacArthur hearings. But they were also concerned by a White House decision in May to tighten the economic blockade of China and even to bomb Manchurian air bases in the event of a massive Chinese air attack on UN forces from Manchuria.[50]

Beyond their concerns about administration policy, however, even these critics came to share some of the same doubts about the President's leadership that Truman's more strident opponents were expressing. If they were less engaged in character assassination than the latter, their conclusion was often much the same—that President Truman was a disaster. "Nothing like the present collapse of Administration control in Congress has been seen since Hoover's day," the *New Republic* thus remarked toward the end of May. "All that was happening in 1933 was the collapse of the banks, but today a war is on. . . . Truman's prestige is near bottom; what exists is a stalemate, a sit-down strike . . . the Ship of State drifts. Nobody is in control."[51]

Unquestionably, Truman's firing of MacArthur had been one of the most courageous and important actions by any President in the twentieth century. By his peremptory dismissal of a figure who, for many, had become a symbol of national destiny, Truman had reaffirmed the fundamental principles of executive control over foreign policy and the President's role as commander-in-chief of the armed services. But with twenty-one months left before Truman would leave office and with the Korean war dragging on from month to month, only a relatively few Americans sensed the long-term implications of what the President had done.

As the Korean War entered its second year, in fact, the optimism of February and March, when UN forces had contained the Communist drive in Korea and begun an offensive of their own, had largely disappeared. By this time, the war had turned into a military deadlock without an apparent end. In the minds of many Americans the one military genius who might have snatched victory from disaster had been relieved of his command by one of the nation's most inept Presidents. The national mood was thus one of dissatisfaction and disillusionment. Yet even before the MacArthur hearings had ended, new hope for a negotiated end to the war developed, when the Soviet delegate to the United Nations, Jacob Malik, indicated that the Soviet Union was ready for a cease-fire in Korea. From this first intimation would follow the opening of peace talks in July.

Notes

1. Roy E. Appleman, *Ridgway Duels for Korea* (College Station, TX, 1990), 38–132; James F. Schnabel, *Policy and Direction: The First Year* (Washington, DC, 1972), 326–327 and 333–334; *Time*, 57 (January 15, 1951), 21–23.
2. Appleman, *Ridgway Duels for Korea*, 83–84 and 120–132; *Time*, 57 (January 8, 1951), 15–16; *ibid.* (January 29, 1951), 28–29; Edgar O'Ballance, *Korea: 1950–1953* (London, 1969), 73–76.
3. Appleman, *Ridgway Duels for Korea*, 29; David Rees, *Korea: The Limited War* (New York, 1964), 184–191; Schnabel, *Policy and Direction*, 333–339; *Time*, 57 (February 5, 1951), 19; *ibid.* (February 26, 1951), 28; *Life*, 30 (February 19, 1951), 25 and 34.
4. Appleman, *Ridgway Duels for Korea*, 147–148 and 579–580; *Life*, 30 (February 19, 1951), 25; *Time*, 57 (March 5, 1951), 26–28.
5. D. Clayton James, *Refighting the Last War: Command and Crisis in Korea, 1950–1953* (New York, 1993), 54–63; Appleman, *Ridgway Duels for Korea,* 147–192; O'Ballance, *Korea*, 82–83; *Time*, 57 (March 5, 1951), 26–28.
6. James F. Schnabel and Robert J. Watson, *The History of the Joint Chiefs of Staff*, III, *The Korean War* (Wilmington, DE, 1979), 439–440.
7. Appleman, *Ridgway Duels for Korea*, 218–314; Schnabel, *Policy and Direction*, 339–340; *Time*, 57 (February 26, 1951), 28.
8. Appleman, *Ridgway Duels for Korea*, 315–449; Schnabel and Watson, *The History of the Joint Chiefs of Staff*, III, *The Korean War*, 466; Schnabel, *Policy and Direction*, 354–364; *Time*, 57 (March 26, 1951), 28–29; Rees, *Korea: The Limited War*, 191–193.

9. *FR*, 1951, VII, 152–153 and 165–167; Dean Acheson, *Present at the Creation: My Years in the State Department* (New York, 1969), 517; Schnabel, *Policy and Direction*, 350–351.

10. Schnabel, *Policy and Direction*, 350–351.

11. "Memorandum for the Secretary of Defense," February 27, 1951, Box 16, Selected Records Relating to the Korean War.

12. "Memorandum of Conversation," March 6, 1951, Box 3, Selected Records Relating to the Korean War; *FR*, 1951, VII, 202–203 and 211–213; Schnabel and Watson, *The History of the Joint Chiefs of Staff*, III, *The Korean War*, 477. For a somewhat different view, which emphasizes the pressures in Washington to expand the war, including even operations against China, see Rosemary Foot, *The Wrong War: American Policy and the Dimensions of the Korean Conflict, 1950–1953* (Ithaca, NY, 1985), 128–134.

13. *Life*, 30 (March 12, 1951), 64–68; *ibid.* (April 16, 1954), 44–45; *Nation*, 172 (March 24, 1951), 264; *New Republic*, 124 (March 26, 1951), 5–6 and 13–16.

14. *Nation*, 172 (March 10, 1951), 218 and 223; *Commonweal*, 53 (March 9, 1951), 534; *Atlantic Monthly*, 187 (March 1951), 13; Peter Lowe, "The Frustrations of Alliance: Britain, the United States and the Korean War, 1950–1951," in James Cotton and Ian Neary (eds.), *The Korean War in History* (Atlantic Highlands, NJ, 1989), 93–96.

15. *New Yorker*, 27 (March 24, 1951), 88–91; *Atlantic Monthly*, 187 (March 1951), 6–8; *Commonweal*, 53 (March 16, 1951), 555.

16. Stephen Ambrose, *Eisenhower: Soldier, General of the Army, President-Elect, 1890–1952* (New York, 1983), 500–504; *New Republic*, 124 (April 16, 1951), 5–6.

17. *FR*, 1951, VII, 223–226; Harry S. Truman, *Years of Trial and Hope: Memoirs* (New York, 1965), 497.

18. *FR*, 1951, VII, 246–247, 251, and 264–265; Schnabel, *Policy and Direction*, 357; Truman, *Years of Trial and Hope*, 498–499.

19. Acheson, *Present at the Creation*, 517.

20. *FR*, 1951, VII, 255–256.

21. *Ibid.*, 731–732 and 785–786; Schnabel, *Policy and Direction*, 357; Truman, *Years of Trial and Hope*, 498–499.

22. John W. Spanier, *The Truman-MacArthur Controversy and the Korean War* (Cambridge, MA, 1959), 201–202; Schnabel, *Policy and Direction*, 358–359.

23. Unsigned Memorandum, March 24, 1951, Box 66, Acheson Papers; Acheson, *Present at the Creation*, 519; *Life*, 30 (March 9, 1951), 36.

24. Acheson, *Present at the Creation*, 519; *FR*, 1951, VII, 267.

25. William Manchester, *American Caesar: Douglas MacArthur, 1880–1964* (Boston, 1978), 638; *FR*, 1951, VII, 299.

26. Michael Schaller, "Douglas MacArthur: The China Issue, Policy Con-

flict, and the Korean War," in Kim Chull Baum and James I. Matray (eds.), *Korea and the Cold War: Division, Destruction, and Disarmament* (Claremont, CA, 1993), 187–190; Roger Dingman, "Atomic Diplomacy During the Korean War," *International Security*, 13 (Winter, 1988–89), 69–75.

27. Richard H. Rovere and Arthur Schlesinger, Jr., *The MacArthur Controversy and American Foreign Policy* (New York, 1951), 172; Acheson, *Present at the Creation*, 521.
28. Acheson, *Present at the Creation*, 521–523; Truman, *Years of Trial and Hope*, 508–509; Rovere and Schlesinger, Jr., *The MacArthur Controversy and American Foreign Policy*, 175–176.
29. Rovere and Schlesinger, Jr., *The MacArthur Controversy and American Foreign Policy*, 170; Trumbull Higgins, *Korea and the Fall of MacArthur: A Precis in Limited War* (New York, 1960), 110.
30. Cabell Phillips, *The Truman Presidency: The History of a Triumphant Succession* (Baltimore, 1969), 336; Robert J. Donovan, *Tumultuous Years: The Presidency of Harry S. Truman, 1949–1953* (New York, 1982), 311–312; Robert H. Ferrell, *Harry S. Truman and the Modern American Presidency* (Boston, 1983), 188–189.
31. Spanier, *The Truman-MacArthur Controversy and the Korean War*, 211–212.
32. Donovan, *Tumultuous Years*, 358–359; *Time*, 57 (April 23, 1951), 26; David M. Oshinsky, *A Conspiracy So Immense: The World of Joe McCarthy* (New York, 1983), 194; Phillips, *The Truman Presidency: The History of a Triumphant Succession* (New York, 1966), 345.
33. *Nation*, 172 (April 4, 1951), 337; *New Republic*, 124 (April 23, 1951), 5–6; *New Yorker*, 27 (April 21, 1951), 106; *Congressional Quarterly Almanac*, VII (1951), 243.
34. Phillips, *The Truman Presidency*, 347–348; Spanier, *The Truman-MacArthur Controversy and the Korean War*, 217; *Nation*, 172 (April 28, 1951), 388.
35. Rovere and Schlesinger, Jr., *The MacArthur Controversy and American Foreign Policy*, 179–182.
36. *New York Times*, April 20, 1951; Spanier, *The Truman-MacArthur Controversy and the Korean War*, 217; Phillips, *The Truman Presidency* (Baltimore, 1969), 348; *Nation*, 172 (April 28, 1951), 388.
37. "Memorandum on Questions for MacArthur Hearings," Box 341, Lyndon Baines Johnson Papers, U.S. Senate, 1949–1961, Lyndon Baines Johnson Library (Austin, Texas).
38. *Ibid*.
39. U.S. Congress, *Military Situation in the Far East*, Hearings Before the Joint Senate Committee on Armed Services and Foreign Relations, 82nd Congress, 1st Session, 11–13, 22–26, 29–30, 39–40, 54–55, 67–68, and 136–137.

40. *Ibid.*, 11–20, 25–26, and 45–48.
41. *Ibid.*, 76; "Some General Observations on the Hearings," n.d. Box 341, Johnson Papers, U.S. Senate, 1946–1961. See also Higgins, *Korea and the Fall of MacArthur*, 160–161.
42. Senate Hearings, *Military Situation in the Far East*, 324–325; *New York Times*, May 5, 1951. See also James, *Refighting the Last War*, 216–217.
43. Senate Hearings, *Military Situation in the Far East*, 324–325.
44. *Ibid.*, 730–744. See also "Analysis of May 15 Testimony," n.d. Box 341, Johnson Papers, United States Senate, 1949–1961.
45. Senate Hearings, *Military Situation in the Far East*, 1375–1390.
46. *Ibid.*, 1673–1714, 1756, 1765–1766, 1837–1885, 1945–1947, 1994–1996, and 2008–2010; Acheson, *Present at the Creation*, 525.
47. Senate Hearings, *Military Situation in the Far East*, 2338–2342 and 2827–2856.
48. "Individual Views of Certain Members . . . ," Senate Hearings, *Military Situation in the Far East*, 3567–3575.
49. *Time*, 57 (June 25, 1951), 21–22; *New Republic*, 124 (June 25, 1951), 6; *Life*, 30 (June 25, 1951), 40–42.
50. *Time*, 57 (June 25, 1951), 18; *New Yorker*, 27 (May 19, 1951), 71; *New Republic*, 124 (May 21, 1951), 5–6; *ibid.* (May 28, 1951), 5; *Nation*, 172 (May 26, 1951), 481. See also *Life*, 30 (May 14, 1951), 40.
51. *New Republic*, 124 (May 21, 1951), 3; *Atlantic Monthly*, 187 (June 1951), 4; *Nation*, 172 (March 31, 1951), 300–301; *ibid.* (April 14, 1951), 341.

CHAPTER FIVE

Negotiations

Although the Soviet Union originated the series of events that led to the opening of cease-fire talks in July 1951, pressure on the Truman administration to arrange a cease-fire in Korea had been mounting among America's European allies and at the United Nations since the President fired General MacArthur in April. While the White House and State Department generally agreed that the United States should undertake a peace initiative following the lines of the statement the President had intended to issue in March, before MacArthur had torpedoed the plan, they also felt strongly that no peace proposal could be made until after the outcome of a military offensive that the Communists had launched on April 22. Otherwise, it would appear the United States was merely acting from a position of military weakness.[1]

Begun in the early evening of April 22, after a four-hour artillery barrage, the Chinese attack turned out to be their greatest military effort of the war. Striking in massive numbers and employing their now familiar tactic of human wave assaults accompanied by shouting and loud bugle blowing, they sought to envelop and isolate Seoul from the north and northeast. But the heaviest fighting was just south of the Imjin River, about twenty-five miles northwest of Seoul, where the heavily outnumbered British Twenty-ninth Infantry brigade and a small contingent of other UN forces beat back the enemy for almost three days before being ordered to withdraw toward Seoul. By the time the fighting ended, the Twenty-ninth had suffered more than a thousand casualties, and only thirty-nine officers and men were left of the 622 men comprising its famed Gloucestershire Regiment.[2]

Fighting in other sectors along the front was also fierce. To the

115

right of the Twenty-ninth, the American Third Division, which had retreated to the Imjin River, came under heavy attack by Chinese forces, many of whom had been newly outfitted and rearmed. Farther east, in the Marine and ROK zone of IX Corps, two ROK artillery units were overrun after losing all their equipment. To preserve his forces, General James Van Fleet, who had taken over the Eighth Army after General Ridgway assumed MacArthur's duties in Tokyo, ordered a withdrawal of up to twenty-five miles to a new line, NO NAME, running roughly from Seoul along the north bank of the Han River.[3]

The withdrawal of UN forces, however, was much different from the disorderly retreat of the previous winter. In the first place, the attack had been expected. Although its scope and intensity had not been predicted, military intelligence knew that the Chinese were building up their forces for a spring offensive. As a result, UN forces were better prepared when the Chinese did strike; they had built their defensive positions on the best possible terrain and surrounded them with minefields and wire entanglements. Second, even though they were forced to give ground before the sheer numbers of the enemy, they retreated in good order, fighting at favorable spots and inflicting maximum casualties on the Chinese through superior air and fire power.[4]

By the end of April the Communist offensive had spent itself. Efforts to outflank Seoul failed. The historic capital remained in UN hands. General Van Fleet had his army intact at the NO NAME line and was even holding back some reserves. Its food and ammunition exhausted, the enemy withdrew in the face of UN firepower. For a maximum gain of thirty-five miles, the Chinese had suffered an estimated 70,000 casualties, as opposed to 7000 casualties for UN forces.[5]

On May 16 the Chinese launched the second phase of their spring offensive, but this too failed. Suffering enormous losses as they moved against defenses heavily protected with mines, barbed wire, interlocking machine gun fire, an enormous wall of artillery fire power, and drums of napalm that could be detonated electronically, the Chinese achieved only a relatively narrow penetration on a secondary front. The carnage was the worst of the war. Chinese losses were estimated at 90,000 for the week of May 17 to May 23 alone and in excess of 200,000 for both phases of the spring offensive. Furthermore, instead of having his men dig in after beating back the enemy, Van Fleet went on the offensive. Within five days UN forces and tanks had once more crossed the 38th parallel. In every sector the Chinese were falling back, their spring offensive having been routed.[6]

How far above the 38th parallel UN forces might have advanced had they been permitted to do so is difficult to determine. On the one hand, the Chinese were disorganized and demoralized. For the first time in the war they were surrendering in large numbers—more than 17,000 in the last two weeks of May. Certainly Van Fleet felt his forces should have been allowed to move farther north. "[W]e had the Chinese whipped," he later remarked. "They were definitely gone. They were in awful shape." On the other hand, more than one million Communist troops still remained in North Korea, and as the UN armies moved north toward the Iron Triangle, enemy resistance stiffened considerably. Any move into the Iron Triangle would almost certainly have meant enormous UN casualties.[7]

Political considerations, even more than military factors, however, were responsible for the decision to limit the UN offensive into North Korea. Responding to mounting world opinion against prolonging the war and believing that it could now negotiate from a position of strength, the Truman administration decided to halt the UN advance in order to test the chances for peace. Its decision represented a sharp departure from its initial response to the Chinese offensive, which had been to ask the United Nations for a select embargo on war goods for China, including oil, and to authorize General Ridgway to institute retaliatory bombing of Chinese bases in Manchuria in the event they were used for a massive attack against UN forces.[8]

Although the United States gained the support of its coalition partners in Korea for both these resolutions, it did not come easily. While the British, for example, were willing to go along with a partial embargo, they made clear their opposition to a complete embargo, which the administration would have preferred but which would have impacted adversely on its colony of Hong Kong. But even more touchy was the possible use of air power against Chinese air bases in Manchuria. General Ridgway had first raised the question of bombing the Manchurian air bases in March when he asked the Joint Chiefs of Staff for authority to retaliate against the bases if they were used to attack his forces.[9]

By this time, the Chinese were far along in building a considerable force of MiG-15 jets and other fighter planes able to strike against UN forces from bases in Manchuria. On April 12, eighty of these MiG fighters attacked forty-eight B-29s and their escorts. Once again, the Far East commander asked for authority to retaliate against the Manchurian air bases if the Chinese launched a major air attack against UN forces, and this time President Truman approved Ridgway's request. Although the British agreed to go along "in principle" with the President's decision, they had made clear throughout the months in which the question of bombing had been under review their serious reservations about attacking Manchuria, which, they feared, could lead to a world war. Furthermore, they insisted that any decision for retaliation against China should be made by the President rather than by the Joint Chiefs and should have London's approval.[10]

England's reluctance to go along with the United States on the bombing issue and on an embargo against China added to the larger malaise that characterized America's relations with its European allies in the spring of 1951. Washington and London remained extremely close allies, of course. While the occasion for much heated language both in England and the United States, the conflict over Far East policy was part of what the respected British economist John Cleveland referred to as the "growing pains of Anglo-America," which allowed the two countries to engage in mutual self-criticism.[11]

Yet it was not only on the issues of the Korean war and America's Far East policy that substantial differences had developed between London and Washington. Another was the costs of rearmament. In fact, the Labor Party had split over this question. In April, Aneurin Bevan, the leader of the Labor left, even resigned from the Cabinet because of it. In explaining to Parliament the reasons for his resignation, Bevan bitterly assailed the United States. "We have allowed ourselves to be dragged too far . . . behind the anarchy of American competitive capitalism," he told the House of Commons.[12]

Other Europeans expressed similar sentiments. Indeed, opposition to the costs of rearmament was even greater in France than in England. The French believed that they had still not recovered sufficiently from the shattering economic effects of World War II to divert as large a proportion of production for defense as the United

States or even England. Many Frenchmen also complained of undue American pressure to rearm. In elections in June, Charles de Gaulle's Rassamblement du Peuples Francais gained the largest share of deputy seats in the National Assembly, 117 of 627, on a program that included resistance to American demands.[13]

Nevertheless, the Korean war remained the outstanding issue in world politics. Like the British, America's other coalition partners in Korea and most neutral and Third World nations at the United Nations opposed any military action that might continue, or even escalate, the war indefinitely. Although America's allies understood the symbolic importance of Korea in terms of resisting Communist expansion, most of them did not impute the same sense of crisis to the conflict as Washington did. Furthermore, they had to weigh other problems and commitments. The European powers continued to worry, especially about becoming further mired in an Asian conflict while the Soviet Union had the capacity to strike somewhere in Europe. Neutral and Third World nations also remained concerned that the Korean war could escalate into a much larger nuclear confrontation involving the world's two superpowers.[14]

Responding to this growing pressure of world opinion and confident that it could negotiate from a position of military strength, the Truman administration decided to make a new effort at arranging a cease fire. On instructions from the State Department, George Kennan held two meetings in May with Jacob Malik, the Soviet ambassador at the United Nations, during which he made clear the United States' desire to arrange an armistice or cease-fire. Nothing was heard from the Soviets for more than two weeks. But perhaps responding to hints from Washington that the United States would accept the 38th parallel as a dividing line between UN and Communist forces and undoubtedly anxious to end a war in which the chances of victory had grown slim, Moscow made a surprise move. On June 22, Malik delivered a speech in which he said that the Soviet people believed the Korean conflict could be ended.[15]

By speaking in terms of the "Soviet people" rather than the Soviet government and by remarking that discussions were only "a first step" toward ending the Korean conflict, Malik semed to hedge a little in his speech. But Acheson decided that while the United States should act with great care, it should enter into negotiations. Earlier Kennan had warned him that if the United States continued to advance into North Korea without making an effort to achieve a cease-fire, the Soviet Union would "see no alternative but to intervene themselves [in Korea]." From Moscow Ambassador Alan G. Kirk reported that Malik's remarks represented a "significant new turn in [the] Soviet approach to Korea." Remarks in Chinese newspapers indicating that Chinese authorities approved of Malik's statement strengthened the argument for pursuing this apparently new opportunity to end the war. A peace initiative also had strong support in the American press.[16]

The question that faced Acheson and others within the administration was how to proceed with negotiations. The State Department and the Pentagon concluded that it would be best for the military commanders in the field to arrange a cease-fire. Not only would that avoid the thorny question of negotiating with two governments not recognized by the United States, China and North Korea, it would also make it easier to exclude sensitive political questions from the talks. On June 30, Tokyo time, General Ridgway therefore broadcast a message to the Chinese, stating that if, as reported, they and their North Korean allies desired to negotiate a cease-fire and armistice, he was prepared to appoint a representative to meet with them.[17]

What happened over the next ten days was a harbinger of things to come. In Moscow Deputy Foreign Minister Andrei Gromyko had led the United States to believe that negotiations would involve only military issues and not political or territorial matters. But in their response to Ridgway's message, the Chinese indicated that they wanted broader negotiations involving a peace settlement. Meanwhile, Ridgway, who was against any proposal to halt hostilities prior to reaching an armistice agreement, dueled with the Joint Chiefs of Staff. The Joint Chiefs agreed with Ridgway that hostilities should continue until an armistice agreement was reached, but they also ordered him not to do anything else that might cause the enemy to change its mind about beginning negotiations.[18]

Carrying out his orders, Ridgway agreed to both the time (July 10) and the place (Kaesong) recommended by the Communists for the beginning of talks. But in another appeal to the Joint Chiefs of Staff he urged that UN forces not be required by any final cease-fire agreement to withdraw farther south than the KANSAS LINE. "Any position taken by our government," Ridgway told the Joint Chiefs of Staff, "which would compel me to abandon the Kansas line or deny me a reasonable outpost zone for its protection would vitally prejudice our entire military position in Korea."[19]

News that negotiations to end the war would soon begin created new hope in the United States and overseas. In Congress a number of Republicans did express reservations and suspicions about the administration's efforts to begin cease-fire talks. But attempts to cut foreign spending and eliminate all wage and price controls began almost immediately after it was learned that Communist and UN negotiators would soon meet at the negotiating table. Overseas one journalist reported from London that the "moves toward peace in Korea [had] filled Londoners with hope as bright as the deep, blue mid-summer skies that are now arching over the city," while another commentator wrote from Rome that the Italians, tied as they were to the inflated American dollar, hoped that "international financial tensions [would] abate with a Korean truce."[20]

In contrast, South Korea expressed alarm at the prospect of an armistice with the Communists that would leave Korea divided. At the time arrangements were concluded to hold peace talks, the ROK government was faced with enormous economic and social problems. Much of South Korea had, of course, been ravaged by the fighting, but along with the war had also come a large refugee problem, major concerns about health and sanitation, and skyrocketing inflation. In the first weeks of the Chinese invasion, close to one million refugees had fled south to Seoul and its environs. By June there were probably between three and six million displaced persons in South Korea. All over the south, refugee camps were set up to provide shelter for the homeless, but they were not enough. Although a number of relief organizations, such as the World Health Organization and the Red Cross, were effective in inoculating refugees against such killers as smallpox and typhus, medical facilities in most refugee camps were inadequate to handle the huge number of cases of disease resulting from overcrowding and poor living conditions. Furthermore, the war contributed to a serious inflation. Prices were more than eight times what they had been three years earlier, the tax system was inefficient and poorly administered, and the government was deeply in debt. As for the government, President Rhee remained despotic and highly unpopular.

Nevertheless, most South Koreans joined Rhee in opposing any plan that divided Korea at the 38th parallel. To reestablish the 38th parallel, American Ambassador John Muccio thus told Secretary of State Acheson "would bring a violent explosion from all Koreans and we would have [the] greatest difficulty keeping them within bounds and controlling ROK forces." Rhee wanted nothing less than to continue military operations once more to the Yalu River, and his government made clear to Washington that anything less would invite another invasion of South Korea by the Communists. His government's security would become impossible, and the Korean people would become demoralized and disillusioned with the United Nations.[21]

Anticipating the Korean reaction to the news of cease-fire negotiations, Acheson sent Muccio a virtual shopping list of points that he should use in presenting the American position regarding talks with the Communists. All of them indicated the hard line the administration intended to take toward any South Korean resistance to peace. They also underscored just how far the United States had traveled from the heady days of late October and November 1950, when the military reunification of Korea seemed all but assured.

Thus Acheson instructed Muccio to make clear to Rhee that his government never had any international recognition north of the 38th parallel; that while an independent and unified Korea had been American policy since 1941 and a UN aim since 1947, neither the United States nor the United Nations had ever assumed that unification should be achieved by force regardless of the circumstances; and that the situation in Korea had changed dramatically since October 7 when the North Korean armies were falling apart and the presumption could be made that neither the Soviet Union nor the People's Republic of China would intervene in Korea. Furthermore, Muccio was instructed by the secretary of state to tell Rhee, in what amounted to a thinly veiled threat, that if, by his intransigence, provocations, and inflammatory statements, he jeopardized an acceptable peace settlement, he could "expect a revulsion of feeling" against Korea by the American people, who had saved his country from destruction at a cost of nearly 100,000 battlefield casualties.[22]

Nothing that Muccio told Rhee did much to deter the aged president from his conviction that the war in Korea had to continue until the Communists were defeated and the country was unified under his leadership. Nevertheless, the United States went forward with its plans to hold talks with the Communists, and, bowing to

American pressure, the South Korean government agreed to be represented at the negotiations, which both the UN and Communist sides said would begin at Kaesong, the ancient capital of Korea, on July 10.[23]

The first two meetings on July 10 and 11 revealed the considerable differences in negotiating positions between the two sides. The UN delegation, headed by Admiral C. Turner Joy, commander of naval forces in the Far East, sought to limit the talks to purely military matters, to obtain a militarily defensible cease-fire line, and to establish a Military Armistice Commission to supervise the truce. The North Koreans and Chinese, led by General Nam Il of the Korean People's Army and General Hsieh Fang of the Chinese People's Volunteers, responded with a plan calling for a cease-fire line at the 38th parallel (in other words, a return to the *status quo ante bellum*) and the withdrawal of all foreign forces from Korea. Joy rejected both items, maintaining that the first amounted to a conclusion that should be the subject of negotiations, not a preliminary to them, and that the second involved a political issue beyond the scope of the talks.[24]

Very quickly the talks broke down over fundamental issues of protocol and procedure. First, the Communists attempted to confine the UN negotiators to a house in Kaesong and a well-guarded pathway from there to the conference building. Then they raised a question of the UN delegation's freedom to communicate with its base at Munsan, located a short distance from Kaesong, when they refused to allow a UN courier to pass through their lines. Finally, they challenged the right of the United Nations to decide the composition of its own delegation by refusing to permit a group of American newsmen to come to Kaesong even though they allowed a number of their own photographers to take pictures of the conference room over the protest of the UN delegation.[25]

Responding to these provocations, Admiral Joy broke off negotiations on July 12, telling the Chinese and North Koreans that if the talks were to continue, both sides would have to receive equal treatment at Kaesong, which would have to be demilitarized. The next day, Ridgway broadcast a message to the Communists outlining the new terms for resuming negotiations. Not only did they agree to Ridgway's demands, but once the talks resumed on July 17, they made a major concession by consenting to eliminate from the agenda any reference to the 38th parallel. In subsequent meetings, they also agreed not to make the withdrawal of foreign troops from Korea an agenda item. Instead, they consented to a new item, which allowed issues like foreign troop withdrawals to be included as recommendations that the negotiators would make "to the governments of the countries concerned."[26]

As a result of this substitution, the agenda for the rest of the talks was completed. It had taken ten meetings and long hours of staff negotiations, but now the negotiators could get down to the first substantive issue between them, fixing a cease-fire line. As far as the UN delegation was concerned, prospects for a successful conclusion of the war seemed good. Morale was high, the Communists had indicated a surprising willingness to compromise on the agenda, and UN forces held a strong defensive position. In many respects the need to keep their troops alert and their guard up when peace seemed so near was the most difficult problem facing UN officers.[27]

But there were other problems as well. In the first place, the enemy was being reinforced constantly, thereby increasing its capacity for launching still another offensive against South Korea. General Ridgway cautioned his commanders that an attack could come at any time the negotiations broke down or during the Japanese peace conference scheduled for September. Chinese air strength was also growing, so that for the first time they had effective control of the air over northwest Korea. Second, the South Koreans remained highly disturbed at the prospect of a permanently divided Korea, and President Rhee agitated openly against any compromise with the Communists, leading President Truman to warn the Korean leader that "the most serious consequences" would follow any attempt on his part to undermine the talks. Finally, while the Chinese and North Koreans had made several concessions on the agenda for negotiations, they were certain to bring up again the issues of the 38th parallel as a cease-fire line and the withdrawal of all foreign forces from Korea. And the UN negotiators were as certain to reject the Communist position on both these matters.[28]

Indeed, as soon as the substantive talks began, the Chinese and North Koreans insisted on the 38th parallel as the demarcation line. The UN negotiators responded by advocating a line north of the battle line to compensate for the cessation of air and naval activity as far north as the Yalu River that would take place after a cease-fire. Weeks passed without any progress toward ending the war.

Newspaper and radio reports became increasingly more pessimistic as to when a breakthrough in the talks would come. Increasingly, Americans began to lose interest in the truce negotiations, and coverage of them was taken off the front pages of newspapers. Major stories in the press included a Senate investigation of racketeering in the United States, new charges of corruption and malfeasance in the Truman administration, the national myopia of McCarthyism, and the Presidential elections still more than a year away. One might have expected the last two of these items to have been tied closely to the administration's conduct of the war, including its handling of the peace negotiations. For the most part, however, the Korean war was incidental to both these stories.[29]

Even in terms of foreign news, there were a number of recent developments, particularly in the Middle East, that competed with Korea for national attention. Of these the most important was the Iranian seizure of the Anglo-Iranian Oil Company (AIOC), a wholly owned firm of the British government that had a monopoly on oil production in Iran. This action was widely perceived in the United States as part of a much larger problem involving a growing tide of nationalism in the Middle East that threatened such vital interests as access to the region's oil and control over the Suez Canal and which posed the danger of Soviet expansionism. At the same time, the fact that the Kremlin did not take advantage of the dispute between Iran and AIOC to attack London or to interfere in Iran's internal affairs was seen by some as part of another development, a Soviet peace campaign, which was also much commented on in the summer and fall of 1951.[30]

Such stories as these and others still less connected with the war in Korea diverted public interest away from the tedious negotiations at Kaesong. Much of the summer, in fact, was frittered away with accusations by each side that the other had violated the neutral zone around Kaesong. Finally, on August 24, after accusing the UN command of bombing the conference site at Kaesong and displaying evidence, which, they alleged, proved their claim, the Chinese and North Koreans suspended the cease-fire talks indefinitely.[31]

Why the Communists chose to break off the truce talks at that time is not entirely clear. Perhaps, as General Ridgway suggested, they did so because they wanted more time to rebuild their forces or sought a propaganda ploy for internal Communist consumption. More likely, the Chinese and North Koreans suspended the talks because they wanted to mesh the resumption of negotiations with the forthcoming Japanese peace treaty conference in San Francisco in the hope of gaining more bargaining leverage, particularly in terms of preventing Japanese rearmament and alignment with the United States.

Of all the non-Communist areas of the Far East, Japan remained strategically the most direct threat to the Soviet Union and Communist China. Not only did it possess the only significant industrialized economy and skilled labor force in the region, it was the principal operational base for carrying out the war in Korea. But the danger from Japan extended far beyond Korea, for as a CIA intelligence estimate concluded in November, "from operational bases in Japan, anti-Communist forces [could] dominate the approaches to the Soviet Far East and northern China and could attack by air or sea all major industrial and military targets in the Communist-held areas of the Far East."[32]

For this reason, Beijing and Moscow attached great importance to preventing the rearmament of Japan and any military ties it might develop with the United States. By breaking off talks at Kaesong until the opening of the San Francisco Conference and then making concessions at Kaesong while the San Francisco conference was taking place, it seems the Communists hoped that they would appear as champions of world peace; they then could argue that peace could be achieved more expeditiously if threats of strategic alliance and Japanese rearmament were put aside.[33]

If this was their purpose, however, they badly miscalculated. An attempt by Soviet Deputy Foreign Minister Andrei Gromyko to have Communist China invited to the San Francisco meeting failed miserably. If anything, Gromyko's presence at the conference, along with representatives from Poland and Czechoslovakia, caused delegates from the other forty-nine countries represented at San Francisco to close ranks and muffle their own representatives about the peace treaty for fear of being identified with the Soviet opposition.[34]

Nor did the San Francisco conference have much effect on the negotiations at Kaesong, except, perhaps, to delay the resumption of talks a little. In fact, the delay was a mutual one, involving the UN Command as well as the Communist negotiators. General Ridgway was determined not to resume peace talks until the Communists agreed to a new location for negotiations, one where incidents of the kind that had led to the suspension of talks at Kaesong would not recur. Militarily, the UN commander felt he could be firm with the enemy. Although the North Koreans and Chinese were being reinforced with new troops, and China was becoming an increasingly dangerous factor in the air war over northwestern Korea, UN troop strength was also growing. In addition, Ridgway's forces were by now seasoned veterans, their position along the KANSAS LINE was becoming stronger each day, and the war was turning into a protracted stalemate. Lastly, the Chinese were believed anxious to avoid having to spend another winter on the battlefield. They were reported short of food and clothing, and China's industry was understood to be suffering severely from the Western embargo. Ridgway was convinced, therefore, that he could force the Communists to make concessions.[35]

Apparently he was right. Once again, the Chinese and North Koreans, who clearly wanted to end a war that had become extremely costly to them without much chance of victory, proved willing to make concessions. On October 7 they agreed to change the location for negotiations, just as Ridgway had predicted they would. Instead of Kaesong, they proposed that the new site for the talks be the village of Panmunjom, about five miles to the east. On October 25 UN and Communist negotiators met at Panmunjom for the first time since discussions had broken off two months earlier.[36]

Once the talks were resumed, the Chinese and North Koreans very quickly dropped their demand that the 38th parallel be the line of demarcation; instead they acknowledged the UN claim that the cease-fire line be the military front, or the point of contact between the two forces at the time the hostilities ended. In contrast, Ridgway insisted that Kaesong, which was strategically located across the approaches to Seoul, come into UN hands or be neutralized. But the administration refused to go along with Ridgway. In what was to become a familiar pattern, the Joint Chiefs of Staff warned the UN commander against being too inflexible and told him, with the President's approval, that the United Nations' minimum position remained the security of the KANSAS LINE. Everything else having to do with a cease-fire was negotiable.[37]

Simply put, the administration was under intense pressure both at home and abroad to reach a peace settlement. Having suffered a series of setbacks in the Middle East, including announcements by Cairo that it planned to break the treaty under which the British garrisoned the Suez Canal and by Baghdad that it intended to negotiate the agreement by which the British maintained air bases in Iraq, London was eager to end the war in Korea. In the United States, there was also a rapidly growing demand to negotiate a peace settlement. The *New York Times* stated that it could not understand why the UN delegation was making an issue "over a seeming trifle," such as Kaesong, when it had already won agreement on the "big issues" involved in a cease-fire line.[38]

Pointing out that public opinion opposed any disruption in the cease-fire negotiations, particularly in view of the concessions already made by the other side, the Joint Chiefs of Staff instructed Ridgway to accept the present line of contact as the demarcation line for a demilitarized zone, with the understanding, however, that it would be renegotiated if other issues were not settled within a reasonable time—a month or so. Despite this last provision, the Joint Chiefs were compromising perhaps even more than they realized. In effect, they were agreeing to a thirty-day *de facto* cease-fire, since neither side in the war would be willing to risk military action when any gains they might achieve would have to be given up at the end of a thirty-day period. This was a substantial change from the Joint Chiefs' previous position that the demarcation line must be the final line of contact at the time the fighting stopped.[39]

Ridgway's response to his latest orders from the Pentagon was immediate. "I feel there is substantial possibility," he told the Joint Chiefs, "that announcement to the Communists of the course you have directed will increase Communist intransigence and weaken our future p[o]s[itio]ns on every substantive point. . . . We stand at a crucial point. We have much to gain by standing firm. We have everything to lose through concessions. With all my conscience I urge we stand firm."[40]

But the UN commander's argument got him nowhere. On November 27, the UN Command accepted a cease-fire line very much like the one the Chinese and North Koreans had proposed after they dropped their demands on the 38th parallel. What followed was a thirty-day *de facto* cease-fire that, from all military reports, worked to the advantage of the North Koreans and Chinese. For example, General Ridgway instructed General Van Fleet to assume the "active defense," limiting offensive operations to the seizure of ground necessary to protect his position and to establish an outer zone of three to five thousand yards. Meanwhile, the Communists began construction of a fourteen-mile defensive network, deeper than any on the Western Front in World War I, which protected their armies for the rest of the war.[41]

Certainly there were legitimate reasons why the Joint Chiefs agreed to a *de facto* cease-fire. Not only was the administration under tremendous pressure, particularly from its European allies, to negotiate an end to the war, but the Chinese and North Koreans had made several important concessions at the negotiating table, such as over the demarcation line at the time of a cease-fire and the withdrawal of foreign troops from Korea after the fighting ended. Any negotiating process involves a certain amount of give-and-take, and it was not unreasonable for the administration to agree to an effective halt in the fighting for a limited time if that might hasten a cease-fire agreement.

Nevertheless, Ridgway's frustration at the restrictions placed on him and the UN team at Panmunjom in bargaining with the enemy is understandable and, at least to a certain extent, justifiable. "[T]he delegation and indeed General Ridgway never knew," Admiral Joy later commented, "when a new directive would emanate from Washington to alter our basic objective of obtaining an honorable and stable armistice agreement. . . . It seemed to us that the United States Government did not know exactly what its political objectives in Korea were or should be. As a result, the United Nations Command delegation was constantly looking over its shoulder, fearing a new directive from afar which would require action inconsistent with that currently being taken." General Lawton Collins of the Joint Chiefs admitted much the same thing by also acknowledging later that instructions from Washington were sometimes "vacillating" and showed "a lack of firmness" that distressed Ridgway and the UN delegation.[42]

Meanwhile, the military stalemate that had developed in Korea during the summer of 1951 continued into the fall and then the winter of 1952. The Chinese and North Koreans continued to reinforce their defense lines, digging and fortifying a growing complex of trenches, bunkers, and caves that honeycombed the ridges looking down on the UN forces just below. They also brought up their own heavy artillery and stockpiled ammunition. By the end of January General Van Fleet was reporting that the Chinese and North Koreans had more artillery than did the UN forces and that their supplies of ammunition and equipment were mountainous. Although the Communists had lost an estimated 45,000 men since the end of their unsuccessful spring offensive, Van Fleet believed their units had been brought up to full strength, and military intelligence reported that they could launch a major offensive at any time.[43]

Against these well-entrenched forces, UN troops were content mostly to straighten out their own defense lines and refurbish their own supplies. At the end of October an American division did capture the strategically valuable heights above Kumsong, which lay just east of the Iron Triangle. The next month fierce fighting took place over a hill near Yonchon, where American forces, caught by surprise, were first driven off the hill by the Communists. Before reclaiming it forty-one hours later, they had to beat off an entire Chinese division at an estimated cost to the Chinese of 1500 men. American casualties were also high.[44]

For the most part, however, UN forces did not engage the enemy in any sustained action after the negotiators at Panmunjom had agreed on November 27 to a tentative cease-fire line. Instead UN commanders in the field attempted to carry out General Ridgway's orders that they assume the "active defense," engaging in no major attack above battalion strength without prior approval. In most cases Ridgway's directive corresponded with their own assessment of battlefield conditions and the likely outcome of the peace negotiations at Panmunjom. By the time agreement had been reached on a demarcation line, many of the battle-wise troops and officers, who had successfully fought off the great Chinese offensive of the previous spring and had moved to the offensive, had begun to be rotated home. Although fresh reserves arrived from the United States, they were not accustomed to the rigors of the Korean winter. Unschooled in such basics as keeping spare dry socks on hand and changing them often, they suffered untoward incidents of frostbite and other cold-related injuries. The contrast between them and their North Korean and Chinese counterparts, who were acclimated to the seasonal harshness of Manchuria and northern Korea and were able to function routinely, was striking.[45]

Even more important, UN commanders in the field shared Ridgway's reluctance to take any action that might unnecessarily endanger their forces or cause loss of life when any gains that might be achieved on the battlefield were likely to be returned to the enemy as soon as the armistice was reached. They followed this policy even after the *de facto* cease-fire expired thirty days later without a settlement on all outstanding issues. For the remainder of the conflict, in fact, the war on the ground became a military stalemate and a war of position as UN forces pursued the active defense, engaging mostly in routine patrol duty, probing actions, and occasional forays against strategically located enemy positions.[46]

In the air, the situation was substantially different. Almost overnight the Chinese developed into a major air power. By the end of November they were reported to have as many as 1400 planes. Of these, about 700 were estimated to be MiG-15s. Able to maneuver at supersonic speeds and to outrun and outclimb the F-86, America's best jet fighter, at 25,000 feet, the MiG-15 was also believed by a number of military leaders to be better armed and equipped than the F-86. Operating from bases just across the Yalu River, the Chinese increasingly challenged UN supremacy over North Korean skies. Indeed, General Ridgway and Far East Air Force Commander General Otto P. Weyland, who once had favored allowing American pilots to cross into Manchuria in "hot pursuit" of enemy aircraft, changed their minds. "Buildup of Communist fighter strength . . . makes the disregarding of the Yalu River as a boundary to fighter action meaningless," they told the Joint Chiefs of Staff.[47]

Complicating the problem for American fliers over North Korea was the growing effectiveness of Chinese and North Korean anti-aircraft fire. A case in point was OPERATION STRANGLE. In an effort to interdict Communist supplies from reaching the front and to sever the enemy's lines from the rest of North Korea, the UN Command had launched the operation in the summer of 1951. The Communists responded to the UN aircraft with radar-directed searchlights and artillery, which sent up huge clouds of deadly flak that sometimes struck as high as 25,000 and 30,000 feet. In January, the worst month of the air war for the United Nations, forty-four planes alone were reported downed by flak.[48]

By the end of January more than 600 Air Force, Navy, and Marine aircraft had been lost to the enemy either from combat in the air or, far more frequently, from ground fire. Loss of enemy planes was about half of that. In several respects the figures were misleading. Most of the losses were older, less maneuverable, piston engine planes like the B-29 bomber, which was particularly vulnerable. Also, Communist aircraft rarely came out in strength beyond "MIG Alley" in northwest Korea, so fewer downed planes were to be expected. But the growing intensity of the air war over North Korea was cause for increased concern within the UN Command and among military experts and commentators in the United States.[49]

By the end of January, moreover, the hope, which had existed even within the administration just two months earlier, that peace was at hand had been largely shattered. The talks at Panmunjom were not going well at all. The thirty-day period for a cease-fire expired with the negotiators deadlocked over the issue of the machinery necessary to administer an armistice. The UN minimum position was that there should be no increase in the number of military personnel in Korea and that a military armistice commission should be established with the right of inspection at selected ports and communication centers to ensure compliance with the armistice. But although the Chinese and North Koreans agreed to the establishment of an armistice commission and in other ways appeared conciliatory, they rejected caps on the number of military personnel or the free access for the commission insisted upon by the UN negotiators; such demands, they argued, constituted interference in their internal affairs. They also insisted on the right to construct military airfields in Korea, something which the UN team absolutely opposed.[50]

Throughout these exchanges at Panmunjom, Washington's position remained one of avoiding a breakdown in negotiations, a policy that continued to annoy and frustrate both the UN negotiating team and General Ridgway. Above all, Ridgway wanted the Joint Chiefs of Staff, from whom he received his instructions, to determine a firm negotiating position and then stick to it. Even President Truman was losing patience with what he regarded as the shilly-shally posture being assumed by the UN negotiators. In particular, he objected, as unnecessary and unwise, to a UN concession on the rehabilitation of communication and transportation facilities other than airfields, which he pointed out could be used in time of war. The Chinese and North Koreans made all the demands and "we the concessions," he even told the Joint Chiefs of Staff during one White House meeting.[51]

The Joint Chiefs also sympathized with Ridgway's position. In early November, they proposed to bomb Chinese air bases in Manchuria whenever Chinese air attacks threatened the security of UN forces. Nevertheless, they remained convinced that the UN negotiators must not break off negotiations with the Communists, and together with the State Department, which strongly opposed any expansion of the war into Manchuria, they were able to convince the President that they were right. Part of the reason they were successful was a new policy statement on Korea, NSC-118/2, prepared by the National Security Council, which satisfied the President that the United Nations could be conciliatory in negotiating with the enemy without increasing the chances of renewed aggression after a peace was finally concluded. According to the document, Korean reunification by military means would require a substantial increase in ground and air forces, a naval blockade of China, and, possibly, even the use of atomic weapons. Not only would the United States lack sufficient resources to expand the conflict in Korea well into 1952, but the deployment of forces to Korea would delay the buildup of forces in Europe and deplete the Army's reserves. Also, other countries would probably refuse to support an expansion of the war, which would increase tensions in the Far East and might lead even to war between the United States and the Soviet Union.[52]

For these reasons, NSC-118/2 concluded that the United States should continue its limited war on Korea while seeking an armistice. But it should make clear to the Chinese that if an armistice was reached and then broken by them, China would be subject to attack by the United States and its allies. "The publicly expressed determination of the United States and our principal allies to retaliate against China in case of renewed aggression would serve notice on the communist world which they would regard with the greatest seriousness. It thus would become the 'greater sanction,' the strongest deterrent to aggression which we could devise, and therefore worth the risk."[53]

Believing that a warning to Beijing along the lines of the "greater sanction" statement would minimize the danger of Chinese aggression in Korea, the Joint Chiefs were also convinced that the United Nations could be flexible in negotiating with the Chinese at Panmunjom, and they were able to persuade President Truman on this point as well. Not only had his administration formulated the "greater sanction" concept, Truman was also well aware of the currents of world opinion on reaching an armistice, and he recognized that in order to satisfy America's own allies, the UN Command needed to project an image of moderation and conciliation in negotiating with the Communists. After being reminded by the Joint Chiefs of Staff, therefore, that a military agreement might be "the only agreement we will have for a long time" and that it "would be impossible to deny for any appreciable time" the rehabilitation of facilities essential to the Korean economy, he agreed to permit the rebuilding of these facilities in Korea other than airfields. Even in the case of airfields, he opened the way for further concessions by agreeing to reconsider the matter if it became the last obstacle to an armistice.[54]

In formulating the "greater sanction" policy, the United States had consulted closely with England, and the policy won the approval of the new Conservative government headed by Winston Churchill, which had defeated the Labor Party in October. Earlier the Labor government had agreed "in principle" to the "greater sanction" policy, and during a visit to Washington at the beginning of January 1952, Churchill made clear that he would honor Labor's pledge. London even consented to State Department language that "should aggression be committed again in Korea, the consequences would be so grave that it would, in all probability, not be possible to confine hostilities within the frontiers of Korea."[55]

The British agreed to such a declaration because they regarded it as the lesser of two evils, the other being a naval blockade of China, which would threaten its tenuous hold on Hong Kong and which, they thought, would probably be ineffective. They were also concerned about the buildup of Communist forces in Korea under the cover of the truce talks. Even so, they continued to differ on the precise steps to take against the Communists if they breached an armistice agreement. The Americans wanted to attack airfields north of the Yalu River. The Labor government had indicated its support for such bombing missions, but again "in principle" only, and it expected to be advised before any military action was actually taken against China. This was essentially the same position that Churchill and his foreign minister, Anthony Eden, who accompanied the British prime minister to Washington, insisted on in their talks with the Americans.[56]

In fact, despite the warm reception that Churchill received from the American people, who still remembered his gallantry and heroism during World War II, Washington and London remained far apart on a number of issues, including proposals to rearm Germany as part of a European Defense Community (EDC) and to open disarmament talks with the Soviet Union. Despite American support for measures aimed at promoting European unity, Churchill made clear that he would continue his predecessor's opposition to British participation in any form of European federation, including the EDC. Moreover, he emphasized the importance of negotiations with Moscow in order to resolve world differences, and he strongly supported arms reductions. All of this placed him at odds with Washington's own policy of "peace through strength."[57]

To the extent, however, that Churchill's visit to the United States and his endorsement of the "greater sanction" policy raised the possibility of turning a limited war in Korea into a much larger regional—and even international—conflagration, it alarmed Britons. Leftists especially accused Churchill of "selling out" to the Americans by aligning Britain to U.S. policy in the Far East. They also charged that the prime minister had given the Americans practically a blank check in an area where American policy had been, to say the least, dangerously haphazard. Churchill was able to quiet some of these misgivings by telling the British people that nothing had been agreed to during his Washington trip. But doubts still remained as the Labor opposition prepared to take on the Conservatives in a debate over foreign affairs that promised to be sweeping and unusually acrimonious.[58]

The "greater sanction" policy, around which so much of the response to Churchill's visit to the United States revolved (although, it must be pointed out, Washington never publicly acknowledged its existence) infuriated General Ridgway. To depend upon a warning at the time of an armistice in order to keep the peace in Korea and at the same time not to take a firmer negotiating stand at Panmunjom on such matters as the rehabilitation of airfields seemed to him the height of folly. "In my opinion," he told the Joint Chiefs of Staff in early January, "the retributive potentiality of UN military power against Red China would be noneffective unless the full results of precipitating World War 3 were to be accepted, and the use of atomic weapons authorized."[59]

Privately President Truman continued to share Ridgway's desire to take a firmer stand against the Communists, and in his private journal, which he often used to vent his anger, he expressed some of his exasperation at the desultory course of the negotiations. Blaming Moscow for the stalemate in Korea, he wrote that he would serve the Soviets with an ultimatum. The ultimatum would "mean all out war," he noted. "Moscow, St. Petersburg, Mukden, Vladivostok, Peking, Shanghai, Port Arthur, Dairen, Odessa, Stalingrad and every manufacturing plant in China and the Soviet Union will be eliminated."[60]

In fact, the President had never discarded the nuclear option. In April 1951, following the renewed Chinese offensive, he approved the deployment of additional nuclear-configured aircraft to Guam. A liaison team from the Strategic Air Command (SAC) was sent to Tokyo to coordinate plans for a possible nuclear operation against the Chinese. In June, reconnaissance aircraft flew over Manchuria and Shantung to gather data on possible nuclear targets. Without ever overtly threatening the Chinese with a nuclear strike, the administration also made clear to the Chinese through intermediaries that the United States had the ability to set back its development for decades, a message that was strong enough to raise concerns in Beijing about America's nuclear intentions.[61]

Following the defeat of the Chinese offensive, however, Truman recalled the B-29s he had sent to Guam. Never entirely discarding the nuclear option, the White House nevertheless looked to the bargaining table as the way to end the war once negotiations began in July 1951, and it steadfastly adhered to a policy of avoiding any position that might jeopardize the peace talks. Consequently Ridgway's appeals for a stronger negotiating position were again turned down. Instead the Joint Chiefs instructed him to proceed with a settlement on the outstanding issues having to do with administering an armistice, leaving only the question of rehabilitating airfields for later discussions. And even this issue, the UN commander was told, should not be the sole obstacle to a cease-fire agreement.[62]

One question that the Joint Chiefs could hardly have imagined would delay such an agreement for more than a year, but that had come up in the negotiations at Panmunjom and was already causing considerable difficulty, involved the repatriation of prisoners of war (POWs). Simply stated, the issue was one of voluntary repatriation, whether all POWs should be repatriated regardless of their wishes or whether there were groups of prisoners who, for one of a number of reasons, did not want to and should not be repatriated. Among these were former South Koreans and Nationalist Chinese soldiers who had been captured and then forced to serve in the captor's armies and thousands of Chinese troops who wanted to go to Formosa rather than back to China. There were also thousands of South Korean civilians who had been taken prisoners by the North Koreans during the early part of the war and had been forced to work as laborers. Although they were not legally POWs, the UN Command categorized them as such.[63]

Treatment of POWs was prescribed by the Geneva Convention of 1949, which called for quick and compulsory repatriation. Intended to avoid a recurrence of the situation after World War II, when the Soviet Union kept captive a large number of German and Japanese prisoners in order to help in the country's massive reconstruction, the Geneva agreement did not provide for those prisoners who did not want to be repatriated. The problem was that UN forces had begun to take large numbers of prisoners who fit into this category, maintaining that they would be physically harmed or even executed if sent back to China.

At the time the POW issue was first raised at Panmunjom in December, the administration had still not reached any final agreement on the POW question. President Truman, who took an abiding interest in the POW question, opposed forced repatriation—or an all-for-all exchange of POWs—unless it was part of a larger package that included major (but unspecified) concessions. At the same time, though, Secretary of State Acheson, the Joint Chiefs of Staff, and UN negotiators at Panmunjom believed that the United States should not countermand the Geneva Convention. The UN negotiating team also believed that the fastest way to get the UN prisoners back was to agree to an all-for-all exchange.[64]

Over the next several months, the administration moved more and more in the opposite direction. Just as President Truman believed that the United States had made a moral commitment to prevent South Korea from falling to the Communists, so he felt the United States could not morally allow Chinese and North Korean POWs to be returned home against their will; to permit that, he said, "would be unthinkable." The administration also saw a propaganda advantage in having thousands of Communist prisoners refuse repatriation, and it hoped that the granting of asylum to these POWs might lead to wholesale defections from enemy ranks and act as a deterrent to future Communist aggression.[65]

Yet the White House had still not finally and completely committed itself against forced repatriation. For all its concern about the morality of such an action and the potential advantages to be gained by rejecting an all-for-all exchange, the administration still refused to take an irrevocable stand against forced repatriation. As on all other matters, the Joint Chiefs of Staff instructed Ridgway on this issue to be rigid only as a last resort and only after all other possibilities had been exhausted.[66]

These latest orders from Washington thoroughly demoralized Ridgway and the UN negotiators at Panmunjom, who never seemed to know just how far to go in sticking to a negotiating position. Having been opposed to the policy of voluntary repatriation, Ridgway and the UN team were nevertheless fully prepared—or so at least Ridgway maintained—to defend that position against the Communists just so long as it was a final position and they could take a stand on an issue confident that they would not be undermined in Washington. Instead, their instruction made the UN negotiating position seem unnecessarily weak and vacillating.[67]

That changed toward the end of February when Truman and Secretary of State Acheson agreed to a plan worked out within the administration involving UN concessions on airfield reconstruction in return for Chinese and North Korean acceptance of voluntary repatriation. If the Communists refused such a *quid pro quo*, then General Ridgway was instructed to begin preparations for the release of those POWs who feared personal harm if repatriated.[68]

Ridgway strongly opposed the plan. The "premature release of POWs," he told the Joint Chiefs, "could result in retaliation against our [UN] prisoners" and would constitute a "breach of faith of the principles which have guided us through the negotiations." Tokyo and Washington also continued to wrangle over a number of other issues being negotiated at Panmunjom, such as the postwar rotation of troops and the composition of a proposed neutral commission that would supervise a postwar armistice. But at least the period of indecision and waffling on the POW question had come to an end, and for the remainder of the war the UN negotiators at Panmunjom would maintain a firm position against forced repatriation.[69]

In arriving at this decision, neither President Truman nor Secretary of State Acheson ever believed that it would produce a lengthy stalemate in the war. They thought that by steadfast negotiations and perhaps bombing of selected targets in North Korea they could break the impasse. At most a settlement would be delayed a few months, certainly not more than a year, as proved to be the case. In fact, there was good reason for optimism. By the beginning of April, the differences between the UN and Communist negotiators at Panmunjom had been narrowed to three major issues: rehabilitation of airfields, voluntary repatriation of POWs, and the constitution of a military armistice commission. Also, the two sides at Panmunjom agreed at the beginning of April, after two months of disagreement, to screen their POWs in order to see how many prisoners were willing to accept repatriation. It was widely believed that any figure over 100,000 repatriates would be acceptable to the Chinese and North Koreans, since they had been informed by the UN negotiators that they could expect about 116,000 returning POWs, and previous discussions indicated that anything over 100,000 would not represent too great a loss of face for them. On April 8 UN forces began the screening process.[70]

With the number of issues between the UN and Communist delegations thus narrowed to only three by the beginning of April and with the process of screening POWs already started, it was not surprising that some observers believed an armistice was near. But for many others the mood was much more somber. In the first place, within the first three days of screening, it became apparent that far fewer than the 116,000 repatriates indicated to the Communists would choose voluntary repatriation. With about half the 132,000 POWs still to be screened, 40,000 already indicated that they would forcibly resist repatriation. Second, the military stalemate that dragged on while both sides continued to negotiate at Panmunjom seemed to many Americans to favor the enemy, which was engaged in a heavy military buildup, including the continued development of a powerful air force capable of striking behind UN lines.[71]

Finally, Korea remained just one theater of the ongoing struggle against Communist aggression, a struggle that seemed to be going not particularly well for the Western democracies. In addition to pessimistic reports from Indochina, there seemed to be problems throughout Southeast Asia and, indeed, throughout the Far Pacific. Beyond Asia, the Middle East, in the turmoil of nationalist uprisings and social unrest, became more and more a cause for concern. In Europe progress continued to be made on rearmament and the building of a defense force against Communist attack, but only slowly, fretfully, and in the face of increasingly well-organized resistance against German rearmament. Even in England, America's staunchest ally, Prime Minister Churchill, was able to beat back a vote of no confidence on his foreign policy only by turning away from the Anglo-American solidarity on China that seemed to have been achieved during his January visit to the United States. Adding to the growing national despair was the fact that 1952 was a Presidential election year, and opponents of the administration were already playing on the unpopularity of the war for political purposes.

Notes

1. Memorandum for Mr. Murphy, April 24, 1951, Box 76, Elsey Papers; *FR*, 1951, VII, 291–292 and 296–298.
2. Roy Appleman, *Ridgway Duels for Korea* (College Station, TX, 1990), 449–479; David Rees, *Korea: The Limited War* (New York, 1964), 247–251.
3. Appleman, *Ridgway Duels for Korea*, 478-496; T. R. Fehrenbach, *This Kind of War: A Study in Unpreparedness* (New York, 1964), 473–490.
4. Appleman, *Ridgway Duels for Korea*, 489–493; *New Yorker*, 27 (May 5, 1951), 94; *ibid*. (May 26, 1951), 64–66; *Life*, 30 (May 7, 1951), 33–34.
5. Appleman, *Ridgway Duels for Korea*, 493-498; Rees, *Korea: The Limited War*, 245–251; *Time*, 57 (May 7, 1951), 29.
6. Appleman, *Ridgway Duels for Korea*, 509–552; *Life*, 30 (June 4, 1951), 27–28; *Time*, 57 (May 28, 1951), 30; Rees, *Korea: The Limited War*, 251–255.
7. Appleman, *Ridgway Duels for Korea*, 553–569; Rees, *Korea: The Limited War*, 258–259; *Life*, 30 (June 4, 1951), 27–28; *ibid*. (June 11, 1951), 43; *Time*, 57 (June 18, 1951), 30.
8. Briefing of Ambassadors on Korea, May 1, 1951, Box 3, Selected Records Relating to the Korean War; Acheson to Certain Diplomatic Officers, May 1, 1951, Box 11, *ibid*.
9. *FR*, 1951, VII, 390–394 and 427–431; *Yearbook of the United Nations: 1951* (New York, 1952), 226–228.
10. Some of the Chinese planes were flown by Soviet pilots who had secretly been flying over North Korea since November 1950. See Steven J. Zaloga, "The Russians in MiG Alley," *Air Force Magazine*, 74 (February, 1991), 74–77; Rees, *Korea: The Limited War*, 193–194; *FR*, 1951, VII, 338–342, 385–387, and 427–431; Livingston Merchant to the Secretary of State, May 5, 1951, and memorandum for General Bradley from Mr. Acheson, May 12, 1951, Box 11, Selected Records Relating to the Korean War; M. L. Dockrill, "The Foreign Office, Anglo-American Relations and the Korean Truce Negotiations, July 1951–July 1953," in James Cotton and Ian Neary (eds.), *The Korean War in History* (Atlantic Highlands, NJ, 1989), 102–103; Rosemary Foot, *The Wrong War: American Policy and the Dimensions of the Korean Conflict*, 1950-1953 (Ithaca, NY, 1985), 145–147.
11. *Commentary*, 11 (May 1951), 407–414. See also *Commonweal*, 28 (May 11, 1951), 113–114.
12. *New Republic*, 124 (May 28, 1951), 10; *Atlantic Monthly*, 187, (June 1951), 16–17.

13. *Ibid.; Nation*, 172 (May 12, 1951), 440–443; *New Yorker*, 27 (June 30, 1951), 42.

14. Walter G. Hermes, *Truce Tent and Fighting Front* (Washington, DC, 1966), 14.

15. Dean Acheson, *Present at the Creation: My Years in the State Department* (New York, 1969), 532–533; *FR*, 1951, VII, 460–462, 483–486, and 507–511; Rosemary Foot, *A Substitute for Victory: The Politics of Peacemaking* (Ithaca, NY, 1990), 37.

16. *FR*, VII, 1951, 536–538, 551–554, and 560–561; Daily Opinion Summary, Department of State, n.d., Box 76, Elsey Papers; Acheson, *Present at the Creation*, 533–534; *Commonweal*, 54 (July 6, 1951), 300–301.

17. *FR*, 1951, VII, 577–578, 593–595, and 610–612; Acheson, *Present at the Creation*, 533–535; Message to the Commander in Chief, Communist Forces in Korea, June 30, 1951, Box 3, Selected Records Relating to the Korean War; Briefing of Ambassadors on Korea, July 3, 1951, Box 8, *ibid.*

18. *FR*, 1951, VII, 610–612.

19. Ridgway to Joint Chiefs of Staff, July 4, 1951, Box 243, Korean War File, President's Secretary File, Truman Papers.

20. *Nation*, 173 (July 7, 1951), 4; *ibid.* (July 14, 1951), 21; *New Republic*, 125 (July 9, 1951), 6; *New Yorker*, 27 (July 14, 1951), 62.

21. *New Yorker*, 27 (June 30, 1951), 60–65; *FR*, 1951, VII, 416–419 and 496–497.

22. *FR*, 1951, VII, 610–612.

23. Message to the Commander in Chief, Communist Forces in Korea, June 30, 1951, Box 3, Selected Records Relating to the Korean War; Briefing of Ambassadors in Korea, July 3, 1951, Box 8, *ibid.*

24. Department of State, "Far East: Progress in the Korean Truce Talks," Box 76, Elsey Papers; *FR*, 1951, VII, 649–656; Foot, *A Substitute for Victory*, 46.

25. *Ibid.*

26. *FR*, 1951, VII, 658–665, 671–673, 682–684, 687–688, and 704–706; Department of State, Far East: Progress in the Korean Truce Talks, Box 76, Elsey Papers; Briefing of Ambassadors on Korea, July 18, 1951, Box 8, Selected Records Relating to the Korean War.

27. *FR*, 1951, VII, 711–718 and 735–737; Hermes, *Truce Tent and Fighting Front*, 34.

28. Hermes, *Truce Tent and Fighting Front*, 34; *FR*, 1951, VII, 738–739, 745–747, 763–765, and 774–776.

29. Briefing of Ambassadors on Korea, August 1, 1951, Box 3, Selected Records Relating to the Korean War; *FR*, 1951, VII, 753–760; *Nation*, 173 (August 4, 1951), 81; *New Republic*, 125 (August 13, 1951), 10; *ibid.* (August 20, 1951), 5; *ibid.* (September 24, 1951), 5; *Atlantic Monthly*, 188 (September 1951), 8 and 11; *Nation*, 173 (September 1, 1951), 166-167; David M. Oshinsky, *A Conspiracy So Immense: The World of Joe McCarthy* (New York, 1983), 214–217.

30. *Life,* 30 (July 30, 1951), 18 and 20; *Nation,* 173 (August 11, 1951), 112–113; *ibid.* (August 18, 1951), 122–123 and 131–132; *Atlantic Monthly,* 188 (August 1951), 4–7; *Commonweal,* 54 (August 17, 1951), 445.

31. *FR,* 1951, VII, 795–798 and 811–812; Foot, *A Substitute for Victory,* 47–48.

32. *Ibid.* See also *Atlantic Monthly,* 187 (April 1951), 11; *New Republic,* 125 (August 27, 1951), 15.

33. *New Republic,* 125 (September 3, 1951), 8; *Commonweal,* 54 (September 7, 1951), 515; Foot, *A Substitute for Victory,* 49–50.

34. *Time,* 58 (September 24, 1951), 24; *New Yorker,* 27 (October 6, 1951), 97; *New Republic,* 125 (September 24, 1951), 3; *Commonweal,* 54 (September 14, 1951), 539.

35. *FR,* 1951, VII, 937–944 and 952–955; Briefing of Ambassadors on Korea, September 21, 1951, Box 3, Selected Papers Relating to the Korean War; Foot, *A Substitute for Victory,* 50–53.

36. Briefing of Foreign Government Representatives on Korea, September 21, 1951, Box 3, Selected Papers Relating to the Korean War.

37. Joint Chiefs of Staff to Ridgway, November 6, 1951, Box 16, *ibid.;* FR, 1951, VII, 1071–1072, 1074, 1092–1093, and 1126; Foot, *A Substitute for Victory,* 58.

38. *Nation,* 173 (October 20, 1951), 319–320; *ibid.* (October 13, 1951), 300–302; *New Yorker,* 27 (October 27, 1951), 17; *ibid.* (October 15, 1951), 3; *Commonweal,* 55 (October 26, 1951), 51.

39. *FR,* 1951, VII, 1131–1133 and 1186–1188; Hermes, *Truce Tent and Fighting Front,* 119; *New Republic,* 125 (October 1, 1951), 3; *New York Times,* November 11, 1951.

40. *FR,* 1951, VII, 1128–1130.

41. *Ibid.,* 1131–1133 and 1186–1188; Hermes, *Truce Tent and Fighting Front,* 119; Henry Kissinger, *Nuclear Weapons and Foreign Policy* (New York, 1957), 50–51; Rees, *Korea: The Limited War,* 301.

42. Admiral C. Turner Joy, *How Communists Negotiate* (New York, 1955), 173–174; J. Lawton Collins, *War in Peacetime* (Boston, 1969), 331. See also D. Clayton James, *Refighting the Last War: Command and Crisis in Korea, 1950–1953* (New York, 1993), 96–98.

43. Hermes, *Truce Tent and Fighting Front,* 175–178.

44. *Time,* 58 (December 3, 1951), 26.

45. Hermes, *Truce Tent and Fighting Front,* 178–181.

46. *Nation,* 173 (December 8, 1951), 489; *Time,* 58 (December 10, 1951), 19; Rees, *Korea: The Limited War* (New York, 1964), 301–303.

47. *Time,* 58 (December 3, 1951), 19; *FR,* 1951, VII, 974–975.

48. Hermes, *Truce Tent and Fighting Front,* 192–194; Rees, *Korea: The Limited War,* 370–378; Time, 59 (February 11, 1952), 36.

49. Hermes, *Truce Tent and Fighting Front,* 199–201; Max Hastings, *The Korean War* (New York, 1987), 258–269; *Atlantic Monthly,* 189 (February 1952), 14–16.

50. Briefing of Foreign Government Representatives on Korea, November 27, 1951 and January 18, 1952, Box 3, Selected Records Relating to the Korean War; *FR*, 1951, VII, 598–600; Hermes, *Truce Tent and Fighting Front*, 121; Foot, *A Substitute for Victory*, 77–78.

51. *FR*, 1951, VII, 1130–1131, 1281–1282, and 1290–1296; Ridgway to Joint Chiefs of Staff, December 18, 1951, Box 16, Selected Records Relating to the Korean War.

52. Foot, *The Wrong War*, 153–156. On the possible consequences of an embargo or naval blockade against the Chinese Communists, see CIA, "Special Estimate # 20," December 15, 1951, Box 243, Korean War File, President's Secretary File, Truman Papers. For the various drafts accompanying the formulation of NSC 118/2, see File NSC-118, Records of the National Security Council, Record Group 429 (National Archives, Washington, DC).

53. *Ibid.*; Foot, *A Substitute for Victory*, 77–79.

54. *FR*, 1951, VII, 1142–1143, 1281–1282, 1290–1296, and 1377–1381; James Webb to American Embassy Rome, November 26, 1951, Box 4267, Records of the Department of State, RG 59, 795.00/11-2651. See also Foot, *The Wrong War*, 158–171.

55. Anthony Eden, *Full Circle: The Memoirs of Anthony Eden* (Boston, 1960), 18–10; "Memorandum of Conversation at Dinner at British Embassy," January 7, 1953, Box 66, Acheson Papers.

56. Eden, *Full Circle*, 18–20.

57. *New Yorker*, 27 (November 10, 1951), 96–97; *ibid.* (November 24, 1951), 149–150; *ibid.* (December 22, 1951), 51–52; New Republic, 125 (November 5, 1951), 5; *ibid.* (November 26, 1951), 9; *ibid.* (December 17, 1951), 9; Eden, *Full Circle*, 36–41; Acheson, *Present at the Creation*, 597–603. See also Anthony Seldon, *Churchill's Indian Summer, The Conservative Government, 1951–1955* (London, 1981), 388–389; Robert McGeehan, *The German Rearmament Question: American Diplomacy and European Defense after World War II* (Urbana, IL, 1971), 126–141; David S. McLellan, *Dean Acheson: The State Department Years* (New York, 1976), 357.

58. *New Republic*, 126 (January 28, 1952), 5; *Time*, 59 (February 4, 1952), 20; *New Yorker*, 27 (February 9, 1952), 59.

59. *FR*, 1952–1954, XV, 10–12 and 17–18.

60. Barton J. Bernstein, "Truman's Second Thoughts on Ending the Korean War," *Foreign Service Journal*, 57 (November 1980), 31–32.

61. Roger Dingman, "Atomic Diplomacy During the Korean War," *International Security*, 13 (Winter, 1988/89), 75–79.

62. Joint Chiefs of Staff to Ridgway, January 27, 1952, Box 16, Selected Records Relating to the Korean War.

63. Barton J. Bernstein, "The Struggle Over the Korean Armistice: Prisoners or Repatriation?" in Bruce Cumings (ed.), *Child of Conflict: The Korean-American Relationship, 1943–1953* (Seattle, WA, 1983), 274–275.

64. *FR*, 1951, VII, 1073 and 1377–1381; Ridgway to Joint Chiefs of Staff, July 21, 1951, Box 16, Selected Records Relating to the Korean War; Hermes, *Truce Tent and Fighting Front*, 135–141; Joy, *How Communists Negotiate*, 150–152.

65. *Public Papers of the Presidents of the United States: Harry S. Truman, 1952–1953* (Washington, DC, 1966), 321.

66. *FR*, 1952-1954, XV, 178–179; Joint Chiefs of Staff to Ridgway, April 28, 1952, Box 16, Selected Records Relating to the Korean War.

67. Joint Chiefs of Staff to Ridgway, January 15, 1952, Box 3, Selected Records Relating to the Korean War.

68. Foot, *A Substitute for Victory*, 101–102. See also Memorandum of Conversation, February 25, 1952, Box 4277, Records of the Department of State, RG 59, 795.00/2-2552.

69. *FR*, 1952–1954, XV, 66–67; Briefing of Foreign Government Representatives on Korea, February 1, 1952, Box 3, Selected Records Relating to the Korean War; Ridgway to Joint Chiefs of Staff, February 12 and March 28, 1952, Box 16, *ibid*.

70. *FR*, 1952–1954, XV, 80–81, 88–91, 95–107.

71. *Atlantic Monthly*, 189 (March 1952), 17; *New Republic*, 126 (February 18, 1952), 6; Hermes, *Truce Tent and Fighting Front*, 169–170.

CHAPTER SIX

Prisoners, Propaganda, and Politics

Although the war in Korea remained a military stalemate as spring finally came to the country in April and May of 1952, the latest reports from the front indicated that the enemy was daily increasing in strength, particularly in terms of air power. While American ground strength dropped slightly in the six months from November 1, 1951, to April 30, 1952, declining from about 265,000 to 260,000, enemy troop strength was estimated to have grown in the same period from approximately 502,000 to 866,000. Nor was this offset by a slight increase in the contribution of the other UN countries (from about 34,000 to 36,000) and a 60,000 troop jump in ROK forces (from about 282,000 to 342,000). Also, enemy armored strength increased from practically nothing to one North Korean and two Chinese armored divisions and one mechanized division, with an estimated 520 tanks. Few if any military leaders thought the Communists had the capacity to sustain another major offensive. But the enemy buildup on the ground was worrisome all the same, and the UN Command doubted that it could launch a major offensive of its own without substantial increases in troop strength.[1]

Of even greater concern to many military experts than the ground buildup was the growth of enemy air power. By April 30 the Chinese had an estimated 1250 planes in Manchuria, of which about 800 were Soviet jets. Although the jets remained in Manchuria for the most part and were too short-ranged to strike at UN lines from behind the Yalu River, General Hoyt Vandenberg, the Air Force chief of staff, believed that the United Nations was losing its air supremacy in Korea. Others feared that if the truce talks dragged on and the Communists were able to complete major bases under construction in North Korea, they could strike in force at UN lines, inflicting heavy casualties. Some Air Force officers even proposed bombing railroads, ports, and marshaling yards throughout China in order to force the Communists to disperse their concentration of air power in Manchuria. But the very strength of the Chinese Air Force made such recommendations seem dubious even for many of those who had earlier advocated such attacks.[2]

Still another matter that a growing number of Americans found disturbing was their perception that the West was losing its struggle to contain the worldwide Communist threat. Of course, many Americans had felt the same way just before war had broken out in Korea in 1950 and again after the Chinese had invaded Korea in November 1950. A significant number had continued to share this view even in the eighteen months that followed, particularly after the war had begun to stalemate, after the negotiators at Panmunjom had failed to reach a quick cease-fire, and after the conflict in Indochina had turned clearly against the French, all of which had occurred by the end of 1951. But between that time and the spring of 1952 the world situation appeared to deteriorate even more.

In Asia Communism seemed to pose a threat not only in Korea and Indochina but throughout Southeast Asia. In some respects this was odd, because the internal situation in several of the countries that concerned Americans was actually better than it had been at any time since World War II. For example, Burma had been torn by a Communist-led insurgency and then by a civil war for more than a year after gaining its independence from England in 1948. But in 1952 the government of U Nu, which had supported the United Nations' action in Korea in 1950, seemed firmly in charge of the country. Similarly, in the Philippines the government of Elpidio Quirino had restored relative stability to the nation after more than a year of economic, political, and military crisis.[3]

Despite this progress, many Americans still remained worried that Burma, the Philippines, and the rest of Southeast Asia might yet fall to the Communists. Part of the reason for this was an early version of what later became known as the "domino theory," the theory that if Indochina were forfeited by the French, there would be nothing to prevent Communism from spreading to the neighboring states, reaching eventually into Burma. Also there was concern that China might actually invade a border country like Burma. Such concerns contributed to the general pessimism that seemed to grip the nation in the spring of 1952. *Time* even drew a map of Asia as seen from the Soviet city of Irkutsk and remarked, "On the southern border of Red China, Russia now stands on the threshold of one of the world's greatest prizes: the rich green valleys of Communist-infested Indo-China and Malaya, and the immense unexploited riches of the islands beyond."[4]

As many of these same Americans turned to the Middle East and North Africa, they found the situation there not much better. The two largely Arab and Moslem regions remained torn by political turmoil and rampaging nationalism that continued to be hostile to the West because of the West's colonial heritage. While the French were fighting in Indochina, the British were in similar trouble in Iran, where, to the anger of the Iranian people, they maintained a complete embargo of that country's oil because of Iran's nationalization of the British-owned Anglo-Iranian Oil Company. In Egypt, rioting against the British had taken place in January because London refused to withdraw its garrison guarding the Suez Canal (at least until Egypt agreed to join a Middle East defense pact) or to turn over to the Egyptians the Sudan, which Egypt claimed as its own.[5]

Meanwhile, in Tunisia, militant nationalism, which had been smoldering for more than half a century against French sovereignty, burst into flames in February following the arrival of a new French resident-general. Demonstrations and riots resulted in eight Arabs dead and twenty wounded. Even in relatively prosperous and tranquil French Morocco, where the United States was spending millions of dollars building five huge air bases, Moslem nationalism and the demand for greater autonomy were beginning to pose a threat to French rule. Indeed, the Sultan of Morocco, thought to be a safe man for France, dispatched a letter to Paris in March demanding more local autonomy.[6]

Reacting to the discontent evident throughout the Arab and Moslem world, some Americans saw the long arm of Moscow reaching out to threaten Western interests in the oil-rich Middle East, along the strategically vital Suez Canal, and throughout the long coast of North Africa that faced into the all-important Mediterranean. Even Secretary of State Acheson, who generally understood the causes of the disaffection and disorder taking place in the Middle East and North Africa and who urged England and France to rid themselves of their past colonial habits, commented to Anthony Eden in February on "the new xenophobic ferment, fanned from

Moscow," that was growing daily in the Middle East. Similarly, a secret report prepared in February by the North Atlantic Treaty Council presented a picture of intensified Cold War activities by the Soviet Union ranging from efforts "to prevent harmony in ideas between Western Europe and the United States" to attempts at "foment[ing] tension in Southeast Asia," sapping Western influence in the Middle East, and "encourag[ing] anti-imperialist moves in such areas as Egypt and Morocco." But even for those who did not make such links, the situation looked ominous, particularly when joined with developments in Southeast Asia and elsewhere. "The whole Middle East has ceased to be governed by the old British and French arrangements," *Life* thus commented toward the end of March. "But the Arabs hate America too—especially Truman—on account of Israel. . . . Everywhere our policy both puzzles and alarms allies and neutralists alike. It is neither a 'strong' policy nor one of appeasement. It brings us the advantages of neither—but the penalties of both."[7]

Another problem which contributed, in *Life*'s words, to the "black[ness of the] big picture" was the uninterrupted deterioration of the British economy. Faced with a worsening balance-of-payments problem and high defense costs, Prime Minister Churchill announced that he was cutting the country's rearmament program by a third. But Churchill's problems were as much political as economic and involved the growing influence within the Labor Party of its more radical Bevanite wing. Although Churchill was able to defeat the Labor challenge to his government and, in the process, further the rift within its ranks, the cost was a virtual abandonment of the Anglo-American agreement on Far East policy that had been hammered out during the British prime minister's visit to Washington in January. During one of the most dramatic foreign policy debates since the end of World War II, Churchill pointed out that the Labor government before him had covertly made the very foreign policy commitment to the United States—a possible extension of the Korean war—that Labor leaders accused him of making. Furthermore, he denied that he intended to be bolder in Asia or more in accord with Washington's policy toward Beijing than those before him. "The fact is," Churchill said, "that there is no change in our policy. Nothing could be more foolish than for the armies of the U.S. or the U.N. to become engulfed in the vast areas of China."[8]

By revealing the secret agreements that the Labor Party had made with Washington, Churchill also increased the power and influence within the Labor Party of Nye Bevan and his anti-American followers. Taking the floor of Parliament after Churchill had sat down, Bevan blasted Britain's rearmament program and its alliance with the United States. "Behind the guise and facade of the United Nations," he said, "the Americans are waging an ideological war with weapons against the Soviet Union." "We do not want any differences of opinion between us and the U.S. to encourage hopes of a [Communist] military adventure anywhere," he concluded, "but we do not want such subservience to American opinion . . . that there is no hope for them except through another blood bath." Although Labor leader Clement Attlee was able to put down a challenge to his leadership from the Bevanite faction within the party, few could dispute the fact that Bevan had emerged from the debate in Parliament stronger than ever, and that antiwar—if not anti-American—sentiment had become a major political force in England, threatening even to capture one of the two major political parties. That prospect was hardly comforting to many Americans already disturbed by Churchill's apparent bending to Britain's political winds.[9]

Much the same was true with respect to the slow progress that was being made in rearming Europe and developing Atlantic solidarity. To be sure, there was some headway on both these matters. In February a major breakthrough occurred when a NATO defense system was ratified by the North Atlantic Treaty Council meeting in Lisbon. In addition, the NATO foreign ministers endorsed the European Defense Community (EDC) and established future military strength levels for NATO, which could not be reached without Germany furnishing a substantial number of troops. Progress was also made on a number of other issues—such as the relative size of the French and German troop levels in the EDC and the community's relation to NATO—which had plagued efforts at establishing a European army but which had to be settled before agreement could be reached on an EDC. Commenting on the achievements of the Lisbon meeting, Secretary Acheson remarked that a "new day" was dawning for the West, while Foreign Secretary Eden referred to the meeting as the "beginning of a new era."[10]

Yet as many observers pointed out, a number of these agreements had been reached only by ignoring or glossing over major differences that still separated the European powers. Also, many of the targets set at the meeting were simply unrealistic, so that the glitter of February became the gloom of March and April. For example, no mention was made in any of the Lisbon accords about what France had always considered a basic principle of a European army—political unification within which the German danger would dissolve. In addition, the understanding reached at Lisbon to spend $300 billion for mutual defense during the next three years ignored a number of economic and political realities, including Europe's shaky economy, Congress's growing reluctance to foot much of the bill for European rearmament, the party differences over rearmament in England, and the movement for disarmament growing throughout Europe.[11]

Within a week the transparency of many of the agreements reached at Lisbon became apparent when the French government of Edgar Fauré fell after losing on a tax bill designed to finance France's $4 billion rearmament program. The French people also began to react very quickly against the restoration of German power, afraid that with much of their own military strength tied up in Indochina, Germany would have a preponderance in European economic and military matters. In Germany, the government of Konrad Adenauer had its own trouble gaining support for the Lisbon accords. Opponents claimed that by making concessions on such matters as military finances, security controls to be imposed on Germany, and limits to be placed on the production of certain war materials, Adenauer had given away too much. In England the London *Times* referred to the European army created at Lisbon as the "phantom army" and deplored what it called "a mistaken attempt to combine military security with political propaganda." Similarly, the view continued to grow throughout Europe that the United States was attempting to subvert the truly internationalist and democratic goals of European unity with a specifically military and predominantly American pattern of Atlantic cohesion. Complicating matters even more, the Soviet Union offered the West a new proposal for a neutralized and unified Germany with its own national army. Obviously intended to prevent Germany from aligning militarily with the West and even becoming a member of NATO, the Soviet proposal nevertheless enjoyed considerable support throughout Europe.[12]

Together these developments shattered much of the optimism about a united and militarily unified Europe, including Germany, which had been evident just after Lisbon. They also contributed to the atmosphere of despair and even crisis that existed in the United States in the spring of 1952. Republicans in a Presidential election year sought to exploit this general malaise in America for partisan purposes. Seeking his party's nomination, Robert Taft made the White House's alleged mismanagement of the Korean conflict a campaign issue. Republicans in the House and Senate, many honestly convinced that the Communists were using the peace talks at Panmunjom to screen an ever-increasing escalation of the war, pressured the administration to terminate its limited war policy. Rejecting the limited war concept and a negotiated peace for Korea, they called for a decisive military victory and the development of a deterrent power, based on increased air and sea power, to prevent further Communist aggression of the kind that had taken place in Korea.[13]

Almost invariably, attacks on the White House's handling of the Korean war turned into renewed charges against the Democrats' entire conduct of foreign policy since the end of 1951, and this in turn rekindled old accusations of "Communists in government" and internal subversion. McCarthyism became a potent political force once more as Republicans flayed away at the administration, firing the political caldron, raising the temper of political discourse, and exacerbating the doubts and fears of many Americans.

Republicans in Congress, of course, had never stopped attacking the White House for its policies toward the war, particularly after the conflict stalemated in the late spring of 1951. But these attacks intensified considerably after Senator Taft announced in September 1951 that he would once more seek his party's nomination for President, having lost the nomination in 1948. Although Taft had been publicly attacking the administration's handling of the Korean war since the beginning of the year, at one time he had appeared to moderate his position, even telling a group of Republicans in July that a "stalemate peace at the thirty-eighth parallel [was] better than a stalemate war at the thirty-eighth parallel." But that changed once the Ohio senator began to campaign in earnest for the nomination. Now Taft denounced the administration for not following the recommendations of General MacArthur, "especially the bombing of

Communist air fields and the use of Chinese Nationalist Government troops for diversionary raids on South China." Much to the annoyance of his critics, he also began referring to the UN intervention in Korea as a "useless war" and as "Truman's war."[14]

Significantly, Taft also repeated familiar charges about America's failed policy in the Far East, which he linked to an internal Communist conspiracy. Communists in government, the labor unions, and "the writing fraternity in Hollywood and New York," he said, were in a position to affect public opinion or public policy. By December, Taft was once more embracing McCarthy and seeking his support despite the fact that he had been moving away from the Wisconsin senator since McCarthy's insinuation the previous June that former Defense Secretary George Marshall had been guilty of conspiracy or treason. Taft's new endorsement of McCarthy reflected the fact that the Red Scare and fear of internal subversion remained very much alive as issues during the 1952 elections.[15]

Korea never figured prominently among the charges of internal subversion made against the administration during the campaign. Efforts to link the outbreak of the war and Communist infiltration of government had generally been dropped during the last half of 1951 because of the White House's conduct of the war, and they were never renewed. But McCarthy himself began to attack the administration's Korean policy. In February he denounced the State and Defense departments for their fear that if the United States adopted a policy of victory, it would become involved in a war with the Soviet Union. Other of his allies labeled the conflict in Korea "a treadmill war" and repeated charges that the White House was following a "no-win" policy. The attacks by the Republican right wing against the administration and their demands for victory in Asia—which clearly meant an invasion of China either by American or Chinese Nationalist forces—became so intense and shrill that Republican renegade Wayne Morse of Oregon took the Senate floor to speak out against what he referred to as a "growing war clique [who proposed] that we commit an act which constitutes for the first time in American history an aggressive act of war against a foreign power."[16]

The important point remains, however, not so much the opposition of the Republican right wing to the administration's conduct of the war or their demand for victory, neither of which was particularly new, but the fact that McCarthy and his allies promised to play a major role in the forthcoming election, particularly if Taft received the Republican nomination. Furthermore, there was every reason to believe that Korea would be just one issue of a larger assault on President Truman's entire foreign policy since the end of World War II and that while the war itself might not be linked to charges of internal subversion, the administration's general conduct of foreign policy, especially in Asia, would be. For those who abhorred McCarthy as an unprincipled demagogue and saw in the Red Scare a challenge to basic American freedoms, or who were convinced an escalation of the Korean conflict might lead to World War III, the American political scene in the spring of 1952 held out the most frightening prospects of all.

Oddly enough, most Americans still did not pay the same attention to the Korean war as they had six or eight months earlier, when there still appeared to be a chance that a quick end to the conflict could be reached at Panmunjom. Although the war had already become an important issue in the Presidential campaign, the press did not give it that much more coverage than it did other issues, such as the war in Indochina or the nationalist uprisings in the Middle East and North Africa. Domestic matters, such as further reports of corruption within the Truman administration and growing speculation over whether Eisenhower would resign his NATO command and return to the United States in order to campaign against Taft, captured far more headlines than Korea. A Roper poll conducted in May concluded that although the Korean war still topped the list of concerns expressed by the American people, there was an increasing interest in domestic events. Six months earlier the people polled mentioned international problems over domestic ones by a five-to-four margin; now the ratios were exactly reversed.[17]

Still, major news stories from Korea did attract considerable public interest, and in the late winter and spring of 1952 no news stories received more attention than Communist allegations of bacteriological warfare in Korea by UN forces and a major prison riot by Chinese and North Korean POWs on the island of Koje-do. Although the Communists had been claiming for months that Americans were spreading smallpox germs in North Korea, the campaign against alleged bacteriological warfare began in earnest on February 18 when Moscow radio accused the United States of spreading smallpox and typhus bacteria and of secretly sending lepers into North Korea. By March 8 the Chinese were charging that the United

States had dropped insects, rats, shellfish, and chicken feathers containing disease germs on Chinese as well as North Korean territory.[18]

On March 11 Secretary of State Acheson asked the International Red Cross to investigate the Communist accusations, but the North Koreans and Chinese rejected such an investigation, insisting that the Red Cross was dominated by Americans. Instead, they joined with Moscow in a stepped-up propaganda campaign against the United States. In Moscow, Leningrad, Kiev, Minsk, and other cities and villages throughout the Soviet Union, workers were pulled from their jobs to be inoculated against American bacteriological weapons, while in Beijing newspapers printed photographic "proof" of weird insects and rotting food. Two American fliers captured by the Chinese read confessions—obviously made under duress and later recanted—in which they said that they had dropped "germ bombs . . . against the people of Korea and the Chinese Volunteers." According to a State Department intelligence report, the bacteriological warfare campaign represented the single greatest effort ever undertaken by the Communists to discredit the United States.[19]

Speculation in the United States and in Europe as to why the Communists decided to launch such a propaganda barrage varied considerably. Some officials theorized that springtime was a period of epidemic in North Korea and China, and that the Communist leaders were merely preparing their people for plagues. Along the same lines, others speculated that China was in very bad shape because the Korean war had drained the country economically and an "anticorruption" campaign had terrorized much of the country. According to this view, the propaganda against the United States was intended to distract the Chinese people from these internal problems. Some British diplomats even thought that since the Soviet Union was now making atomic bombs, they had to create some other dastardly form of warfare that they could claim was a Western monopoly.[20]

Although the Chinese clearly manipulated the charges of bacteriological warfare for propaganda purposes, there is ample reason to believe that they were sincere in their conviction that the United States was engaging in bacteriological warfare. Furthermore, while the evidence to support such a claim remains unpersuasive, a circumstantial case could be—and was—made to support their charges. In the first place, Chinese and North Korean forces were suffering from a high incidence of typhoid, smallpox, and a disease characterized by high fever, backache, headache, and running sores. Also, the United States had an ongoing germ research program that it had accelerated after 1950, and both Moscow and Beijing were aware that Washington employed a number of Japanese scientists in this program who had conducted experiments in germ warfare during World War II. They also knew that the UN Command had been monitoring incidents of epidemic in North Korea; a United Press International (UPI) headline even detailed the story of an American general who had gone behind enemy lines to learn if communist forces were suffering from the plague. It was not unreasonable for the Chinese to conclude, therefore, that the United States was responsible for their infliction.[21]

Regardless of the merits of the Chinese charges, their accusations of bacteriological warfare were highly effective in weakening America's moral weight in Europe, particularly among neutralists, and in stirring worldwide reaction against the United States. Communists in France, Italy, Belgium, Holland, and West Germany held large protest parades against the United States. And in Tehran, Communist youths, shouting "germ warfare," touched off a large riot that left 12 dead and 250 wounded.[22]

Even more harmful to the image of the UN Command than accusations about germ warfare, though, was a riot by Chinese and North Korean POWs on Koje-do island, about twenty miles southwest of Pusan. This barren and rocky piece of land housed about 130,000 Koreans and 20,000 Chinese troops crowded together into compounds intended to hold between 700 and 1200 prisoners but actually holding about five times that number. Conditions in the compounds made them virtually impossible to control, and on February 18, 1952, guards entering a prisoner compound were attacked by 1500 prisoners brandishing homemade weapons, including iron bars, clubs, and barbed wire. In the melee that followed, 77 POWs were killed and another 140 wounded. Similar prisoner riots took place in the weeks that followed, albeit none as serious as that of February 18, and the Communist negotiators at Panmunjom used them to accuse the UN Command of barbarous treatment of POWs. They also charged that the UN Command was resorting to force to prevent the POWs from choosing early repatriation.[23]

Insofar as they concerned mistreatment of POWs, these accusations contained considerable substance. Chinese Nationalist troops were sometimes used as guards in the Chinese camps, and they frequently brutalized the prisoners to "encourage" them to renounce Communist China. The chief UN negotiator at Panmunjom, Admiral Joy, recorded in his diary that on one occasion, when prisoners were asked to decide whether they wished to be repatriated to the People's Republic of China (PRC), "those doing so were either beaten black and blue or killed." "[Th]e majority of the POWs were too terrified to frankly express their choice," Joy said. General Ridgway, who would shortly be named to replace Eisenhower as commander of NATO, even warned the Joint Chiefs that a "potentially explosive atmosphere" existed at Koje-do, which, he said, was "capable of developing to such a point [that] it might result in heavy loss of life and great discredit to the US and UNC."[24]

That potential turned into frightening reality when on May 7 prisoners in Compound 76 seized the commander of the island, Brigadier General Francis T. Dodd, while he was talking to them through the compound's gate, and demanded, as a condition of his release, that the UN Command admit it had practiced inhumane treatment of POWs. In response and acting on his own authority, Brigadier General Charles F. Colson, who had assumed command of Koje-do following Dodd's capture, made a statement meeting most of the prisoners' demands. Following Colson's statement, the prisoners released Dodd as they had promised. Later both he and Colson were demoted to the rank of colonel, Dodd because he had allowed himself to be seized and Colson for the unauthorized statement that he made.[25]

The Communists used the incident at Koje-do to launch a second propaganda barrage against the United States, which the Joint Chiefs of Staff described as equal in intensity, ferocity, and vulgarity to that directed against Germany during World War II. Together the charges of barbarous treatment of Communist POWs and the bacteriological warfare campaign put the UN Command on the defensive in its negotiations with the Communists. In an effort to regain the diplomatic initiative and to break new ground in the negotiations at Panmunjom, the UN went ahead with a package proposal to the Chinese and North Koreans that had been in the works since the middle of March. As General Ridgway explained the package, it represented an effort to reach an agreement on the three unresolved issues separating the UN and Communist negotiators: airfield reconstruction, the composition of a neutral armistice commission, and the repatriation of POWs. By its provisions the restrictions on airfield construction and rehabilitation would be deleted; the proposed composition of the neutral nations commission would be four mutually acceptable nations, excluding the Soviet Union (something that Ridgway had always insisted upon); and the exchange of POWs would reflect the principle of "no forced repatriation."[26]

The package was presented to the Communist negotiators on April 28 in an atmosphere of mutual distrust compounded not only by the question of UN treatment of Communist POWs and the bacteriological warfare charges, but by the Communist shock at the small number of POWs the UN Command offered for repatriation. Although the UN negotiators had informed the Chinese and North Koreans before the screening of POWs had begun in April that as many as 116,000 POWs might be repatriated, after the screening was complete it was determined that only about 70,000 prisoners wished to return home. The Communists termed this figure totally unacceptable and, for a time, even suspended talks.[27]

On May 2, however, the enemy negotiators returned to Panmunjom and, after some jockeying, accepted the UN terms on airfield reconstruction and the composition of an armistice. But they insisted that all Communist POWs must be repatriated. So now the differences between the two sides in the negotiations had been reduced to one issue: prisoner repatriation. But on this issue little progress had been made. Worse, the United States had taken a final and irrevocable position, and so, apparently, had the Chinese and North Koreans.[28]

News of the failure to break the deadlock in the talks at Panmunjom was made public on May 7. It coincided with the arrival in Tokyo of General Mark Clark, whom President Truman had named to succeed General Ridgway following the President's appointment of Ridgway as the new NATO commander. A tough field commander like Ridgway, Clark had helped plan the North African campaign in 1942, and at age forty-six he had been appointed the youngest three-star general up to that time. A hero of the Italian campaign, he had fought at Anzio, Rapido River, and Cassino. Described as "straight-backed and broad-shouldered" and believing in what he referred to as the "calculated risk," he had been much criticized by his men because of the heavy casualties they had taken in Italy.[29]

Scarcely had Clark taken command when he was confronted with a major political crisis inside South Korea. Internally the country remained in a state of economic, social, and political chaos. By the spring of 1952 one of every nine South Korean men, women, and children had been killed as a result of the war. Of a population of 30 million before the war, at least 5 million had suffered casualties, and an equal number had been displaced. Millions of people were homeless, most of the country's factories had been leveled, its schools had been either wrecked or requisitioned by the military, inflation was spiraling, and agricultural production had fallen by a third. Seoul remained the most battle-scarred city in the world.[30]

South Korea was also faced with its most serious political challenge since the war began in 1950 as a result of President Syngman Rhee's determination to remain in power despite widespread disaffection with his regime. Ever since the opening of peace negotiations in July 1951, the South Korean leader had remained a thorn in the side of the UN Command. In simplest terms, Rhee demanded the unification of Korea by military means if necessary, even though the UN Command had many months before abandoned unification as a military objective of the war. By the end of February 1952 the obstreperousness of the Korean president had become such that President Truman warned him that unless he moderated his public statements in opposition to the peace negotiations at Panmunjom, South Korea would lose American support. The degree of military and economic assistance that his government could expect to receive from the United States, Truman told Rhee, would be influenced "by the sense of responsibility demonstrated by your government, its ability to maintain the unity of the Korean people, and its devotion to democratic ideals."[31]

It was precisely the devotion of the Rhee regime to democratic ideals that was in question during the spring and early summer of 1952. Political opposition had been mounting steadily in South Korea throughout 1952, spurred on by inflation, resentment at Rhee's autocratic methods, and internal dissension within his own cabinet over various domestic issues. When it appeared in May that the National Assembly, which elected the president, would not return Rhee to office, he declared martial law in the area around

Pusan and arrested a number of his opponents in the Assembly, accusing them of treason and complicity in a Communist conspiracy.[32]

Rhee's purpose was to have a new Assembly elected, which would then change the Korean constitution so that there would be a popular election of presidents. Rhee would then have an excellent chance in a "popular vote" watched over by the police, the armed forces, and the terroristic Tae Han Youth Corps. Potential legislative opposition could be blocked by a division of the Assembly into two chambers. Rhee may even have reasoned that his proposal for the popular election of the president would have considerable appeal to the Americans, since they elected their presidents the same way.[33]

If the South Korean president thought this, however, he was badly mistaken, for his declaration of martial law evoked widespread disapproval in Washington. Both the State and Defense departments warned of the danger of increasing political instability in Korea as a result of imposing martial law. From Tokyo, General Clark even raised the possibility of a military coup against Rhee. Although he hoped that Rhee would be persuaded "to listen to reason," Clark warned the Joint Chiefs of Staff that the "[o]nly alternative would be to take over and establish some form of interim gov[ernment]." In the event that "serious internal disturbances . . . interfere with mil[itary] operations, it will be necessary for me to assume control."[34]

On June 2, Washington learned that Rhee was preparing to present the Assembly with an ultimatum—either to agree to his constitutional amendment or be dissolved—even though he lacked the constitutional authority to do that. Truman warned the South Korean president against taking such "irrevocable" action, and Rhee backed down. But the crisis remained far from over, for Rhee then organized mass demonstrations, which became increasingly vituperative and anti-American in character. In response, the Joint Chiefs issued a directive, prepared by the State Department and approved by President Truman, instructing Clark and American Ambassador John Muccio to prepare a contingency plan for military intervention against the South Korean president. "It is hoped the necessity for implementation of [the] plan can be foreseen sufficiently in advance to permit implementation [by the] highest gov[ernmen]tal authority," the Joint Chiefs told Clark. "However, in

[the] event [of a] sudden outbreak of violence, civil disorder or an emer[gency] necessitating immed[iate] action, [you] will be authorized to implement the plan without further authority."[35]

The coup was never executed. Instead, Rhee cowered the National Assembly into approving a constitutional amendment on July 3 that provided for the popular election of a president and vice-president and established a second legislative chamber. First, the South Korean president broke up a meeting of fifty prominent South Korean businessmen, labor leaders, scholars, and politicians who had met to discuss ways of getting rid of him. Then, after holding martial law over the heads of the National Assembly for five weeks and having at least eleven assemblymen put in jail and others threatened by the police, he had the assembly renew his presidency for an indefinite term. Finally, he had 600 of his supporters besiege the assembly, catching eighty anti-Rhee members inside and demanding that they resign. Thoroughly intimidated, the assembly caved in the next day and gave Rhee the constitutional amendment he had wanted. In return, imprisoned legislators were released from custody.[36]

Not until July 28 did Rhee lift martial law, but now firmly in control of the government, the South Korean leader was overwhelmingly retained in office on August 5 as the first popularly elected president of Korea, receiving more than 5.2 million of the 7 million votes cast without making a single speech. Although the UN Command had not been happy at how Rhee had intimidated the National Assembly, it was pleased by the relative honesty of the election and by the fact that the immediate political crisis seemed resolved. However, its fundamental difference with the South Korean president over the military unification of Korea remained, and General Clark completed his contingency plans for a coup, which he filed "for future use if neces[sary]."[37]

While this political drama in Korea was unfolding, the war remained stalemated. Fighting a war of position, each side continued to strengthen its bunkers and interior lines. Conditions on the front came to resemble those of World War I, with deep dug emplacements, trenches, barbed wire defenses, and an extensive outpost line where most of the combat took place. Throughout the summer and into the fall, there were occasional bursts of activity as the enemy made fierce efforts to capture UN outposts, particularly near Chorwon and Kumhwa, two legs of the Iron Triangle. Communist artillery activity also increased markedly as Air Force and Navy planes were unable to prevent an enemy artillery buildup. But heavy rains prevented any significant fighting for most of July and August, and whatever action took place hardly altered the battle line at all.[38]

In the United States there was increasing demand from Republican members of Congress and other opponents of the administration to increase the military pressure on the ground against the Communists, and the argument, frequently made during the summer, that the failure to do this removed the only Communist incentive for settling the war was by no means an unreasonable one. But as General Ridgway told the Joint Chiefs before leaving for his new command at NATO, there was little justification for launching a major military offensive when UN forces lacked the capacity to inflict a decisive military defeat. Despite Republican calls for a decisive military victory, moreover, it is highly unlikely that either the American people or Congress would have gone along with such a beefing up of America's military effort in Korea even if the White House had been willing. The war and the president had become too unpopular for that.[39]

Most certainly, America's allies would never have accepted an expansion of the war involving attacks on Manchuria, which Clark stated would have been necessary to achieve a military victory in Korea. Proof of that fact was their reaction when the UN Command did, in fact, expand the air war in June by attacking hydroelectric facilities on the Korean side of the Yalu River. The largest of these power plants, Suiho, was so badly damaged that North Korea was blacked out for two weeks. By reducing casualties, American planners had hoped the air war would make the Korean conflict more palatable at home while punishing the enemy and forcing him to agree to peace. President Truman may have agreed to the attacks because of his own continued frustration with the deadlocked negotiations at Panmunjom. Once more conjuring up a situation in which he served the Communists with an ultimatum threatening them with nuclear holocaust, he ruminated privately in his diary, "[y]ou either accept our fair and just proposal or you will be completely destroyed."[40]

Whatever the reasons for the attacks or their military effect, however, the bombings infuriated opinion throughout Europe. For the millions of Europeans still anxious for a four-power conference with the Soviet Union to resolve the German question and to settle other world problems, including ending the Korean war, the raids along the Yalu River represented a dangerous escalation of the war that imperiled the already slim chances for world peace. In no country was the reaction against the bombing any stronger than in England. Attacking power plants on the Manchurian frontier without first consulting London was too much even for the Churchill government, which had to admit to the opposition Labor Party that it had not been told of the bombings in advance. Although Churchill and Foreign Secretary Eden reluctantly supported the action, privately Eden rebuked Secretary Acheson, who happened to be in London, for his discourtesy and more or less obliged him to apologize to a group of British leaders of both parties at a private meeting at Westminster.[41]

The most far-reaching damage of the bombings, however, was not the strained relations it caused between Washington and Churchill's conservative government as much as it was the powerful ammunition it gave to the Bevanites within the Labor opposition. By making Churchill and Eden appear as unprincipled stooges of the United States, Bevan and his followers were able to argue that this kind of undisciplined action by the United States amounted to as great a threat to world peace as Soviet aggression. Even those Laborites violently opposed to Bevan and his views were taken back by the American action, for, as one correspondent reported from London, even they were "genuinely alarmed by the idea that a decision could be taken somewhere, maybe without their knowledge, that would drag them willy-nilly into a third world war."[42]

Despite the enormous reaction against the United States, particularly in England, that America's bombing of the Yalu power plants had caused, the UN Command continued its escalation of the air war. General Clark claimed that the Yalu raids had been a necessary military measure, and in the next few months American planes stepped up their attacks on North Korean targets, even hitting an oil refinery only eight miles from the Soviet border, as a primary means of bringing military pressure on the enemy. In July the Joint Chiefs also approved a request from Clark for a squadron of F-84s with an atomic delivery capability, which he had asked for in response to a buildup in the Far East of Soviet and Chinese air power. According to Clark, there were now approximately 1100 Communist bombers in the areas adjacent to Japan and Korea, with an additional 590 bombers in striking range of these two countries. At least some of these bombers were believed capable of delivering atomic weapons, and they were protected by an effective radar network and a fighter force now estimated to include 1500 jet and more than 2000 conventional-type fighters. The Joint Chiefs of Staff doubted that the threat of an air strike against the Far East Command was any greater than against other commands. But they promised Clark a fighter squadron by August, and meanwhile they made available to him planes from the Strategic Air Command in case an emergency developed requiring the use of atomic weapons.[43]

By now the UN Command in Tokyo and military planners at the Pentagon were totally frustrated. The war remained stalemated not only militarily, but also diplomatically. At Panmunjom no progress was made concerning the issue of prisoner repatriation, still the only issue preventing an end to the war. Also frustrated, the State Department even considered dealing directly with the Soviet Union in Moscow, but it was discouraged from doing so by George Kennan, now America's ambassador to the Soviet Union, and by General Clark and Clark's adviser in Tokyo, Ambassador Robert Murphy. Instead, all three officials favored intensifying the bombing of North Korea, which, they believed, was undercutting North Korean and Chinese morale, even though it seemed to have no discernible effect on the negotiations at Panmunjom. The State Department then went so far as to recommend a Presidential statement offering an armistice based on the points already agreed to at Panmunjom as well as an exchange of those POWs willing to be repatriated, leaving the disposition of the others to be resolved later. But the Pentagon argued that the issue of prisoner repatriation was too important to be left unresolved, and toward the end of September President Truman personally decided against any new approaches to the Communists.[44]

Instead, Truman directed that General William K. Harrison, Jr., who had replaced Admiral Joy as the chief UN negotiator at Panmunjom at the end of May, offer the United Nations' package proposal once more to the enemy, allowing ten days for a reply. If the Chinese and North Koreans rejected the proposal, the UN Command would then recess the talks indefinitely and "be prepared to do such things as may be necessary." On October 8 the Communist negotiators formally rejected the United Nations' package proposal, whereupon General Harrison declared the talks indefinitely recessed.[45]

Frustrated at this total lack of progress at ending the war, the Pentagon reviewed its military options. In fact, since February the Joint Strategic Plans Committee, an advisory group to the Joint Chiefs of Staff, had taken up the very question of what options to adopt in Korea in case of an indefinite prolongation or breakdown in the talks at Panmunjom. Later, in response to a new assignment to consider possible military alternatives against North Korea and Communist China, the committee had concluded that it would be necessary to authorize the use of atomic weapons in the Far East. The Joint Chiefs decided that the committee placed too much emphasis on atomic weapons and asked that the question be studied more carefully.[46]

Meanwhile, the Joint Chiefs asked General Clark for his advice on military options. The armistice negotiations had been unsuccessful, Clark responded on September 29, not because of the POW issue but because the UN Command had not "exerted suf[ficient] mili[tary] pressure to impose the r[equire]m[en]t for an armistice on the enemy." Furthermore, the UN commander distinguished between intensified military action, on the one hand, and the type of military offensive necessary to bring about a final peace in Korea, on the other. Simply to increase military pressure on the enemy or even to march to the narrow waist of the peninsula, a possibility raised by the Joint Chiefs, would be counterproductive. Any contemplated course of action had to include "provision for carrying the battle all the way to the Yalu in the event that a mili[tary] victory cannot be achieved short of the line." Would an expansion of the war lead to Soviet intervention or possibly World War III? Clark did not think so. He believed "that World War III [would] not be brought about by action on our part, that conflict would commence only when the USSR so determines on her appraisal, unaffected by US or UNC actions." Two weeks later Clark told General J. Lawton Collins that while he did not include the use of tactical nuclear weapons in his planning, he recommended that he be given authority to do so.[47]

Clark was under no illusion that the Joint Chiefs, much less the White House, would approve the kind of military action he had in mind, particularly the lifting of restrictions on the use of atomic weapons. But Clark's remarks were important, nevertheless, for in responding to the Joint Chiefs and in writing Collins, Clark expressed some of the exasperation he and his subordinates felt in being forced to fight a limited war with minute supervision from Washington. In fact, the sentiment was widespread at Clark's headquarters in Tokyo and among his commanders in Korea that the armistice negotiations had constituted a colossal blunder on the part of the United Nations. Like the UN commander, his staff at headquarters and his commanders in the field believed that the Communists had been "on the ropes" after the failure of their spring offensive in 1951, and the staff and the commander were convinced that what had been called for was a decisive military initiative rather than a decision to seek an armistice. Similarly, Clark and his commanders, such as General James Van Fleet of the Eighth Army and General Otto P. Weyland of the Far East Air Force, expressing views similar to General Douglas MacArthur before them, emphasized that the United States had to recognize that it was a great Pacific power as well as an Atlantic power and that the Korean war was part of the global conflict being waged by the Communists against the United States so that America's security interests demanded that it win the war.[48]

Of course, most Americans shared the same frustrations that Clark and his commanders felt over a seemingly endless war that offered little hope of a battlefied victory. Many of these same Americans had also expressed the same view as they did about the need for the United States to give the Pacific region greater priority in its struggle against Communist aggression. Certainly this had been a recurring theme of the war almost since the time the North Koreans first crossed the 38th parallel in June 1950. What lent particular weight to the frustrations and grievances of so many Americans in the summer and fall of 1952, however, was that in a Presidential election year the issues of ending the war and setting future directions for American foreign policy were bound to be decisive in determining the outcome of the campaign. Actually Dwight Eisenhower, the eventual Republican nominee and President-elect, offered far less in terms either of bringing peace to Korea or changing the course of the nation's foreign policy than did his principal Republican rival, Senator Taft. But it was largely because he promised to be more moderate than Taft in the conduct of foreign policy while appearing to have new ideas about ending this most unpopular of all wars, that he was able to win his party's nomination in July and then go on to a relatively easy election victory in November.

Notes

1. Briefing of Foreign Government Representatives on Korea, May 13, 1952, Box 3, Selected Records Relating to the Korean War; *Time*, 59 (March 17, 1952), 36; *ibid.* (March 31, 1952), 28; Walter G. Hermes, *Truce Tent and Fighting Front* (Washington, DC, 1966), 198–199.

2. Hermes, *Truce Tent and Fighting Front*, 199-200; *Time*, 58 (December 3, 1951), 19; *New Republic*, 126 (February 18, 1952), 5.

3. John F. Cady, *The United States and Burma* (Cambridge, MA, 1976), 201–205; David Joel Steinberg, et al., *In Search of Southeast Asia: A Modern History* (New York, 1971), 345–346 and 375–376.

4. Steinberg, et al., *In Search of Southeast Asia*, 346–347, 367–368, and 382; *Commonweal*, 55 (January 25, 1952), 387; *New Republic*, 126 (March 10, 1952), 39-40; *Time*, 59 (March 10, 1952), 39–40.

5. *Life*, 32 (February 4, 1952), 17–18; *Atlantic Monthly*, 190 (July 1952), 4–6; Robert W. Stookey, *America and the Arab States: An Uneasy Encounter* (New York, 1975), 83-84 and 132–135.

6. *Commonweal*, 55 (February 8, 1952), 435; *ibid.* (February 15, 1952), 465; *New Yorker*, 27 (January 12, 1952), 47–49; *ibid.* (February 9, 1952), 98; *Time*, 59 (March 31, 1952), 32–37.

7. *FR*, 1952–1954, XV, 280–288; *Life*, 32 (March 17, 1952), 36; David S. McLellan, *Dean Acheson: The State Department Years* (New York, 1976), 386–395; Dean Acheson, *Present at the Creation: My Years in the State Department* (New York, 1969), 600.

8. *Nation*, 173 (December 15, 1951), 509 and 512–513; *New Republic*, 125 (December 17, 1951), 10–12; *New Yorker*, 27 (February 9, 1952), 59; *Time*, 59 (February 18, 1952), 28; *ibid.* (March 10, 1952), 32–33.

9. Michael Foot, *Aneurin Bevan: A Biography*, II (2 vols., London, 1973), 361–366; *New Yorker*, 28 (March 15, 1952), 50–51; *ibid.* (March 29, 1952), 102–104; *Nation*, 174 (March 15, 1952), 247–248; *Atlantic Monthly*, 189 (May 1952), 17–21; *New Republic*, 126 (March 3, 1952), 8; *ibid.* 126 (May 19, 1952), 8.

10. Robert McGeehan, *The German Rearmament Question: American Diplomacy and European Defense After World War II* (Urbana, IL, 1971), 188–198; Acheson, *Present at the Creation*, 622–627; *Time*, 59 (March 3, 1952), 17 and 23.

11. McGeehan, *The German Rearmament Question*, 192–193; *Time*, 59 (March 3, 1952), 23; *Commonweal*, 55 (March 14, 1952), 555; *New Republic*, 126 (March 24, 1952), 3.

12. *New Republic*, 126 (March 17, 1952), 8; *ibid.* (May 19, 1952), 8–9; *Nation*, 174 (March 22, 1952), 263; *ibid.* (May 17, 1952); *Time*, 59 (March 24, 1952), 37; *Commonweal*, 55 (March 28, 1952), 604.

13. *Nation*, 174 (May 17, 1952), 466–468.

14. Ronald J. Caridi, *The Korean War and American Politics: The Republican Party as a Case Study* (Philadelphia, 1968), 182; *New Republic*, 126 (February 11, 1952), 33; *Time*, 59 (February 18, 1952), 24; *Commonweal*, 55 (February 29, 1952), 509.

15. *Nation*, 174 (February 2, 1952), 98–99; *ibid.* (February 16, 1952), 151–152; *ibid.* (May 17, 1952), 473–475; New Republic, 126 (January 14, 1952), 16–17; *ibid.* (March 17, 1952), 11–12; Time, 58 (November 19, 1951), 23.

16. Caridi, *The Korean War and American Politics*, 183–184.

17. *New Republic*, 126 (May 19, 1952), 7.

18. *FR*, 1952–1954, XV, 79–80; Briefing of Foreign Government Representatives on Korea, March 4 and 18, 1952, Box 13, Selected Records Relating to the Korean War.

19. "Intelligence Report," March 27, 1952, Box 13, Selected Records Relating to the Korean War; *Time*, 59 (April 7, 1952), 30; John Toland, *In Mortal Combat: Korea, 1950–1953* (New York, 1991), 537.

20. *Life*, 52 (April 7, 1952), 52; *Time*, 59 (April 7, 1952), 30.

21. Callum MacDonald, *Korea: The War Before Vietnam* (New York, 1986), 161–163; John Toland, *In Mortal Combat: Korea, 1950–1953* (New York, 1991), 416–419 and 536–537; Mark Ryan, *Chinese Attitudes Toward Nuclear Weapons* (New York, 1990).

22. *Time*, 59 (May 19, 1952), 23–24.

23. *FR*, 1952–1954, XV, 136–138; Ridgway to Joint Chiefs of Staff, April 3, 1952, Box 10, Selected Records Relating to the Korean War; Hermes, *Truce Tent and Fighting Front*, 233–234 and 237–239; *Time*, 59 (January 28, 1952), 21; *Time*, 59 (March 3, 1952), 34–36; *ibid.* (March 24, 1952), 30; *Life*, 32 (March 31, 1952), 92–98.

24. Ridgway to Joint Chiefs of Staff, April 3, 1952, Box 10, Selected Records Relating to the Korean War; Rosemary Foot, *A Substitute for Victory: The Politics of Peacemaking at the Korean Armistice Talks* (Ithaca, NY, 1990), 109–120; Barton J. Bernstein, "The Struggle Over the Korean Armistice: Prisoners of Repatriation?" in Bruce Cumings (ed.), *Child of Conflict: The Korean-American Relationship, 1943–1953* (Seattle, WA, 1983), 284–285.

25. *Time*, 59 (May 19, 1952), 36–37; Hermes, *Truce Tent and Fighting Front*, 244–245.

26. *FR*, 1952–1954, XV, 136–138 and 308–310; *Time*, 59 (June 9, 1952), 25; *ibid.* (June 23, 1952), 23; *Life*, 32 (June 23, 1952), 32–33; *Intelligence Report*,

March 27, 1952, Box 13, Selected Records Relating to the Korean War; Foot, *A Substitute for Victory*, 101–102.

27. *FR*, 1952–1954, XV, 145–154.

28. Briefing of Foreign Government Representatives on Korea, April 29 and May 2, 1952, Box 3, Selected Records Relating to the Korean War.

29. D. Clayton James, *Refighting the Last War: Command and Crisis in Korea, 1950–1953* (New York, 1993), 102–103; *Time*, 59 (May 19, 1952), 36.

30. *Ibid.*, 59 (March 10, 1952), 29; *ibid.* (April 21, 1952), 30; *ibid.* (May 26, 1952), 30; *Nation*, 174 (February 2, 1952), 107–109; *Commonweal*, 56 (June 13, 1952), 236–237; *ibid.* (June 25, 1952), 383–385.

31. *FR*, 1952–1954, XV, 74–76.

32. Ridgway to Joint Chiefs of Staff, May 3, 1952, Box 16, Selected Records Relating to the Korean War: Memorandum for the Secretary of Defense from the Joint Chiefs of Staff, March 26, 1952, Box 3, *ibid.*; Special Korean Briefing, June 6, 1952, Box 16, *ibid.*

33. *FR*, 1952–1954, XV, 281–285; *Nation*, 174 (February 9, 1952), 132–134.

34. Joint Chiefs of Staff to Clark, May 30, 1952, Box 17, Selected Records Relating to the Korean War; *FR*, 1952–1954, XV, 274–276 and 281–285.

35. *FR*, 285–286, 301–305, and 358–360.

36. *Time*, 59 (June 30, 1952), 24; *ibid.*, 60 (July 7, 1952), 25.

37. Clark to Joint Chiefs of Staff, August 8, 1952, Box 17, Selected Records Relating to the Korean War.

38. Edgar O'Ballance, *Korea: 1950–1953* (London, 1969), 126; Hermes, *Truce Tent and Fighting Front*, 292–296.

39. Rees, *Korea: The Limited War* (New York, 1964), 303–305; *New Republic*, 126 (March 24, 1952), 3; Robert J. Donovan, *Tumultuous Years: The Presidency of Harry S. Truman, 1949–1953* (New York, 1982), 382.

40. Robert F. Futrell, The United States Air Force in Korea, 1950–1953 (New York, 1961), 451–453 and 480–487; *Time*, 59 (June 30, 1952), 24; Bernstein, "The Struggle Over the Korean Armistice," 292–293.

41. *Time*, 59 (June 23, 1952), 26; *ibid.*, 60 (July, 7, 1952), 3–4 and 26; *Nation*, 174 (June 14, 1952), 575–576; *ibid.*, 175 (July 5, 1952), 1 and 3–4; *Life*, 33 (July 7, 1952), 27.

42. *Nation*, 175 (July 5, 1952), 3–4; *New Yorker*, 28 (July 19, 1952), 64.

43. Clark to Joint Chiefs of Staff, June 23, 1952, Box 17, Selected Records Relating to the Korean War; Memorandum for the Commander-in-Chief, Far East, July 9, 1952, *ibid.*

44. *FR*, 1952–1954, XV, 364–367, 386–398, 421–427, 430–436, 446–447, 514–521, and 522–525; Henkins to Kitchen, November 4, 1952, Box 4284, Records of the Department of State, RG 59, 795.00/11-452; Truman to Clark, September 26, 1952, Box 17, Selected Records Relating to the Korean War; Rosemary Foot, *The Wrong War: American Policy and the Dimensions of the Korean Conflict, 1950–1953* (Ithaca, NY, 1985), 176–180; Foot, *A Substitute for Victory*, 146–150.

45. *FR*, 1952–1954, XV, 554–557.
46. James F. Schnabel and Richard J. Watson, *The History of the Joint Chiefs of Staff*, III, *The Korean War* (Wilmington, DE, 1979), 929.
47. *FR*, 1952–1954, XV, 548–550; James, *Refighting the Last War*, 119–211.
48. *FR*, 1952–1954, XV, 548–550; Schnabel and Watson, *The History of the Joint Chiefs of Staff*, III, *The Korean War*, 932–933; Frank Pace, Jr. to President Truman, October 15, 1952, and attachments, Box 243, Korean War File, President's Secretary File, Truman Papers.

New President, New Initiatives

Dwight D. Eisenhower won the Republican Party's nomination for the Presidency because a group of moderate Republicans, determined to prevent the right wing of the party from gaining the nomination for Robert Taft, saw in General Eisenhower an extremely popular alternative whose international orientation, commitment to the principles of collective security, and belief in the Atlantic alliance coincided with their own views on foreign policy. Although Eisenhower did not formally enter the Presidential race until he resigned his NATO command at the end of May, the effort to draft him, led by Senator Lodge of Massachusetts, had been going on since late 1951, and it had become increasingly clear since the March primary in New Hampshire that Eisenhower would be receptive to a draft "Ike" movement. One of the questions raised by those speculating on whether Eisenhower would be a candidate for the Republican nomination was his views on the Korean war.

As president of Columbia University at the time the conflict broke out in Korea and then as commander of NATO forces in Europe after 1951, Eisenhower had said or written very little about the war. At the outset he did state publicly his support for American military intervention, remarking that "there was no recourse but to do what President Truman did." Indeed, he expressed dismay that the administration was not doing enough to martial the nation's forces to resist Communist aggression in Korea. Following a meeting with President Truman and Defense Secretary George Marshall shortly after North Korea invaded South Korea, he noted in his diary that there appeared "to be no disposition to begin serious mobilization." "Truman's military advisers are too complacent," he also wrote. He made it clear to the administration that it needed to begin a rapid rearmament program. This enabled him to argue later that he had urged the White House to do more in Korea but had been ignored.[1]

What was noteworthy about Eisenhower's views on Korea, however, was how little he said or wrote about the war following the initial outbreak of hostilities. Convinced that Korea was part of Moscow's plans for world domination and firmly committed to the principles of international cooperation and collective security, Eisenhower remained strongly supportive of the UN action in Korea. But from June 1950 until the time he returned to the United States from Europe two years later, he concentrated almost exclusively on promoting the Atlantic alliance.[2]

Not until he formally launched his bid for the nomination in June, with a speech and news conference in his hometown of Abilene, Kansas, did he begin to speak out on the Korean war. His comments differed substantially from the statements being made by Taft and his supporters, who bitterly attacked the administration's war policies and called for a decisive military victory. In contrast, Eisenhower told reporters, "I do not have any prescription for bringing the [war] to a decisive end." "I believe we have to stand firm and take every possible step we can to reduce our losses, and try to get a decisive armistice out of it." Precisely because his views seemed so moderate, Eisenhower appeared to many Americans—and Europeans—an attractive alternative to the extremism associated with the Taft wing of the Republican Party. [3]

After he won the nomination, however, Eisenhower began to speak out harshly against the Democrats' handling of the Korean war; this was part of a general attack on the administration's entire foreign policy. During a campaign stop in Philadelphia in September, for example, he blamed the war on the administration's "failure to observe some of the principles for preventing war," and tied this to its "loss" of China. "We are in [Korea]," he said, "because this Administration abandoned China to the Communists. . . [and] announced to all the world that it had written off most of the Far East as beyond our direct concern." By October the Republican nominee was even denouncing the Korean peace talks as a Communist "bear-pit" into which the Democrats had fallen and arguing that if there were to be wars in Asia, the United States should let Asians fight them.[4]

In contrast to Eisenhower, the Democratic nominee, Governor Adlai Stevenson of Illinois, appeared a model of urbanity and sobriety. Defending the very principles of moderation that Eisenhower had seemed to abandon, Stevenson charmed audiences with his wit, manner, and reasoned judgment. Forced to defend the administration's foreign policy and its conduct of the war, the Democratic candidate did so with sophistication and eloquence. Nevertheless, the Republican nominee remained the overwhelming favorite of the electorate, and to the extent that the Korean war was decisive in the election, it worked overwhelmingly to Eisenhower's advantage. A Gallup poll taken in September on which Presidential candidate could best handle the Korean war found that 67 percent of the voters believed Eisenhower could do a better job than Stevenson, while only 9 percent believed otherwise.[5]

The high point of the campaign, however, came in Detroit on October 24 when Eisenhower incorporated into a speech he was making a pledge suggested by one of his speech writers, Emmet John Hughes, to go to Korea if elected. "Only in that way," he told his audience, "could I learn how best to serve the American people in the cause of peace. I shall go to Korea." There is some disagreement among political analysts as to just how important this pledge was to the election's outcome. Most analysts agree that Eisenhower's personal popularity with the voters would probably have ensured his victory regardless of any campaign issues. The very lack of a systematic and comprehensive dialogue on the war until the final weeks of the campaign also suggests that it might not have been the decisive issue that some have maintained. Finally, the election involved a number of issues other than Korea, including corruption within the administration and McCarthyism. A poll taken after the election by the Survey Research Center of the University of Michigan found that domestic issues such as these were far more important to the voters than was foreign policy.[6]

But while the war might not have been the decisive issue of the campaign, it seems beyond doubt that it was of paramount importance in determining Eisenhower's *margin* of victory, for it persuaded many Americans that the Republicans would soon end a war that had become extremely unpopular. It was not only the inconclusive and seemingly endless nature of the war that disturbed many Americans, but also a series of related issues, such as the nation's high inflation rate, which was attributed directly to the war, and the recalling of World War II reservists, particularly pilots, to active duty. Many of those recalled, having to leave their families and successful civilian careers, felt they were being unfairly assigned dangerous combat missions while their regular Air Force counterparts were being given cushy office assignments. At the same time, Americans were incensed about the drafting of young men to fight in Korea, while the Republicans were able to turn to their own advantage Democratic boasts that the American people were enjoying unparalleled prosperity by countering that the Korean war was at the root of this prosperity and that good times were "being bought by the lives of our boys in Korea."[7]

"So long as a single American soldier faced enemy fire in Korea," Eisenhower remarked in Pittsburgh as the campaign was coming to a close, "the honorable ending of the Korean war and the securing of honorable peace in the world must be the first—the urgent and unshakable—purpose of a new administration." A few days later the voters delivered their verdict, overwhelmingly electing him President by a margin of almost 55 percent to Stevenson's 44.3 percent. Although neither Eisenhower nor the Republican Party had a concrete program for ending the war, it was widely speculated in Washington and throughout the nation that Eisenhower would soon say or do something in Korea that would lead to a resumption and early conclusion of the truce talks.[8]

Such hopes were quickly shattered by developments at the United Nations, where Soviet Ambassador Andrei Vishinsky delivered an angry speech blasting an Indian peace initiative that, ironically, had also been opposed by the United States. First circulated by India's Krishna Menon toward the middle of November, the resolution provided for the establishment of a neutral nations repatriation commission to handle the repatriation problem until peace was restored in Korea. Then the political conference that was supposed to be called after the armistice would decide the final fate of those prisoners of war still resisting repatriation. Secretary of State Acheson spoke out strongly against the resolution because he believed it would leave the repatriation question unresolved at the time of the armistice. Instead, the United States pushed an earlier twenty-one-nation resolution that it had co-sponsored calling on Communist China and North Korea to agree to an armistice based on voluntary repatriation.[9]

Although Acheson referred to the Indian proposal as a "dangerous idea" that was also conceptually vague, it nevertheless had the support of most of America's allies. Not only did countries like England and France consider the resolution a way to break the dead-lock in the peace negotiations, they were also deeply concerned about what the new administration would do in Korea once it took office. In England, Foreign Secretary Anthony Eden also had to con-sider the unity of the British Commonwealth, particularly the de-mands of the newer nations of the Commonwealth, who—as in this case—often aligned themselves with neutralist powers against the United States. In France the pressures on the government were more subtle but also concerned a form of anti-Americanism gener-ally associated with neutralism and resistance to German rearma-ment and that ran the gamut from opposition to American high tar-iffs to opposition to American high ideals. At the end of 1952 the French were particularly indignant at America's rigid anticolonial-ism, especially in North Africa.[10]

Aware of the widespread support for the Menon resolution and seeking to gain allied backing for America's own twenty-one-nation resolution, Acheson held a round of talks with allied leaders. The White House also persuaded President-elect Eisenhower to make a statement publicly backing the administration's position on volun-tary repatriation of POWs to show that there would be no policy change on that essential issue after the Republicans took office in January. But the secretary of state failed to change any minds, and the Menon resolution continued to gain such widespread support after it was formally introduced on November 17 that it ceased to be a matter of whether the General Assembly would approve it. As Acheson told President Truman, the only question now was whether the Indian proposal could be amended to make it more ac-ceptable to the United States.[11]

This proved to be just what happened. The crucial amendment in Acheson's view had to do with the question of when POWs re-sisting repatriation would be turned over to the political conference, which was to be held after the armistice. But it was not made clear how much longer they would have to remain incarcerated. The sec-retary of state did not like handing the POWs over to the political conference in the first place, but certainly not for an indefinite pe-riod. Applying the principle of the carrot and stick, in which he ap-peared conciliatory even as he warned America's European allies that their failure to support him on this issue would jeopardize America's support for NATO "and other arrangements of the same sort," the secretary of state was able to bring them around to the

American position. In turn, they prevailed on India to agree to amendments ensuring that within three months after the armistice the repatriation process would end and the final disposition of remaining prisoners would be determined by the United Nations itself.[12]

By this time, however, Vishinsky had taken the floor of the General Assembly to assail the Menon resolution, stating that it was "designed not to put an end to the war but to perpetuate it." By wrecking any prospect of an imminent political settlement of the war, Moscow apparently hoped to put the President-elect in the awkward position of going to Korea for no apparent purpose other than to consider means of expanding the war, a position America's allies would certainly reject.[13]

If this was in fact Moscow's purpose, the Soviets miscalculated badly, for Vishinsky's speech solidified UN support behind the American position, making it appear that Moscow and not Washington represented the roadblock to final peace in Korea. Ironically, Washington now became the driving force behind the Indian initiative. With Washington fully behind it, the General Assembly approved the resolution on December 3 by a vote of 54 to 5. In this way the United States succeeded in turning an unacceptable proposal into a victory for its position on POWs.[14]

But this victory had not been without cost to the principle of allied unity. Indeed Secretary Acheson would later refer to the allied efforts in behalf of the Menon resolution as the "Menon Cabal." And there can be no doubt that for a while at least the Indian proposal strained the united front on Korea that the Truman administration tried so hard to maintain. The fact was that since the United States bore the greatest burden of responsibility in Korea, it expected its views to carry the greatest weight in matters concerning Korea, and it deeply resented when this was not the case.[15]

As the Soviets may also have hoped, their rejection of the Menon resolution just about eliminated any chance that Eisenhower's trip to Korea would produce anything tangible in the way of ending the war. Indeed, what was most noteworthy about the trip was what Eisenhower did *not* do. Keeping his campaign pledge, the President-elect went to Korea at the beginning of December under a blanket of total secrecy. During his trip he flew along the front, toured the battlefields, ate with the troops, visited the wounded, and met separately with President Syngman Rhee and General Clark. But his two meetings with Rhee, who had hoped to turn Eisenhower's visit into a week-long public display of patriotism, parades, dinners, and mass rallies, were kept brief, and Eisenhower refused to appear publicly with him. Nor did the President-elect give Clark, who had prepared elaborate plans for a military victory, an opportunity to outline his proposals. Because driving the Chinese completely off the Korean peninsula, as Clark proposed, required carrying the conflict across the Yalu River, it risked a global war with the Soviet Union, a gamble that Eisenhower was not yet prepared to make.[16]

Nevertheless, the new President's visit to Korea made some lasting and important impressions on him. Above all, he returned home persuaded that the United States "could not stand forever on a static front and continue to accept casualties without any visible result." "Small attacks on small hills," he later commented, "would not end the war." A military gesture of considerable magnitude was warranted. In this sense, those who had always been nervous that Eisenhower's trip to Korea might lead to a military escalation had cause to be concerned.[17]

Following Eisenhower's return to the United States, however, a lull set in as President Truman prepared to turn over his office to Eisenhower and as the talks at Panmunjom remained recessed. President Truman, whose relations with Eisenhower were already strained, took umbrage at a meeting that the President-elect held with General MacArthur following his return. At the meeting in New York, in mid-December, MacArthur recommended "the atomic bombing of enemy military concentrations and installations in North Korea" if the Soviet Union would not agree to a summit conference with the United States in which the two nations would guarantee the neutrality of Germany, Austria, Japan, and Korea. He also proposed the "sowing" of a nuclear shield to prevent the flow of enemy supplies from China into North Korea.[18]

In response, Eisenhower merely thanked MacArthur for his proposal and said he would have to study it in greater detail. Nevertheless, when Truman heard that Eisenhower was going to meet with MacArthur, he turned livid. At a news conference he shot back by doubting whether MacArthur had a feasible proposal for ending the war and by labeling Eisenhower's trip to Korea a piece of demagoguery whose sole purpose was to fulfill a campaign promise. The President's remarks stirred a nest of controversy, but although

Eisenhower was infuriated by Truman's comments, he refused to break openly with the President, preferring to use the time before inauguration day for organizing his new administration.[19]

In Korea, meanwhile, the news was mixed. The truce tents at Panmunjom stayed empty as neither side offered any new proposals to break the deadlock over prisoner repatriation and as the Communists waited to see if the new administration had any fresh approaches toward resolving this problem. On the battlefied, there was a significant increase in activity in October and November as the Chinese apparently sought to pressure the United States out of the war in this election season. Some of the fighting was the heaviest since 1950 and involved sizable contingents of ROK troops, who performed extremely well. In October, for example, ROK forces engaged the Chinese in the battle of White Horse Hill, near the Chorwon corner of the Iron Triangle. In extremely bloody fighting, the South Koreans killed or wounded an estimated 10,000 Chinese during the first six days of the battle alone, and they still retained the hill. Elsewhere along the front, Communist probes were beaten back, and there were no signs of a major enemy breakthrough.[20]

Otherwise, there was little to cheer about. According to Pentagon figures released in November, the United States was taking casualties at the rate of more than 1,000 a week, the heaviest in a year. Since the truce talks had begun sixteen months earlier, more than 44,700 American troops had been killed or wounded. The Pentagon also announced that the United States had already dropped more bombs on Korea than in the first two years of World War II. The Eighth Army had used about the same weight of mortar and artillery shells as in the whole European operation from D-Day to V-E Day. And yet the enemy had gotten stronger, not weaker. By the end of 1952 its forces in North Korea totaled about 1.2 million, and its defensive lines had become virtually impenetrable.[21]

This was the dilemma facing Eisenhower when he took office in January 1953. Although he had not committed himself to any particular program or plan for ending the war, he was determined to take new initiatives to bring the conflict to a close. While he believed the pivot of the Cold War remained Europe and not Asia, he recognized that influential sectors of public opinion favored a more vigorous policy in the Far East. And although he had frowned on suggestions for using nuclear weapons in Korea, his secretary of state, John Foster Dulles, believed that the United States should threaten a nuclear response in case of Communist aggression, a policy that later became known as "massive retaliation."

A highly successful lawyer and diplomat, Dulles had been the recognized Republican spokesman on foreign policy for more than a year. Generally regarded as a moderate Republican because of his internationalist views, he had, beginning with an article that *Life* published in May 1952, made clear his willingness to use America's nuclear power. Our present policies, he said, were "treadmill policies which, at best, might keep us in the same place until we drop exhausted." The way out of this trap was to rely on nuclear deterrence—"that is for the free world to develop the will and organize the means to retaliate instantly against open aggression by Red armies, so that, if it occurred anywhere, we could and would strike back where it hurt, by means of our own choosing."[22]

Eisenhower believed that Dulles's formulation of the doctrine of deterrence was too simple and unqualified. Even so, the new President felt it was important for the Soviets to know that aggression against America's vital interests could produce a nuclear response. And by relying on air power and nuclear deterrence, the United States could avoid spending itself into bankruptcy, an issue that Dulles had also raised in his *Life* article. With certain reservations, therefore, Eisenhower was sympathetic to a foreign policy based on nuclear deterrence, and at no time did he eliminate as an option the use of nuclear weapons in Korea.[23]

In fact, at a National Security Council meeting less than a month after taking office, Eisenhower himself raised the nuclear option. The United States could not continue fighting the war as it had in the past, he stated. Its self-respect and that of its allies were at stake, and if the allies objected to the use of atomic weapons "we might as well ask them to supply three or more divisions needed to drive the Communists back." In making these remarks, Eisenhower was probably just speculating out loud, and he dropped the subject after General Bradley told him how opposed the allies would be to any form of nuclear warfare. But it is clear that as early as February, the new President was already considering adopting a nuclear strategy in Korea.[24]

It is also clear that Eisenhower was determined to end the Korean war quickly. To pressure the Chinese into signing a peace agreement and to appease Old Guard Republicans, the President announced in his first State of the Union message that the "Seventh Fleet [would] no longer be employed to shield Communist China."

Eisenhower stressed that his instructions implied no aggressive intent on his part; in fact, the Seventh Fleet had been assisting the Chinese Nationalists in conducting raids along the coast for some time. But in stopping the fleet's patrolling of the Formosa Strait, Eisenhower was effectively warning Beijing that if a truce was not forthcoming, Chiang Kai-shek's forces might be used against the mainland.[25]

A truce *was* coming but not as fast as the administration had hoped. In December 1952, the UN Command agreed to a proposal by the International Red Cross in Switzerland to an exchange of sick and wounded POWs. Although General Clark anticipated that the Communists would turn down the proposal, to his surprise they agreed to the exchange on March 28, 1953, and even suggested that the truce talks be reopened at Panmunjom. Two days later, Premier Zho Enlai of the People's Republic of China announced over the radio that he was willing to have all nonrepatriates turned over to a neutral state "so as to ensure a just solution to the question of their repatriation."[26]

Apparently Beijing made this major concession on the POW question, a concession that resembled the same Indian plan that China had rejected the previous December, because both the Soviet Union and it were anxious by 1953 to end the war. On March 5 Soviet premier Joseph Stalin died after suffering a brain hemorrhage. Stalin's replacement, Georgi Malenkov, sought to improve relations with the West and, for this purpose, began what reporters and other political observers referred to as a "Soviet peace offensive." On March 15 he announced that there were no disputes between Moscow and Washington "that cannot be decided by peaceful means, on the basis of mutual understanding." Shortly thereafter, the Soviet Union relaxed its controls over Eastern Europe, arrested Lavrenti P. Beria, head of the notorious KGB, and renewed an earlier offer by Stalin in 1952 to consider a reunited, partially rearmed, but neutralized Germany. Anxious to resolve some of its differences with the West, realizing that the war in Korea could escalate into a global conflict, which it wanted no more than the United States did, and also apparently feeling more confident about its own military capability now that it was a strong nuclear power, Moscow probably pressured China and North Korea to end the conflict.[27]

This was most likely not hard to do, for the costs of the war to them were enormous. In 1951, for example, 60 percent of China's tax revenue went to the defense budget, and by the end of 1952 there were more than a million Chinese soldiers in North Korea. Estimates at the end of the war placed China's losses at about 900,000 men. Also, the conflict meant a drain of trained personnel who were badly needed to rebuild a country ravaged by forty years of internal strife. Since Beijing had already achieved maximum prestige by driving UN forces out of most of North Korea, there was little more to be gained from continuing the conflict. As for North Korea, it suffered the loss of nearly 520,000 personnel, while unofficial estimates placed the number of civilian casualties at about a million. Food shortages had become so serious that widespread famine was prevented only by emergency food shipments from other Communist countries, and morale was extremely low.[28]

With China no longer insisting on the repatriation of all POWs, it now appeared that the deadlock on the one issue preventing an end to the Korean war had been broken and that peace was finally at hand. Once more pressure mounted on the United States to accept Zhou Enlai's offer on nonrepatriates and to reopen the armistice talks. But Dulles and Eisenhower felt that before talks were resumed at Panmunjom, the Chinese and North Koreans should first make good on the other part of their proposal: an exchange of sick and wounded. Considering how anxious the Communists now were for an armistice, Dulles also thought the UN Command could obtain a much better agreement than one based on a division of Korea at the 38th parallel. Personally he would have liked to tell the Chinese and North Koreans that unless Korea was divided at the narrow waist of the peninsula that lay ninety miles north of the 38th parallel, the armistice would be called off. President Eisenhower vetoed that idea because it would mean a politically unacceptable renewal of the war in Korea. But he agreed to a National Security Council statement reserving to the United States the right to void any armistice agreement that failed to lead to a political settlement in Korea.[29]

Meanwhile General Clark made contact with the enemy about exchanging sick and wounded prisoners. Like the administration, Clark had remained extremely suspicious of the Communists, warning the Joint Chiefs that it would be "completely naive" not to anticipate "every form of chicanery" in their proposal for a prisoner exchange. But on April 5 the Chinese and North Koreans agreed to meet the next day to work out the details for the exchange, and within the week arrangements were concluded for swapping 5,800

POWs held by the United Nations in return for 600 POWS held by the Communists. All this created tremendous excitement and optimism at the United Nations, in Washington, and throughout Europe that peace was finally at hand.[30]

Yet a number of difficult questions remained unanswered, such as which "neutral" country would take responsibility for prisoners resisting repatriation and whether they would be transferred to that neutral country or remain in Korea. To answer these questions the UN Command agreed to reopen armistice talks with the Communists. So anxious were America's allies to resume the negotiations that the British warned Washington against pressing the Chinese too hard for clarifications of Zhou Enlai's earlier statement. But in South Korea the government responded to the news that truce talks were about to begin again by orchestrating a series of anti-armistice demonstrations, parades, and rallies throughout the country and by pressing the United States for a security pact, which would obligate Washington to assist the South Koreans in militarily expelling the Communists from the Korean peninsula if a post-war conference failed to bring about Korea's political reunification. President Rhee even threatened to march to the Yalu River alone if necessary.[31]

Despite a personal letter from Eisenhower to Rhee in which the American President warned the South Korean leader that any effort on his part to disrupt an armistice would "nullif[y]" America's peaceful efforts in behalf of political reunification, the demonstrations continued in Seoul, Pusan, and other cities and towns throughout South Korea. The demonstrations did not prevent the exchange of sick and wounded POWs from beginning on April 20 and ending on May 3 in an operation known as LITTLE SWITCH. But they did indicate the irascibility of the South Korean president and his determination to thwart any peace agreement that did not include Korean reunification.[32]

Even as LITTLE SWITCH was getting started, negotiations were resumed at Panmunjom. Although they quickly became bogged down over the particulars of a prisoner exchange, on May 7 the Communists offered a new proposal for settling the repatriation issue. They no longer insisted that nonrepatriates be sent out of Korea, and they cut the screening process from six to four months. More important, they proposed in place of a single neutral nation a Neutral Nations Repatriation Commission (NNRC) similar to the one intended in the Indian resolution of the previous December.

Composed of Poland, Czechoslovakia, Switzerland, Sweden, and India, each of which would provide equal numbers of armed personnel, the NNRC would take over custody of nonrepatriates in the camps where they were being held. But the final disposition of the nonrepatriates after the screening process was complete would be determined by the postwar political conference.[33]

The administration's initial response to the Communists' latest offer was one of cautious interest. Although it believed the proposal could be a positive step toward ending the war, it thought the offer could be acceptable only if provision was made for the final disposition of nonrepatriates within a fixed period. It was willing to accept Poland and Czechoslovakia as members of a five-member NNRC, but all decisions on substantive matters would have to be by unanimous vote. Furthermore, it also proposed a complex scheme that would be spread over a five-month period for the disposition of the nonrepatriates. At the end of that period, the NNRC would be disbanded and those POWs who still refused repatriation would become civilians.[34]

When he learned of this counterproposal to the Communists' latest offer, President Rhee was furious. At a meeting with General Clark on May 12, Rhee rejected the introduction of any neutral troops into South Korea, especially Poles, Czechs, or Indians, to whom he referred as political spies, saboteurs, and agitators. Rather than accept Indian troops on Korean soil, he threatened to release the nonrepatriated POWs without consulting the UN Command. He also refused to turn over any Koreans to any neutral commission.[35]

Clark sympathized with much of what Rhee had to say, having earlier warned the Joint Chiefs of the violent reaction the placing of armed Communist personnel in South Korea would create in the country and having his own misgivings about the membership of the NNRC. But the administration ordered him to agree to hand over all Korean as well as Chinese nonrepatriates to the NNRC and to accept the Communist demand that all disputes within the Repatriation Commission be decided by a majority rather than by a unanimous vote, thereby conceding a point on which the UN Command had previously taken a firm position. Clark was also to consent to changes whereby nonrepatriates would remain in the custody of the NNRC for ninety days rather than the sixty days stipulated earlier. Clark found these instructions particularly galling because he had formulated his own proposal, which, if implemented, would have taken a much harder line toward the Communists, including possibly releasing North Korean POWs and increasing military pressure against enemy lines.[36]

Clark's proposal, however, was unacceptable to the administration. In the first place, the renewed talks had been dragging on for nearly a month without any resolution. Word came from India that among the greatest obstacles to a final peace settlement were the very points on which Clark wanted to remain firm, that is, the UN Command's position on Korean nonrepatriates and its insistence on unanimity on substantive issues before the NNRC. The Indian government indicated that prospects for peace would be greater if the United States adhered more closely to its resolution of the previous December, and the State Department agreed, believing that India had some understanding with China on its resolution.[37]

Another reason the administration changed its stand on the armistice talks was simply the ever-present pressure of its allies to reach a settlement of the war, even if that meant making concessions to the Communists. Indeed, in recent weeks the pressure became unrelenting as a number of America's closest friends, including England and France, became more convinced than ever that the United States was becoming obsessed by its terror of world Communism and internal subversion and that President Eisenhower lacked the leadership either to control the saber rattling of his secretary of state or to put an end to the rantings and ravings of Senator McCarthy and his mad followers.

Indeed, many Europeans were convinced that the administration had been taken over by the Republican right wing and that Senator McCarthy as much as anyone else was dictating foreign policy. Europeans had long been perplexed by the phenomenon of McCarthyism, whose broad appeal they found hard to comprehend. But in the spring of 1953 they were concerned that the Wisconsin senator was powerful enough and the President weak enough to jeopardize the very structure of American diplomacy. Now chairman of the Senate's Permanent Subcommittee on Investigations, McCarthy fought the nomination of Charles Bohlen, a distinguished career diplomat and Soviet expert, as ambassador to Moscow, and he cowed the State Department into accepting his nomination of Scott McLeod, a close friend and ally, as its personnel and security officer. He also launched an investigation into subversion in the "Voice of America" and sent his chief counsel, Roy M. Cohn, and a friend, David Schine, to Europe, where they upbraided American diplomats for being "soft on communism" and ordered the removal of "radical" books from United States Information Service libraries.[38]

Precisely because many European leaders were concerned that Eisenhower was not in command of his own administration and that he was being dictated to by extremists within his own party, among whom they often listed Dulles, they concluded it was necessary to press even harder for an end to the Korean war. In England Prime Minister Churchill went a step further. Addressing Parliament, he berated the truce negotiators at Panmunjom for dillydallying, and he taunted Washington for its unwillingness to meet with the Soviets face to face. Expanding on this theme, he said that Stalin's death had apparently induced "a change of attitude and . . . of mind in the Soviet Union," and he called for a "conference on the highest levels . . . between the leading powers without delay." A few days later the leader of the opposition, Clement Attlee, joined Churchill in a bipartisan effort to end the war and to hold a summit conference of world leaders. "[The] American government," Attlee remarked, "[is] not really master in [it]s own house. . . . One sometimes wonders who is more powerful, the President or Senator McCarthy."[39]

Reaction in the United States to Churchill's and, especially, to Attlee's remarks indicated that Anglo-American relations had reached a new low since the outbreak of the Korean war. McCarthy referred to the leader of the Labor Party as "comrade Attlee" and added, "If [the British] are trying to blackmail us into accepting a Communist peace on the ground that if we do not they will withdraw, I say, 'Withdraw and be damned!'" California Senator William Knowland added that the United States was "now face to face with the problem that our chief ally has joined with certain other United Nations members in urging a Far Eastern Munich." But the outpouring against England was by no means limited to the Republican right wing. The Washington *Post*, a good friend of England, compared Attlee's speech to 'Big Bill' Thompson's promise to Chicago voters that he would "'punch King George in the snoot,'" while Democratic Senator Paul Douglas of Illinois stated that "the free world . . . should not move together in acquiescence to tyranny."[40]

It was not only England, however, that objected to the apparent inflexibility and uncompromising position of the United States. The State Department reported that it had received protests or criticisms from Canada, Australia, Belgium, New Zealand, and even Italy, among others. Responding to this worldwide demand for compromise and peace in Korea, the administration decided to agree to terms on the problem of nonrepatriates along the lines of the earlier Indian resolution of December.[41]

What most concerned the White House now was how South Korea would react to the prospects of an imminent armistice agreement, for President Rhee had continued to make clear his determination to accept nothing less than the expulsion of the Chinese Communists from the Korean peninsula and the military reunification of the country. Worried that Rhee might try to sabotage an armistice agreement, the administration instructed General Clark and Ambassador Ellis Briggs in Pusan to confer with the South Korean president in order to warn him not to impede the peace process and to explain why the United States could not give him the security pact he so badly wanted. Meeting with Rhee on May 25, the two Americans tried to reassure Rhee that a bilateral defense pact was not necessary, that it would weaken the "greater sanctions" statement agreed to earlier (which together with an armistice agreement would better ensure Korea's security), and that the United States was prepared to assist South Korea in developing and maintaining a twenty-division army and a marine brigade.[42]

At the same time, however, Clark and Briggs made clear to the South Korean leader that the United States would take a strong stand against any action affecting its policy in the Far East. They also told Rhee that American assistance after the war depended on his firm assurance that South Korea would cooperate with UN troops in Korea. Rhee's government had to refrain from agitating against an armistice. It also had to cooperate in implementing the agreement, and it had to keep its armed forces under the operational control of the UN Command. If South Korea acted unilaterally, they said, Washington might be forced to take "all necessary measures" to safeguard the security of its forces.[43]

Rhee would have none of it. Appearing shocked by the UN Command's armistice proposals and declaring them unacceptable to the government of the Republic of Korea, he informed Clark and Briggs that he would now have to consider making his own proposal, which would include an immediate cease-fire and the simultaneous withdrawal of all Chinese Communist and UN forces from Korea. He also suggested strongly that he would order the release of all North Korean nonrepatriates while turning the Chinese nonrepatriates over to the UN Command. In a personal message to the South Korean president, President Eisenhower tried to reassure him that the United States would not abandon Korea, but Rhee remained unpersuaded.[44]

Rhee's persistent opposition to an armistice agreement and his increasingly bolder threats to pursue a unilateral course persuaded the UN Command and administration officials to prepare plans for the worst possible contingency—a withdrawal of ROK forces from the UN Command. The Eighth Army drew up plan EVERREADY, which envisioned three different scenarios, the most extreme being a situation in which ROK forces and the Korean population became openly hostile to UN forces. Depending on the seriousness of the circumstances, the UN Command would respond with an escalating series of measures up to and including the proclamation of martial law, the seizure of dissident military and civil leaders, and the establishment of a military government. Both Secretary Dulles and Defense Secretary Charles E. Wilson disapproved of plan EVERREADY as being too extreme. But they authorized Clark to take whatever measures were necessary "to insure the integrity of [his] forces," thereby giving him broad powers to act in case of a perceived emergency.[45]

At the same time that the administration considered drastic measures against the Rhee government, however, it also decided to meet one of Rhee's principal demands, a mutual security pact between the United States and South Korea. Although the White House had opposed such a pact on the grounds that it would weaken the "greater sanctions" statement and detract from the UN character of the Korean conflict, it changed its mind at the beginning of June. But the president made the agreement, which he did not want publicized for fear it might become embroiled in the peace talks, contingent on the willingness of the South Korean government to accept an armistice along the lines proposed by the UN Command and to leave Korean forces under the control of the UN Command.[46]

What the administration was doing at the end of May was reconsidering its position with respect to the Korean war. To be sure, its objective remained the unification of Korea by political rather than by military means, and it was searching for ways to resolve the POW question, the last obstacle to peace if the ROK government would agree to armistice terms. For this reason alone the administration had consented to a mutual pact with South Korea. In order to end the war in Korea, however, the President introduced another new element into the equation of peacemaking—the threat of atomic warfare if the Beijing government did not agree quickly to an armistice.

Actually, the White House never gave the Chinese such an explicit warning. But Eisenhower had been considering a nuclear option since at least February when General Clark had requested permission to bomb the area around Kaesong. At the end of March the President again raised the possibility of using atomic weapons during a meeting of the National Security Council. Although recognizing that America's allies would strongly object to the use of such weapons since they would be the battleground in an atomic war between the United States and the Soviet Union, he and Secretary Dulles agreed that "the tabu" that surrounded the use of atomic weapons would have to be destroyed.[47]

In subsequent weeks the Joint Chiefs of Staff sought Eisenhower's permission to employ atomic weapons if the enemy did not agree to the UN Command's latest proposal. The President did not give the Joint Chiefs the authority they wanted, but he agreed that it might be necessary to expand the war outside Korea if the Chinese and North Koreans rejected the United Nations' latest offer. In that case, he recognized the atomic bomb might need to be used, although he was deeply concerned that the Soviet Union might retaliate by bombing Japan. About the same time, Secretary Dulles told Prime Minister Jawaharlal Nehru during a visit to New Delhi that in the absence of an armistice agreement, the war in Korea would be broadened, a message that, Dulles assumed, Nehru would pass on to Beijing.[48]

In other words, Eisenhower did not have to threaten the Chinese directly with nuclear war. Almost certainly they knew that his patience was wearing thin; that he was determined to end the Korean war quickly; that he was under pressure to widen the war; that he did not feel constrained by the policies of the previous administration with respect to any military operation, including the use of nuclear weapons; and that the United States had nuclear weapons on Okinawa. The President did not have to deliver an ultimatum to Beijing—peace or atomic bombs—because they understood he was thinking along these lines anyway.[49]

In response to—or in spite of[50]—the threat of nuclear war, the Chinese and North Koreans broke the deadlock in the peace talks on June 4 by accepting the UN Command's proposals of May 25 with only a few minor changes. Indeed, in some respects—for example, the formula for releasing nonrepatriates to civilian status—the Communist proposals far exceeded the administration's most optimistic expectations. According to the Chinese and North Korean plan, thirty days after the post-armistice political conference, the NNRC would release from prisoner of war status any POWs who had not been repatriated and for whom no other disposition was agreed to by the political conference. For a further thirty days the commission and the Indian Red Cross would offer assistance to those who elected to go to neutral nations, after which the commission would be disbanded.[51]

Barring unforseen developments, then, the POW issue had been finally resolved, and the way seemed open for concluding the armistice negotiations that had dragged on for more than two years. But the Eisenhower administration had still to contend with its South Korean ally, which had already indicated its determination to undermine the delicate peace process.

Notes

1. Stephen E. Ambrose, *Eisenhower: Soldier, General of the Army, President-Elect, 1880-1952* (New York, 1952), 494–495.
2. Chester J. Pach, Jr. and Elmo Richardson, *The Presidency of Dwight D. Eisenhower* (Lawrence, KS, 1991), 16–17.
3. Ambrose, *Eisenhower: Soldier, General of the Army, President-Elect,* 532–535; *New York Times,* June 6, 1952; *Commonweal,* 56 (June 27, 1952), 286.
4. Time, 60 (September 15, 1952), 22–23; *ibid.* (September 22, 1952), 24; *New Republic,* 127 (October 20, 1952), 3; *Commonweal,* 57 (October 31, 1952), 85–90; Richard Whelan, *Drawing the Line: The Korean War, 1950–1953* (Boston, 1990), 342–343.
5. *Time,* 60 (September 15, 1952), 21.
6. Ronald J. Caridi, *The Korean War and American Politics: The Republican Party as a Case Study* (Philadelphia, 1968), 212–213 and 233–236; Robert

A. Divine, *Foreign Policy and U.S. Presidential Elections, 1952–1960* (New York, 1974), 75–76.

7. Caridi, *The Korean War and American Politics*, 182-208; Whelan, *Drawing the Line*, 345. See also Joseph B. Phillips to the Secretary, September 15, 1952, and attachments, Box 4283, Records of the Department of State, RG 59, 795.00/9-1522; *Time*, 60 (November 10, 1952), 21; *Nation*, 175 (November 11, 1952), 315–316.

8. Edward Keefer, "President Dwight D. Eisenhower and the End of the Korean War," *Diplomatic History*, 10 (Summer, 1986), 268–269; Caridi, *The Korean War and American Politics*, 235–245; *Nation*, 175 (November 15, 1952), 437; *New Republic*, 127 (November 17, 1952), 7.

9. Dean Acheson, *Present at the Creation: My Years in the State Department* (New York, 1969), 700–702.

10. *New Yorker*, 28 (November 15, 1952), 175; *ibid.* (November 29, 1952), 164; M.L. Dockrill, "The Foreign Office, Anglo-American Relations and the Korean Truce Negotiations July 1951—July 1953," in James Cotton and Ian Neary (eds.), *The Korean War in History* (Atlantic Highlands NJ, 1989), 110–111.

11. Memorandum of Conversation, October 29 and November 11 and 13, 1952, Box 67, Acheson Papers; Meeting with the President, November 5, 1952, Box 67, *ibid.*; Meeting with the President, November 5, 1952, *ibid.*; Memorandum for the President, November 8, 1952, Box 4284, Records of the Department of State, RG 59, 795.00/11-852; *FR*, 1952–1954, XV, 662-63.

12. *FR*, 1952–1954, XV, 662–686.

13. *New Yorker*, 28 (December 6, 1952), 174–176.

14. *Yearbook of the United Nations: 1952* (New York, 1953), 195–202; Rosemary Foot, *A Substitute for Victory: The Politics of Peacemaking at the Korean Armistice Talks* (Ithaca, NY, 1990), 156–157.

15. Acheson, *Present at the Creation*, 700-705; Dockrill, "The Foreign Office, Anglo-American Relations and the Korean Truce Negotiations July 1951-July 1953," 111–112.

16. Stephen E. Ambrose, *Eisenhower: The President* (New York, 1984), 30–31; Mark W. Clark, *From the Danube to the Yalu* (New York, 1954), 233; Max Hastings, *The Korean War* (New York, 1987), 317.

17. Ambrose, *Eisenhower: The President*, 31; Dwight D. Eisenhower, *Mandate for Change* (New York, 1963), 95; Keefer, "President Dwight D. Eisenhower and the End of the Korean War," 269–270.

18. "Memorandum on Ending the War," December 14, 1952, Box 8, Subject Series, Papers of John Foster Dulles, Dwight D. Eisenhower Library (Abilene, KS); William Manchester, *American Caesar; Douglas MacArthur, 1880–1964* (New York, 1978), 688–689; Ambrose, *Eisenhower: The President*, 31–32 and 34–35.

19. The President's News Conference of December 11, 1952, *Public Papers of the Presidents of the United States: Harry S. Truman, 1952–1953* (Washington, DC, 1966), 1075.

20. *Time,* 60 (December 22, 1952), 20; Joseph C. Goulden, *Korea: The Untold Story of the War* (New York, 1964), 385; Walter G. Hermes, *Truce Tent and Fighting Front* (Washington, D.C., 1966), 311–318; David Rees, *Korea: The Limited War* (New York, 1966), 385–386.

21. Edgar O'Ballance, *Korea: 1950–1953* (London, 1969), 127–129; Hermes, *Truce Tent and Fighting Front*, 366–339.

22. *Life*, 32 (May 26, 1952), 146.

23. Ambrose, *Eisenhower: Soldier, General of the Army, President-Elect*, 547–548; Ambrose, *Eisenhower: The President*, 51–52.

24. *Ibid.*; Discussion at the 131st Meeting of the National Security Council, Box 4, Ann Whitman Files, National Security Council Series, Dwight D. Eisenhower Papers, Dwight D. Eisenhower Library (Abilene, KS); Foot, *A Substitute for Victory*, 161–162.

25. Ambrose, *Eisenhower: The President*, 47; Rees, *Korea: The Limited War*, 405.

26. Hermes, *Truce Tent and Fighting Front*, 411–414.

27. Robert B. Simmons, *The Strained Alliance: Peking, Pyongyang, Moscow and the Politics of the Korean Civil War* (New York, 1975), 227–228; Adam B. Ulam, *The Rivals: America and Russia Since World War II* (New York, 1971), 194–200; Whelan, *Drawing the Line*, 352–354.

28. Robert A. Scalapino and Chong-Sik Lee, *Communism in Korea*, I (2 vols., Berkeley, CA, 1972), 422; Rees, *Korea: The Limited War*, 461; Simmons, *The Strained Alliance*, 213.

29. Memorandum for the President, April 1, 1953, Box 9, Subject Series, Dulles Papers; Memorandum to the Secretary of State from Eisenhower, April 2, 1953, *ibid.*; Discussion at the 139th Meeting of the National Security Council, April 8, 1953, Box 1, Ann Whitman Files, National Security Council Series, Eisenhower Papers.

30. *FR*, 1952–1954, XV, 136–138; Mark W. Clark, *From the Danube to the Yalu*, 245–247.

31. Resumption of Korean Truce Negotiations, April 14, 1953, Box 4285, Records of the Department of State, RG 59, 795.00/4-1453; U. Alexis Johnson to the Secretary, April 8, 1953, *ibid.*, 795.00/4-853.

32. Eisenhower to Rhee, April 23, 1953, Box 1, Ann Whitman Files, International Series, Eisenhower Papers; Memorandum from Young to Robertson, Records of the Department of State, RG 59, 795.00/4-2453; Briggs to Secretary of State, April 23, 1953, *ibid.*, 795.00/4-2353.

33. "UNC in Current Korean Negotiations," April 28, 1953, Box 4285, Records of the Department of State, RG 59, 795.00/4-2853; "Personal for Murphy," from Dulles, May 4, 1953, *ibid.*, 795.00/5-453; Memorandum for the Files, May 11, 1953, *ibid.*, 611.95A24/15-1153; Memorandum of

Conversation, May 8, 1953, *ibid.*, 795.00/5-853; Clark, *From the Danube to the Yalu*, 259.

34. "Korean Truce Negotiations," May 11, 1953, *ibid.*, 795.00/5-853.
35. Clark, *From the Danube to the Yalu*, 264; Briggs to Secretary of State, May 14, 1953, Box 4286, Records of the Department of State, RG 59, 795.00/5-1453.
36. Clark, *From the Danube to the Yalu*, 264–268; Clark to Joint Chiefs of Staff, May 16, 1953, and Joint Chiefs of Staff to Clark, May 23, 1953, Records of the United States Joint Chiefs of Staff, RG 218, 383.21 (Korea 3-19-45) (Section 129).
37. Allen to Secretary of State, May 15, 1953, Box 4285, Records of the Department of State, RG 59, 795.00/5-1553.
38. *New Yorker*, 29 (March 7, 1953), 89; *ibid.* (April 4, 1953), 109–110; *ibid.* (May 16, 1953), 97–98; *Nation*, 176 (April 11, 1953), 202–203; Ambrose, *Eisenhower: The President*, 58–62.
39. *Time*, 61 (May 18, 1953), 32; *ibid.* (May 25, 1953), 28; *New Republic*, 128 (May 25, 1953), 19.
40. *Time*, 61 (May 25, 1953), 19.
41. Allen to Mr. Bonbright and Mr. Merchant, May 18, 1953, Box 4286, Records of the Department of State, RG 59.795.00/5-1553.
42. Memorandum for the President, May 19, 1953, *ibid.*, 795.00/5-19; Smith to Amembassy Pusan and Amembassy Tokyo, May 22, 1953, *ibid.*, 795.00/5-1853. See also John Kotch, "The Origins of the American Security Commitment to Korea," in Bruce Cumings (ed.), *Child of Conflict: The Korean-American Relationship, 1943–1953* (Seattle, WA, 1983), 243–244.
43. *Ibid.*
44. To Secretary of State from Seoul, May 25, 1953, and Smith to Amembassy Pusan and Amembassy Tokyo, May 27, 1953, Box 4285, Records of the Department of State, RG 59, 795.00/5-2553 and 795.00/5-2753.
45. Outline of Plan EVERREADY, May 4, 1953, Records of the United States Joint Chiefs of Staff, RG 218, 383.21 Korea (3-19-45) (Section 130); Collins to Clark, May 30, 1953, *ibid.*
46. James F. Schnabel and Robert J. Watson, *The History of the Joint Chiefs of Staff*, III, *The Korean War* (Wilmington, DE, 1979), 993–994; Telephone Conversation with Senators Wiley and George, June 4, 1953, Box 9, Subject Series, Dulles Papers.
47. *FR, 1952–1954*, XV, 1059–1069; Keefer, "Eisenhower and the End of the Korean War," 270–273; Ambrose, *Eisenhower: The President*, 97–98.
48. *Ibid.*; Whelan, *Drawing the Line*, 360–361.
49. Ambrose, *Eisenhower: The President*, 98. For a different view that plays down the role of the nuclear threat in Eisenhower's strategic thinking, see Roger Dingman, "Atomic Diplomacy During the Korean War," *International Security*, 10 (Winter, 1988/89), 80–89. Compare with Edward

C. Keefer, "President Dwight D. Eisenhower and the End of the Korean War," *Diplomatic History*, 10 (Summer, 1986), 267–268. See also Hastings, *The Korean War*, 319–320.

50. On this point, see especially Foot, *A Substitute for Victory*, 178–183. Compare with Keefer, "Eisenhower and the End of the Korean War," 280–282.

51. Memorandum for the President, June 4, 1953, Box 4286, Records of the Department of State, RG 59, 795.00/6-453; Telephone Conversation with the President, June 4, 1953, Box 10, Telephone Calls Series, Dulles Papers.

CHAPTER EIGHT

Peace Without Victory

Having broken the stalemate in the peace negotiations, the administration's major concerns now shifted to persuading the South Korean government to accept the armistice terms that had been agreed to by the Communists and the UN Command and not to attempt to disrupt the peace process. From the time agreement was reached on an armistice, the UN Command was concerned that at some point South Korea would attempt to engineer the unsanctioned release of North Korean repatriates. President Eisenhower wrote a letter to President Rhee on June 6, 1953 which he released to the press, urging the South Korean leader to accept the armistice terms. If South Korea agreed to the armistice, Eisenhower said, he could reassure Rhee that his administration would not renounce its efforts to bring about the peaceful reunification of Korea. The White House would also go forward with a mutual defense pact and continue to supply economic aid to Korea. But the time had now come to decide whether to seek Korean reunification through military or political means. "We would not be justified in prolonging the war," the President warned Rhee, "with all the misery that it involves in the hope of achieving by force, the unification of Korea."[1]

Still Rhee remained recalcitrant. Anti–cease-fire demonstrations organized by the government grew in intensity as crowds gathered outside the American embassy at Pusan to sing patriotic songs and to chant anti-American slogans. The government also ordered the immediate return of all ROK officers from the United States, took what it termed "pseudo-extraordinary security measures," and recalled the South Korean delegate from the armistice negotiations at Panmunjom. Finally, on June 16 President Rhee responded to Eisenhower's letter of June 6 with a harsh and uncompromising message.

Although Eisenhower's offers of economic and military assistance were highly appreciated by the Korean people, Rhee told the President, they could not induce Korea to agree to an armistice, for "to accept such an armistice is to accept a death warrant."[2]

Despite such indications that the South Korean leader might try to undermine the armistice agreement, White House officials were shocked, nevertheless, when on June 18, the day after Rhee sent his message to Eisenhower, his government orchestrated the mass breakout of more than 25,000 North Koreans POWs from four major prison camps. Korean guards simply stood aside as the prisoners broke out of the compounds. Rhee openly acknowledged his complicity in the breakout, stating that the reason why he acted without consulting the UN Command was "obvious." Even so, Rhee had acted in defiance of the UN Command, and his action gave the Communists a major propaganda issue and a good excuse for breaking off the armistice talks if they were so inclined.[3]

Rhee's freeing of North Korean POWs also aggravated relations between Washington and its European allies, already sensitive to American dictation in foreign policy and its heavy-handed policy toward the Soviet Union, and increasingly alarmed by the menace of McCarthyism across the Atlantic. Indeed, by the time of the June 4, 1953, breakthrough in the armistice negotiations, Europe had become haunted by the specter of the United States in the grip of a hysterical witch-hunt and of a President cowering before the power of Senator McCarthy and his followers. As the *Atlantic Monthly* commented, "[i]t is progressively more difficult to persuade Europeans that McCarthy does not speak for the United States."[4]

Many of the same European leaders who were obsessed by the power of right-wing extremism in the United States found it hard to believe that American officials did not conspire in the release of the North Korean POWs or that they were so naive as not to know of Rhee's plot to free them ahead of time. From England Ambassador Winthrop Aldrich thus wrote that there was "widespread concern" over the freeing of the POWs, ranging from fear that the truce negotiations would be upset to insinuations that the UN Command had been either "negligent, acquiescent or even directly involved" in their release. About the same time, Britain's ambassador to the United States, Sir Roger Makins, told Secretary Dulles that developments in Korea had raised a question as to the language of the "greater sanctions" statement, which might no longer be appropriate in view of the fact that South Korea and not the Communists might break an armistice agreement.[5]

In the United States the National Security Council met in an emergency session and, with the President presiding, agreed that the administration should repudiate the release of the POWs as violating South Korea's agreement with the UN Command. The National Security Council also decided to tell Rhee that unless he agreed to cooperate with the UN Command, including retaining his troops under UN Command, the United States would "have to effect other arrangements." Although the National Security Council never stated what these "other arrangements" might be, it later became clear that the UN Command would proceed with an armistice agreement without the South Koreans and that South Korea would be cut off from American aid after the agreement was signed. One thing that the National Security Council never intended was that the United States would withdraw from Korea, for as Eisenhower later remarked, "[s]uch a result would be surrender to the Chinese, handing them on a silver platter everything for which they had been fighting for three years."[6]

Following the National Security Council meeting, President Eisenhower sent Rhee the strongest note he had written so far to the South Korean leader. Using the same language as at the National Security Council meeting, Eisenhower told Rhee that unless he was "prepared immediately and unequivocally to accept the authority of the UN command to conduct the present hostilities and to bring them to a close, it will be necessary to effect another arrangement." Dulles also sent Assistant Secretary of State Walter Robertson on a special mission to Korea in order to make clear to the South Koreans the United States' determination to conclude a peace with or without the South Korean government. Robertson carried with him an unusually harsh letter from the secretary of state to President Rhee in which Dulles denied that the United States had ever sought the reunification of Korea by military means. The Secretary also charged Rhee with breaking the principle of allied unity at a time when the enemy offered an armistice restoring South Korean authority over a territory somewhat larger than before the North Korean invasion. "It is you who invoked the principle of unity and asked us to pay the price," Dulles scolded Rhee. "We have paid it in blood and suffering. Can you now honorably reject the principle which, in your hour of need, you asked us to defend at so high a price?"[7]

As Robertson began his mission, the situation in Korea was volatile. On the positive side, the Chinese and North Korean negotiators did not use the release of the POWs as an excuse for breaking off the talks as they might have. They did accuse the United States of complicity in their release. The Chinese also sought assurances that former prisoners were not being impressed into the ROK army and that all North Korean POWs had been released. But they seemed satisfied when Washington gave them the assurances they wanted and denied participation in the release of the POWs. From the evidence that was available at the end of June 1953, it appeared that the Chinese were willing to accept Washington's explanations even if they doubted their truthfulness.[8]

On the negative side, however, President Rhee proved unpredictable. In private conversations with Robertson, Rhee insisted that before he would agree to an armistice, all remaining non-Korean repatriates had to be turned over to the Neutral Nations Repatriation Commission at the demilitarized zone (DMZ) and that the postwar political conference agreed to at Panmunjom had to be limited to ninety days. Furthermore, the United States had to reaffirm its pledge to provide economic aid to South Korea and to help build up its army to twenty divisions. Finally, Washington had to conclude a mutual defense pact with his country.[9]

President Eisenhower responded quickly to these terms. He agreed in principle to all of them, although he pointed out that he could not "guarantee" (the term mistakenly used in transmitting Rhee's conditions to Washington) passage of a mutual defense pact since that was up to the Senate, and he made clear that the time limit for the political conference was up to the conferees. But he assured Rhee that if after ninety days no progress was being made at the meeting and the Communists were using the gathering for propaganda purposes, the United States would consider joining South Korea in boycotting it.[10]

Although Robertson was greatly encouraged by the news he received from Washington and was convinced that Rhee would accept a cease-fire if he could do so without losing face, more trouble lay ahead. On June 27, 1953, the South Korean leader stated that President Eisenhower had agreed to all his conditions for an armistice and asked that they be put into writing. But that very same evening he injected new conditions for an armistice agreement. He wanted an army larger than twenty divisions, and, even more unacceptable to Washington, he wanted the United States to agree that it would join South Korea in resuming military operations if the political conference failed to bring about the reunification of Korea within ninety days after the signing of an armistice.[11]

Robertson immediately rejected these new demands. Instead, the administration attempted, through thinly veiled threats and carefully planned leaks, to leave the impression in Korea that the United States would withdraw from that country if Rhee sabotaged the armistice. But Rhee remained defiant, insisting as he had before that the United States must agree to renew hostilities against the Communists if the political conference failed to bring about the unification of Korea within ninety days after the armistice.[12]

In pressing the Rhee government to agree to armistice terms, the administration remained under pressure of its own to conclude a truce without South Korea, most notably from the British and a growing block of congressional leaders. London told Washington that it was becoming increasingly difficult to remain silent while the United States attempted to deal with Rhee. At the same time, reports from Capitol Hill indicated a growing sense of frustration at Rhee's efforts to undermine a truce agreement. Even many Old Guard Republicans sympathetic to Rhee either remained silent or came out in support of a cease-fire. The demand in the United States for ending the war and the reaction against Rhee's unauthorized release of enemy POWs had simply become that great.[13]

At Eisenhower's request, Secretary Dulles conferred with Senate leaders of both parties. They told the secretary that they could still get a defense agreement approved provided there was no further loss of confidence in the ROK government's willingness to cooperate with the United States in the armistice and in the postwar political conference. In fact, by now Dulles was himself so frustrated by Rhee that he advised Undersecretary Robertson to return to the United States. "If, as seems probable, you can be of no further assistance," he instructed his special envoy, "you may terminate your mission at your convenience."[14]

Before leaving Korea, however, Robertson met one last time with the South Korean leader to report on Dulles's conversations with the Senate leaders and to warn him again that arrangements agreed to by the United States were contingent upon the conduct of the South Korean government. Increasingly apprehensive now that the Senate might not ratify a defense pact, Rhee capitulated. The next day he informed Robertson that although his government would not sign an armistice agreement, neither would it obstruct its implementation. Two days later, he repeated his promise in a personal letter to President Eisenhower.[15]

On July 10, 1953, the armistice talks reconvened. The most immediate question insofar as the Communists were concerned was whether the United States could guarantee South Korea's conduct in the post-armistice period. The UN Command negotiators told the Chinese and North Koreans that the UN Command would withdraw all military aid and support if ROK forces violated the armistice agreement. But the Communists took their own measure to ensure the ROK's good conduct by launching a final military offensive against ROK forces along the main lines of resistance (MLR).[16]

Since early in the year the tempo of the war had increased significantly as the likelihood of reaching an armistice agreement improved. In fact, a direct relationship existed between stepped-up military activity by the Communists and the prospects of peace. The closer peace appeared, the more the enemy intensified its military effort. If the Chinese and North Koreans could correlate an armistice with a successful military offensive, they could argue that they had won a military victory. Such a claim would have potentially enormous propaganda value, particularly among Asians. Furthermore, the winter lull in the fighting had given the Communists time to rearm and regroup for an escalation of the war, and victory in the battlefield would improve their bargaining power at Panmunjom. Finally, as peace grew nearer, it behooved the Chinese and North Koreans to "bloody" the ROK army in order to force the Rhee government to accept armistice terms and to make it clear just how costly an independent move north would be.[17]

In March and April there had been a flurry of activity in the Old Baldy-Porkchop area, a complex of hills about twelve miles west of Chorwon on the western front. On March 23, 1953, the Chinese launched a coordinated strike against both Old Baldy and Porkchop Hill. An ugly, barren mass with a flattened top, which jutted out awkwardly in front of the Eighth Army, Old Baldy was attacked after a massive Chinese artillery and mortar barrage destroyed most of the bunkers that had already been weakened by heavy spring rains. Manned by units of the U.S. Seventh Division and a Colombian battalion, the hill was then overrun by a reinforced Chinese regiment of about 3,500 men, advancing in waves through a curtain of their own fire. Despite repeated counterattacks, including the use of tanks, artillery, and air strikes, the enemy held their positions tenaciously. Finally General Maxwell B. Taylor, who had replaced Van Fleet in February as commander of the Eighth Army, ordered that no more attacks be carried out, having decided that Old Baldy was not essential to the defense of the sector.[18]

But the heaviest fighting of the spring and, indeed, one of the heaviest battles of the entire war, began the next month on Porkchop Hill. Although attacked simultaneously with Old Baldy in March, Porkchop was still in UN hands when, on April 16, 1953, the Communists struck back again. Flanked by the Chinese as a result of the loss of Old Baldy, Porkchop overlooked an important part of the main lines of resistance (MLR) northeast of Old Baldy and near White Horse Hill. As a result, both the Communists and the UN Command attached great importance to holding Porkchop. Although American forces managed to hold on to the hill, in the three-day seesaw battle that took place, they engaged the enemy in hand-to-hand combat. At the same time, Eighth Army artillery set a new record for such a narrow front by firing 77,000 rounds in a single day, while each side inflicted heavy casualties on the other.[19]

On July 6, the Chinese launched a massive attack against Porkchop Hill that was even heavier than the battle in April. Determined to take the hill, the Chinese simply overpowered the badly outnumbered American defenders. As the fighting continued into the second and third days and as casualties on both sides mounted, the stakes became higher, and each side committed more and more forces to the battle. But inclement weather prevented the UN Command from launching air strikes against the enemy, and by June 11 General Taylor decided that the Chinese determination to hold the hill, regardless of the cost in casualties, outweighed any tactical advantage Porkchop might have. Reluctantly, therefore, he ordered the withdrawal of the remaining American forces from the hill.[20]

By this time peace talks had already resumed at Panmunjom, and with the approach of a final cease-fire agreement, the Communists launched their largest offensive since the spring of 1951, once more directing the main effort against the ROK army. In the fighting that followed, ROK forces suffered enormous casualties. So intense was the enemy attack and so great were Korean losses that General Clarks and Taylor decided to fly reinforcements from Japan to bolster the front. In all, the Chinese drove ROK forces back as much as six miles before the offensive was halted by combined American and South Korean forces. Some of the ground lost to the Communists was recovered, but before the attack ended, UN Command forces had suffered more than 14,000 casualties, most of them South Korean. In General Clark's view, the main reason for the Communist offensive "was to give the ROKs a 'bloody nose' and [to] show them and the world that 'puk chin'—'go north'—was easier said than done." If this was in fact their purpose, they had succeeded well.[21]

By July 19 the Communist offensive was over. Lines were stabilized, and the enemy, having accomplished its objective and suffering large casualties of its own, was prepared to sign a final agreement. There still remained a number of details to be worked out, such as a revision of the final demarcation line, the delivery of the nonrepatriates to the DMZ, and the signing ceremony. But for the most part, these were settled without too much difficulty.[22]

What difficulty remained was largely with the Rhee government, which for a final few days imperiled the armistice process. On July 20 Beijing radio broadcast a statement by North Korean Lieutenant General Nam Il, senior delegate to the Communist truce team, which Nam had delivered at Panmunjom the previous day. In his statement Nam referred to a number of promises that General Harrison had made to the Chinese and North Koreans over the period between July 11 and 16. These had included assurances that the United States would not support the South Korean army in cases where it violated the armistice agreement, that the South Korean government would abide by the terms of the armistice indefinitely and not just for the ninety-day period of the political conference, and that any personnel who were authorized to enter South Korea in conformity with the armistice agreement would be protected.[23]

Both publicly and privately the Rhee government rejected the promises that Harrison had made. What the government still wanted was the resumption of hostilities in case the political conference failed to bring about Korean unification, American military and "moral" assistance if it resumed hostilities, and American approval of the Korean text of a draft mutual-defense treaty containing an automatic military clause in the event of an attack on Korea by another power (i.e., North Korea or Communist China). Foreign Minister Pyun Tai Yung even told representatives of the American press that his government was "reconsidering her position" as a result of Harrison's statements at Panmunjom. In San Francisco Dr. Yu Chan Yang, South Korea's ambassador to the United States, said that his government would "attack" if Korean unification was not achieved within ninety days after the start of the political conference. And from Korea President Rhee remarked that the guarantees offered to him by Assistant Secretary of State Robertson during his mission to Korea had been "vitiated" by the pledges General Harrison had made to the Communists at Panmunjom.[24]

In Washington the administration responded once more to these threatening remarks with a combination of the carrot and stick. On the one hand, it argued that Harrison was speaking only on behalf of the UN Command and as the military commander responsible for the signing of the armistice. Neither he nor the UN Command could commit the United States to any particular course of action, the White House said. On the other hand, Secretary Dulles and others within the administration made it clear to the South Koreans that the United States could not promise to resume hostilities automatically if the political conference broke up or in any way bind Congress to issue a declaration of war. Nor could it promise material aid to South Korea if its forces sought to unify Korea by military means. Lastly, the administration rejected the South Korean government's request for a mutual defense pact with an automatic military clause in it, offering instead a standard clause that in the event of a future attack on South Korea, the United States would consult on the best means of restoring peace and would make its decision in accordance with its own constitutional procedures.

In the end South Korea had little choice but to agree once more that it would do nothing to undermine the armistice terms even though it would not be a party to the truce. It was simply too dependent on American economic and military aid and too vulnerable to military attack from the north to follow its own course. For a second time, therefore, Rhee told the United States that his government would not obstruct the peace process. But his recalcitrance was rewarded again by renewed promises of support from the United States, including a defense pact, a separate promise from Eisenhower that an "unprovoked attack" upon South Korea would result in an "immediate and automatic military reaction" by the UN

Command, a promise of an immediate $200 million in economic assistance, and a pledge from Secretary of State Dulles that he would meet with Rhee shortly after the armistice was signed to discuss mutual problems and prepare a common negotiating position for the post-armistice political conference.[25]

Finally, July 27 was set as the date for the signing of the armistice at Panmunjom. Now General Clark threatened to delay the signing ceremony until the Chinese and North Koreans removed from the building where the signing was to take place copies of Picasso's "Dove," which had become the Communists' symbol of peace. The Communists agreed to paint over the copies. There was also a last-minute snag over the signing ceremony itself. The UN Command wanted the commanders to sign the agreement at Panmunjom along with the chief negotiators at the talks. The Communists said they would come to Panmunjom only if the UN Command agreed that no South Korean would attend the ceremony in any capacity and that no newsman from Formosa would be admitted into the DMZ on armistice day. The UN Command rejected this demand, with the result that in the end the chief negotiators signed the agreement at Panmunjom, General Harrison for the UN Command and Nam Il for the Communists, while the commanders-in-chief countersigned at their respective headquarters. Apropos of the entire history of the negotiations, first at Kaesong and then at Panmunjom, the signing ceremony was conducted in complete silence. Neither side spoke to the other as they left the building in which they had agreed finally to end the war.[26]

The armistice had been signed and the war ended. But what followed was not a sense of victory or euphoria on the part of most Americans, merely gratification that an unpopular war was over. Instead of jubilation, a widespread feeling existed in the United States that while there was no more war, neither was there peace or victory. For the first time in its history, the United States could not claim victory over its enemies. Also, for the first time in their history, Americans were told that the end of a war meant merely a cease-fire, not a return to peacetime conditions. Certainly this was the message that President Eisenhower conveyed to the American people when, in announcing the end of the conflict, he stated, "there is, in this moment of sober satisfaction, one thought that must discipline our emotions and steady our resolution. It is this:

we have won an armistice in a single battleground—not peace in the world. We may not now relax our guard nor cease our quest."[27]

On the day after the peace was announced, the sixteen nations with armed forces in Korea signed the "greater sanction" statement in which they reaffirmed their intention to resist any renewed attacks on South Korea from the north. The consequence of such a breach of the armistice, they declared, "would be so grave that in all probability, it would not be possible to confine hostilities within the frontiers of Korea." But the statement was not made public until August 7 when General Clark revealed its existence in a report to the UN Security Council. It was done this way because of growing allied opposition to the greater sanction concept. In brief, the allies, particularly the British, had second thoughts about issuing a declaration that appeared warlike, would be unpopular at home, might appear to tie them too closely to the Rhee governmment, and might poison any effort to ease world tensions.

The fact was that throughout Europe widespread disgruntlement continued to be expressed about the irresponsibility of American foreign policy and the failure of the Eisenhower administration to respond to the gestures of peace coming from Moscow since Stalin's death in March, including even the Communists' willingness to end the three-year war in Korea. For example, in May Prime Minister Churchill called for a summit meeting of the Big Four Powers. The Soviets responded by proposing a peace treaty with Germany that would include the reunification and neutralization of that country followed by the holding of free elections. But in July Secretary of State Dulles rejected the Soviet proposals on Germany, maintaining that the holding of elections in that country should precede rather than follow the conclusion of a peace treaty. Once more Europeans made note of the intractability and unreasonableness of American foreign policy. In England the House of Commons devoted two days just before adjourning for a summer recess to a debate on foreign policy, during which considerable displeasure was expressed about Washington's reluctance to negotiate with the Soviets on such questions as the future status of Germany.[28]

Under these circumstances London was loath to follow America's lead in approving a "greater sanction" statement, which could lead to an extension of the Korean war in China itself should the armistice be broken. The British reminded Washington, therefore, that they had been uneasy about the statement since Rhee had freed the POWs on June 18, and they maintained that in terms of world opinion the declaration might do more harm than good. In response to such objections, Secretary of State Dulles agreed not to issue the statement until after the armistice was signed and then to do so without any fanfare.[29]

Still, by the time Dulles visited Korea at the beginning of August, the United States had taken several concrete steps to reassure the Rhee government that it would carry out its promises and pledges. Dulles's main business in Korea was to sign a mutual defense treaty. As the Eisenhower administration had made clear to the South Koreans, it could not agree to a treaty with an automatic military clause in it. Instead, the treaty merely provided that the United States and South Korea would "consult together" whenever their political independence or security seemed threatened. Although this was less than what Rhee had wanted, he accepted the treaty as the best he could obtain. In the final communique of the visit the United States assured Rhee that if the Communists attacked South Korea before the treaty was ratified by the Senate, "the UN Command, including the Republic of Korea forces, would at once and automatically react, as such an unprovoked attack would be an attack upon and a threat to the UN Command itself and to the forces under its command."[30]

Even as Dulles was visiting South Korea, the operation known as BIG SWITCH began, as 75,823 POWs were returned to the Communists in exchange for 12,773 UN Command POWs. This left more than 22,600 enemy nonrepatriates (the majority Chinese) and 359 UN Command nonrepatriates. As agreed in the armistice, the nonrepatriates were turned over to the Neutral Nations Repatriation Commission toward the end of September, several weeks after OPERATION BIG SWITCH had ended. During the time that the NNRC had custody of the POWs, they were given "explanations" in which they were strongly encouraged to return home, but without much success. In the end only 137 of the former Communists elected to go back, while only 10 of the UN Command nonrepatriates chose to return home. The rest were eventually released the following January 1954 after the NNRC handed them back to their custodians, the period for "explanations" having expired on December 23. First, the UN Command let its prisoners go after announcing that the nonrepatriates had been promised their freedom within 180 days after the signing of the armistice. A few days later the Communists, who had been against releasing the prisoners, did the same with the nonrepatriates they held. On February 1, 1954, the problem of the POWS thus having been finally resolved, the NNRC voted to dissolve itself.[31]

By this time plans for the post-armistice political conference, which was supposed to have been held within ninety days after the armistice, had been floundering for several months. The administration felt that the conference should be arranged in such a way that those who had borne the brunt of the fighting predominate; or, in other words, that the United States would not be one among equals representing the UN position. The White House also felt strongly that representation at the conference should be limited to those countries that had actually fought in Korea—with the one exception of the Soviet Union. It was against having "neutral" nations, specifically India, represented, and while it was willing to allow the Soviet Union to participate, it wanted it to do so only as a belligerent, not as a neutral, nation. As Washington interpreted the armistice agreement relating to the political conference, the agreement called for a conference of "both sides," and countries like India, which had been officially recognized as a neutral nation, would thus have no logical place at the gathering.[32]

Not all of America's allies agreed with this interpretation. The French preferred a "round-table" rather than an "across-the-table" conference, or a conference built around the concept of open discussion involving a number of nations rather than one based on the concept of confrontation between two opposing parties. They wanted to invite neutral nations like India to the conference rather than to limit it to the former belligerents only, and they wanted the meeting to discuss a number of issues, including the war in Indochina, rather than to confine discussion strictly to Korea. The British and the Commonwealth countries also favored inviting India and other neutral nations to the sessions.

At the United Nations the United States was able to round up enough votes and abstentions to prevent the two-thirds vote needed to seat India at the conference, so that the UN resolution of August 28, 1953, approving the armistice agreement limited the postwar political conference to the former belligerents only, except for the Soviet Union, which could participate "provided the other side desires it." But many diplomats at the United Nations regarded the vote as the greatest diplomatic defeat the United States had suffered since the end of World War II, the rationale being that for the first time in the history of the United Nations the United States had isolated itself almost completely from its allies and had handed the Communists the best opportunity they had ever had to appear to the Asian masses as champions of international cooperation. The London *Times* even remarked that the United States was beginning to "look more and more like a satellite of South Korea."[33]

Preparations for the political conference did not begin, however, until the end of October 1953, nearly ninety days after the armistice was signed. On October 26 Ambassador Arthur Dean, representing the UN side, met with representatives from the People's Republic of China and North Korea. The exchange of notes and the talks that followed had an all too familiar ring to them. Both sides disagreed over the agenda, the U.S. emissary wanting first to decide the time and place for the conference, the Communists wanting to talk first about participation by Asian neutrals, which, in their view, included the Soviet Union.[34]

America's problems were not with the Communists alone, however. President Rhee continued to cause difficulty for the administration, making emotional outbursts and threatening to renew hostilities unilaterally if the political conference did not bring about Korean unification. At the beginning of November 1953, President Eisenhower wrote Rhee warning him that by his remarks he was endangering Senate ratification of the mutual defense pact that had been negotiated in August. "If I should be forced to conclude that after the coming into force of the [Mutual Defense] Treaty, you might unilaterally touch off a resumption of the war in Korea," the President told Rhee, "I could not recommend its ratification and I am certain that the Senate would not ratify it." The South Korean president did muffle his remarks for the while, and in January 1954 the Senate approved the treaty with Korea. But Rhee remained a thorn in the side of the administration.[35]

Eventually, in 1954, agreement was reached to hold a conference of the Korean belligerents in Geneva in April in order to discuss Korean unification and other related matters. But the meeting deadlocked over the supervision and conduct of elections that were to bring about unification, and it finally broke up in June. As a gesture toward unification, the nations that fought in Korea and the government of the Republic of Korea signed a declaration reaffirming as their objective the holding of carefully supervised free elections throughout Korea. Since no agreement between the two sides had been reached, however, the armistice remained in effect, and the problem of Korean unification reverted to the United Nations, where it remains today. But by June 1954 most of the world's attention had turned to another phase of the Geneva meeting having to do with another area of the world—Indochina.[36]

Notes

1. Memorandum for the President, June 4, 1953, Box 9, Subject Series, Dulles Papers; Letter to President Syngman Rhee of Korea, June 6, 1953, *Public Papers of the Presidents of the United States: Dwight D. Eisenhower*, 1953 (Washington, DC, 1960), 377–380.

2. *FR*, 1952–1954, XV, 1165–1167; Rhee to Eisenhower, June 17, 1953, Box 1, International Series, Eisenhower Papers.

3. Mark W. Clark, *From the Danube to the Yalu* (New York, 1954), 279–283.

4. *Atlantic Monthly*, 192 (July 1953), 9–10. See also *Time*, 60 (June 29, 1953), 12–13; *Life*, 35 (July 6, 1953), 10.

5. Aldrich to Secretary of State, June 18, 1953, Box 4287, Records of the Department of State, RG 59, 795.00/6-1853; Memorandum of Conversation with the British Ambassador, Sir Roger Makins, June 18, 1953, *ibid.*, 795.00/6-185; M. L. Dockrill, "The Foreign Office, Anglo-American Relations and the Korean Truce Negotiations July 1951–July 1953," in James Cotton and Ian Neary (eds.), *The Korean War in History* (Atlantic Highlands, NJ, 1989), 112–113.

6. *FR*, 1952–1954, XV, 1200-1205; Dwight D. Eisenhower, *Mandate for Change* (Garden City NY, 1963), 185–186.

7. *FR*, 1952–1954, XV, 1206–1210 and 1238–1240; Edward C. Keefer, "President Dwight D. Eisenhower and the End of the Korean War," *Diplomatic History*, 10 (Summer, 1986), 284–285; Eisenhower, *Mandate for Change*, 185–186; Dulles to Amembassy Seoul, Amembassy Pusan, Amembassy Tokyo, June 18, 1953, Box 4287, Records of the Department of State, RG 59, 795.00/6-1953.

8. *FR*, 1952–1954, XV, 1234–1236.

9. *Ibid.*, 1276–1277. See also *Time*, 61 (June 22, 1953), 29.

10. *FR*, 1952–1954, XV, 1277–1278.

11. "Personal for Secretary Johnson from Robertson," June 27, 1953, Box 4287, Records of the Department of State, RG 59, 795.00/6-2753; *FR*, 1952–1954, XV, 1280–1286.

12. W.K. Scott to the Secretary of State, June 30, 1953, Box 4287, Records of the Department of State, RG 59, 795.00/6-3053; Telephone Conversation

with Sen. Knowland (and Sen. Smith), Box 9, Subject Series, Dulles Papers.

13. *FR*, 1952–1954, XV, 1331–1332; "Current Discussions with Rhee Re. Korean Truce," July 2, 1953, Box 4287, Records of the Department of State, RG 59, 795.00/7-253; Dockrill, "The Foreign Office, Anglo-American Relations and the Korean Truce Negotiations July 1951-July 1953," 113–114. See also *New Yorker*, 29 (June 20, 1953), 82–84.

14. *FR*, 1952–1954, XV, 1340; Dulles Amembassy Seoul, July 7, 1953, Box 4287, Records of the Department of State, RG 59, 795.00/7-753. See also Telephone Conversation with Stephens and Persons, Box 10, Dulles Phone Calls Series, Dulles Papers.

15. *FR*, 1952–1954, XV, 1352–1359; Keefer, "President Dwight D. Eisenhower and the End of the Korean War," 286–287.

16. Kenneth R. Mauck, "The Formation of American Foreign Policy in Korea, 1945–1953," (unpublished Ph.D. dissertation, University of Oklahoma, 1978), 399.

17. Walter G. Hermes, *Truce Tent and Fighting Front* (Washington, DC, 1966), 459.

18. *Ibid.*, 393–395; *Time*, 61 (April 6, 1953), 34.

19. David Rees, *Korea: The Limited War* (New York, 1964), 409–413.

20. Hermes, *Truce Tent and Fighting Front*, 470–473; Rees, *Korea: The Limited War*, 413–414; *Time*, 61 (June 22, 1953), 28–29.

21. Clark, *From the Danube to the Yalu*, 291. See also Hermes, *Truce Tent and Fighting Front*, 473–478.

22. William Vatcher, *Panmunjom* (New York, 1958), 199–200; Hermes, *Truce Tent and Fighting Front*, 483–484.

23. *New York Times*, July 20, 1953.

24. *Ibid.*, July 22, 23, 24, 1953; *FR*, 1952–1954, XV, 1406–1407 and 1413–1418.

25. *FR*, 1952–1954, XV, 1430–1432; Ohn Chang-il, "South Korea, the United States, and the Korean Armistice Negotiations," in Kim Chull Baum and James A. Matray (eds.), *Korea and the Cold War: Division, Destruction, and Disarmament* (Claremont, CA, 1993), 227–229.

26. *Ibid.*, 1432–1436 and 1442–1444; Clark, *From the Danube to the Yalu*, 294–295.

27. Radio and Television Address to the American People Announcing the Signing of the Korean Armistice, July 26, 1953, *Public Papers of the Presidents of the United States: Dwight D. Eisenhower*, 1953, 520–522. See also *New Yorker*, 29 (August 8, 1953), 53.

28. *Time*, 62 (July 27, 1953), 7-8; *ibid.* (August 24, 1953), 16; *New Yorker*, 29 (July 25, 1953), 48; *ibid.* (August 8, 1953), 69; *ibid.* (August 29, 1953), 64.

29. "Circular Re: Joint Policy Declaration," from Dulles, July 22, 1953, Box 4288, Records of the Department of State, RG 59, 795.00/7-2253.

30. Press Releases, Nos. 424 and 426, August 8, 1953, Box 9, Subject Series, Dulles Papers.

31. Joseph Goulden, *Korea: The Untold Story* (New York, 1982), 647; Rees, *Korea: The Limited War*, 436–437.

32. Telephone Conversation with Ambassador Lodge, June 20, 1953, Box 9, Subject Series, Dulles Papers; "Post Armistice Korean Problems," July 20, 1953, Box 4288, Records of the Department of State, RG 59, 795.00/7-2053.

33. "Political Conference on Korea," July 28, 1953, and Visit of Ambassador Bonnet Regarding Korean Political Conference, July 31, 1953, *ibid.*, 795.00/7-2853 and 795.00/7-3153; *New Yorker*, 29 (September 5, 1953), 77–84; *Time*, 62 (September 7, 1953), 17.

34. U.S. Ambassador Seoul to Department of the Army, October 30, 1953, Box 4032, Records of the Department of State, RG 59, 795B.00(w)/10-3053.

35. *FR*, 1952–1954, XV, 1591–1593.

36. Department of State, *The Korean Problem at the Geneva Conference*, April 26–June 15, 1954 (Washington, DC, 1954).

Conclusion

As the United States Marines retreated from the strategic town of Hargaru-ri after the Chinese Communists had entered Korea in massive numbers in December 1950, they broke into a parody of an old British Indian Army song:

Bless 'em all, bless 'em all,

The Commies, the U.N. and all:

Those slant-eyed Chink soldiers

Struck Hagaru-ri

And now know the meaning of the U.S.M.C.

But we're saying goodbye to them all,

We're Harry's police force on call

So put back your pack on

The next step is Saigon,

Cheer up, me lads, bless 'em all![1]

Certainly the Marines could not have anticipated that American soldiers would be fighting in Vietnam, in defense of the Saigon government, less than fifteen years later. But neither was it entirely fortuitous that the song's refrain should mention Saigon as the next likely area of American combat, for one major consequence of the Korean war was an increase in American military assistance to the French fighting the Vietminh in Indochina to the point where the United States was underwriting about eighty percent of the cost of the war by 1954.

210

At the same time, the Korean war made the United States reluctant in the 1950s to enter into another limited war, such as was being fought in Indochina. Even before President-elect Eisenhower took office in 1953, Secretary of State Dean Acheson had warned against committing American troops in Indochina. It would be "futile and a mistake to defend Indochina in Indochina," Acheson remarked. We "could not have another Korea, we could not put ground forces into Indochina." Similarly, President Eisenhower, sensitive to Truman's fate in Korea, refused to intervene in Indochina in 1954, when the French were on the brink of defeat, without the support of Congress and America's allies. "[I]f the United States were, unilaterally, to permit its forces to be drawn into conflict in Indochina and in a succession of Asian wars," the President told Acting Secretary of State Walter Bedell Smith, "the end result would be to drain off our resources and to weaken our over-all defensive position."[2]

Most of America's military leaders felt the same way. In fact, many high-ranking officers found themselves on the horns of a dilemma as a result of the Korean experience. While Korea revealed much of the futility of limited war, it also made clear to a number of generals and admirals that this was the only type of war feasible in the future. Former General Matthew Ridgway thus wrote in 1967:

> Before Korea, all our military planning envisioned a war that would involve the world, and in which the defense of a distant and indefensible peninsula would be folly. But Korea taught us that all warfare from this time forth must be limited. It could no longer be a question of *whether* to fight a limited war, but of *how* to avoid fighting any other kind.[3]

Different leaders, however, drew different lessons from the experience of the Korean war. For President Lyndon Johnson, who began the buildup of American forces in Vietnam in 1965, the North Korean invasion of June 1950 was a lesson in the dangers of not meeting military responsibilities abroad. "I could never forget the withdrawal of our forces from South Korea," he later wrote, "and then our immediate reaction to the Communist aggression of June 1950."[4] To Assistant Secretary of State William P. Bundy, testifying in 1965 before the Senate Foreign Relations Committee, the Korean war taught three lessons. The first was a recognition that aggression must be met "head-on" or else it would intensify and be harder to contain. The second was that a defense line in Asia limited to an island perimeter, such as existed before Korea, did not adequately define America's vital interests in that region of the world, that what happened on the Asian mainland would bear directly on these interests. The final lesson of the Korean experience was that "a power vacuum was an invitation to aggression" and that in cases of such aggression "there must be a demonstrated willingness of major external power both to assist and to intervene if required." Thus the Korean experience did not keep the United States from engaging in another limited war in Vietnam in the 1960s.[5]

Like the Vietnam war, the Korean war had been a limited war whose object became less than total victory. Truman had gone to war in 1950 because he saw the world in crisis and because he was concerned with maintaining the international credibility of the United States and his own credibility at home. Just months after the loss of China to the Communists and the Soviet detonation of an atomic bomb, much of the world seemed in jeopardy of falling to the Communists and a nuclear war appeared an increasingly dangerous possibility. Moreover, Truman was confronted with a domestic Red Scare and accusations of being "soft on communism," which threatened to unravel his administration. With the world in such a state of crisis and with his own administration's credibility at stake, Truman concluded that he had no choice but to respond to what he regarded as naked aggression in Korea sponsored and directed from Moscow.

That the Korean conflict also involved a civil war both north and south of the 38th parallel was something the White House never fully grasped. It would take another generation of leaders and the Vietnam war to educate Americans about the difference between nationalist movements with leftist (even Communist) orientations and Soviet efforts at global expansionism. Even the way American forces looked upon the Korean people mirrored America's general insensitivity to indigenous forces of change. As the military historian Max Hastings has pointed out, "among all the thousands of reports and assessments in the archives of the United States and her allies, depressingly few pay even lip service to the needs or interests of the Korean people. Korea merely chanced to be a battlefield upon which the struggle against the international Communist conspiracy was being waged."[6]

For the most part, American forces in Korea also viewed their erstwhile comrades-in-arms, the Republic of Korea army, with arrogance and disdain, scarcely hiding their contempt for the Koreans' abilities as soldiers. The irony was that until General Ridgway took over command of the Eighth Army in December 1950, American forces resembled more a ragged army in retreat than a well-honed military force. The first American troops into Korea after the war broke out in June 1950 were from Japan, where as an occupation force, the four undermanned divisions had become soft and undisciplined, lacking adequate leadership, training, and equipment. Despite the success of the Inchon invasion and the breakout from the Pusan perimeter in September 1950, they were hardly prepared for the Chinese onslaught of November and the brutal Korean winter that followed. Had the Chinese been more of a modern military force and less of a primitive army hampered by lack of equipment and poor communications and lines of supply, they may very well have been able to drive UN troops from Korea before they had an opportunity to regroup and take the military offensive. As it was, the Chinese were able to fight a far more modern and better equipped force to a virtual military draw. As a result, they became recognized in world capitals as a major player in the global political arena.[7]

Ultimately, however, China was able hold its own against a technologically far superior military machine only at a huge cost of Chinese lives. Although Mao Zedong continued to insist on human wave assaults, other Chinese military leaders concluded that revolutionary armies, lacking sophisticated military equipment, should never fight Western armies on their own terms; instead, they should probe Western weaknesses, attacking when Western resources and technology were of least value and counting on Western impatience with extended war to bring about ultimate victory.

Unfortunately, the American military drew just the opposite conclusion. As Max Hastings has also commented, "the American Army emerged from Korea convinced that its vastly superior firepower and equipment could always defeat a poorly equipped army if it was provided with the opportunity to deploy them." What they failed to understand was that because the Chinese relied heavily on human and animal labor to supply their forces, they were less dependent than the Americans on Korea's road system. It was precisely America's dependence on trucks and roads for their main supply routes that made them so vulnerable to the Chinese military strategy of flanking operations and road blocks. For this underestimation of the enemy's ability to fight without conventional means of resupply the United States would pay a heavy cost in Vietnam a decade later.[8]

The administration also underestimated the difficulty of sustaining popular support for a war in which total victory (the complete destruction of the enemy) was not the aim and in having constantly to reassure America's own allies of its limited purposes in the war. This point can be easily overstated, for Truman was largely successful in getting the British and America's other allies to cooperate with the administration in Korea and at the United Nations. Nevertheless, as a result of their differences with the Americans over military strategy and war aims in Korea and the heavy costs of rearmament, Washington's closest allies, England and France, were never again to be rushed into a military crusade with the United States against Communist expansion.[9]

One of General MacArthur's problems as UN commander was his failure to understand the limitations and pressures imposed on the United States by its allies. But at the same time, the administration often failed to appreciate the military consequences of its political decisions, with the result that seemingly contradictory orders were sometimes given to MacArthur and his successors, Generals Ridgway and Clark. This included their general instructions, irrespective of any consideration about the safety and security of their forces, to maintain maximum military pressure against the enemy without doing anything that might escalate the war into a larger conflict. For this failure on the administration's part to comprehend fully the military implications of its political actions, the Joint Chiefs of Staff have to assume part of the responsibility. Instead of communicating to the administration the nation's military capabilities and limitations in Korea, it violated a dictum set forth by the military strategist Baron Karl von Clausewitz over 150 years earlier—namely, that the civilian leadership had to be made aware of the imperatives of military operations.

This simply was not the case in Korea. What is striking about the war in Korea, in fact, is the passive role that the Joint Chiefs of Staff often played in formulating political *and military policy* in Korea. The decision to limit the war in Korea after the Chinese invasion was essentially a political one reached with surprisingly little input from the Joint Chiefs. (In fact, throughout the Korean war the role and responsibilities of the Joint Chiefs, even with respect to the Secretary of Defense, remained unclear and ill-defined.[10]) Much the same was true of the military strategy—the active defense—that was subsequently followed notwithstanding pleas from the field for a general offensive above the 38th parallel.

Had greater military pressure been maintained against the Chinese and North Koreans after negotiations began in July 1951, it is quite conceivable that a settlement of the war might have been reached much earlier, long before Eisenhower raised the threat of atomic warfare. But the longer the war dragged on, the more hazardous a general offensive became and the more difficult it was to follow any military strategy other than the active defense. As General Maxwell Taylor, who took over command of the Eighth Army from General James Van Fleet in 1953, later commented, "Our unwillingness to keep military pressure on the enemy during the negotiations had been a mistake, I was sure, but by 1953 it was established policy, and it was too late to try to change."[11]

Nevertheless, the Korean conflict remains one of the decisive events of recent American history. It globalized the Cold War. The United States military presence was extended worldwide. By 1955 the United States had 450 bases in thirty-six countries. The Foreign Aid program became the Mutual Security program whose aim was not primarily economic and social reconstruction but rather the buildup of local defense forces by recipient countries. Most important, the United States no longer viewed the Communist threat as limited largely to Europe and parts of the Middle East. Indeed, as the political situation in Europe stabilized and the Communist threat in Western Europe diminished over the next ten years, the United States became increasingly more occupied with events in Asia, particularly Southeast Asia. Ironically, the Democratic administrations of John F. Kennedy and Lyndon B. Johnson came to share the view promulgated by MacArthur during the Korean war—that the battlefield of the Cold War would be Asia rather than Europe. The result was the Vietnam tragedy of the 1960s and 1970s.[12]

Yet there were significant positive results for the United States—and for many Koreans—as a result of the Korean war. Although Washington failed to bring about by military means the political reunification of Korea, it had prevented South Korea from falling to the Communists. This, in turn, allowed South Korea eventually to become one of the major economic and industrial powers of the Far East and for its citizens to enjoy one of Asia's highest standards of living. Also, while South Korea was to be governed over the next forty years by authoritarian leaders who placed major restrictions on democratic political processes, they escaped falling under the control of the far more totalitarian regime of North Korea. Notwithstanding the undeniably repressive nature of the Seoul government, therefore, it is not unreasonable to conclude that the major beneficiaries of the Korean war have been the South Korean people themselves.

But the United States was also a beneficiary. In the first place, the war provided assurance to Japan's fledging democracy, just emerging from American military occupation, that it could depend on the United States for political and military support. The economic boost from the war also jump-started the Japanese economy, beginning the process that has turned Japan into an economic colossus and model for emulation by other East Asian countries, including South Korea. Thus, despite the Vietnam war, the United States largely achieved its post–World War II policy for the Far East, predicated as it was on an economically vibrant Japan tied closely to the West. In contrast, Moscow's lackluster support for China during the war widened an already developing split between Moscow and Beijing. Indeed, China emerged as a strong rival to the Soviet Union within the Communist bloc and especially among third world countries, which admired and identified with China's successful resistance to what they perceived to be "Western imperialism." In geopolitical terms, therefore, the Soviet Union may have been harmed far more as a result of the Korean war than was the United States.[13]

Perhaps as important as any consequence of the Korean war, however, is the legacy it left in terms of the use of nuclear weapons to fight a war. The Korean war was America's first war fought in the nuclear age. President Truman had considered the nuclear option on several occasions, and President Eisenhower had raised the threat of nuclear war to pressure the Communists into concluding an armistice. The threat of atomic warfare was also basic to the Eisenhower-Dulles doctrine of massive retaliation. Yet the very existence of nuclear weapons had dictated a limited war in Korea. And as the first war the United States had fought since the advent of nuclear weapons, Korea confronted American leaders with the relative powerlessness of a weapon that, in the final analysis, was too terrible to be used.

Notes

1. The quote is from T. R. Fehrenbach, *This Kind of War: A Study in Unpreparedness* (New York, 1973), 294–304.
2. George C. Herring, *America's Longest War: The United States and Vietnam, 1950–1975* (New York, 1986), 22; Dwight D. Eisenhower, *Mandate for Change* (Garden City, NY, 1963), 354. See also Norman Podhoretz, *Why We Were in Vietnam* (New York, 1982), 34–35 and 51.
3. Matthew B. Ridgway, *The Korean War* (Garden City, NY, 1967), vi.
4. Lyndon Baines Johnson, *The Vantage Point: Perspectives of the Presidency* (New York, 1971), 152.
5. Russell H. Fifield, *Americans in Southeast Asia: The Roots of Commitment* (New York, 1973), 150–151.
6. Max Hastings, *The Korean War* (New York, 1987), 338–339.
7. Bevin Alexander, *Korea: The First War We Lost* (New York, 1986), 47.
8. Hastings, *The Korean War*, 334; Alexander, *Korea: The First War We Lost*, 310–311.
9. Hastings, *The Korean War*, 331–332.
10. Doris M. Condit, *The Test of War: 1950–1953* (Washington, DC, 1988), 23.
11. Maxwell D. Taylor, *Swords and Plowshares* (New York, 1972), 137.
12. Lisle A. Rose, *Roots of Tragedy: The United States and the Struggle for Asia, 1945–1953* (Westport, CT, 1976), 239–244; Hastings, *The Korean War*, 338; Charles E. Bohlen, *Witness to History, 1929–1969* (New York, 1973), 294–304.
13. Steven I. Levine, "Breakthrough to the East: Soviet Asian Policy in the 1950s," in Warren I. Cohen and Akira Iriye (eds.), *The Great Powers in East Asia, 1953–1960* (New York, 1990), 296–311; John Toland, *In Mortal Combat: Korea, 1950–1953* (New York, 1991), 594–596.

Suggestions for Further Reading

Over the past ten years, an enormous literature has been published on the Korean war. For a review of some of this literature, see Bruce Cumings, "Korean-American Relations: A Century of Contact and Thirty-Five Years of Intimacy," in Warren Cohen, ed., *New Frontiers in American-East Asian Relations: Essays Presented to Dorothy Borg* (New York, 1983), 237–282; Robert J. McMahon, "The Cold War in Asia: Toward a New Synthesis?" *Diplomatic History,* 12 (Summer, 1988), 307–327; Rosemary Foot, "Making Known the Unknown War: Policy Analysis of the Korean Conflict in the Last Decade," *Diplomatic History,* 15 (Summer, 1991), 411–431. A dated, but still useful annotated bibliography is Keith D. McFarland, *The Korean War: An Annotated Bibliography* (New York, 1986).

Undoubtedly the most important volume on the Korean war in recent years has been Bruce Cumings, *The Origins of the Korean War, II: The Roaring of the Cataract, 1947–1950* (Princeton NJ, 1990). This supplements Cumings' earlier work, *The Origins of the Korean War, I: Liberation and the Emergence of Separate Regimes, 1945–1947* (Princeton, NJ, 1981). Making use of Korean language materials as well as archival and government publications from the United States, Cumings places the origins of the Korean war within the context of a civil war in Korea after World War II. He also spins a web of intrigue in the United States on the part of public and private individuals seeking American military involvement in Asia. Two other important volumes are Rosemary Foot, *The Wrong War: American Policy and the Dimensions of the Korean Conflict, 1950–1953* (Ithaca, NY, 1985), which shows that General Douglas MacArthur was not alone in wanting to extend the war to China, and Foot, *A Substitute for Victory: The Politics of Peacemaking at the Korean Armistice Talks*

(Ithaca, NY, 1990), a multidimensional analysis of the armistice negotiations ending the war, which makes the case that the Communists were more flexible and more willing to make concessions in the talks than was the United States. Particularly good on the geopolitical context of the war are Richard Whelan, *Drawing the Line: The Korean War, 1950–1953* (Boston, 1990), and Peter Lowe, *The Origins of the Korean War* (London, 1986). Also good on major military and diplomatic decisions is D. Clayton James, *Refighting the Last War: Command and Crisis in Korea, 1950–1953* (New York, 1993). The theme of the book is evident from its title.

Still highly useful are David Rees, *Korea: The Limited War* (New York, 1964), for twenty years the standard work on the conflict, and Joseph C. Goulden, *Korea: The Untold Story of the War* (New York, 1982), one of the first books to mine the records of the Joint Chiefs of Staff. Also not to be neglected are several official histories of the war, which, too, are based on military records but which deal at length with the diplomacy of the war. These are James F. Schnabel, *Policy and Direction: The First Year* (Washington, DC, 1972); Roy E. Appleman, *South to the Naktong, North to the Yalu* (Washington, DC, 1961); and Walter G. Hermes, *Truce Tent and Fighting Front* (Washington, DC, 1966). These should be supplemented with Doris M. Condit, *The Test of War, 1950–1953* (Washington, DC, 1988), a thoroughly documented history of the Office of the Secretary of Defense, which is the second volume of a projected multivolume history of that office. Condit makes clear that the role of the Joint Chiefs of Staff "vis-à-vis" Secretary of Defense George Marshall remained unclear throughout the Korean war.

Among other general treatments of the Korean war, especially its military side, are Carl Berger, *The Korean Knot: A Military-Political History* (Philadelphia, 1964); Harry J. Middleton, *The Compact History of the Korean War* (New York, 1965); Edgar O'Ballance, *Korea: 1950–1953* (London, 1969); Robert Leckie, *Conflict: The History of the Korean War* (New York, 1962); T.R. Fehrenbach, *This Kind of War: A Study in Unpreparedness* (New York, 1963); Guy Wint, *What Happened in Korea: A Study in Collective Security* (London, 1954); Martin Lichterman, "To the Yalu and Back," in Harold Stein, ed., *American Civil-Military Decisions: A Book of Case Studies* (University City, AL, 1963), 569–642; Callum A. MacDonald, *Korea: The War Before Vietnam* (New York, 1986); Max Hastings, *The Korean War* (New York, 1987); Clair Blair, *The Forgotten War: America in Korea, 1950–1953* (New

York, 1987); Bevin Alexander, *Korea: The First War We Lost* (New York, 1986); and John Toland, *In Mortal Combat: Korea, 1950–1953* (New York, 1991). A contemporary account of the opening of hostilities is Marguerite Higgins, *War in Korea* (Garden City, NY, 1951).

Important collections of articles, a number of which will be noted individually in the course of this essay, are Frank Baldwin, ed., *Without Parallel: The American-Korean Relationship Since 1945* (New York, 1973); Bruce Cumings, ed., *Child of Conflict: The Korean-American Relationship, 1943–1953* (Seattle, 1983); James Cotton and Ian Neary, eds., *The Korean War in History* (Atlantic Highlands, NJ, 1989); and Kim Chull Baum and James I. Matray, eds., *Korea and the Cold War: Division, Destruction, and Disarmament* (Claremont, CA, 1993). For a broad assessment of the impact of the Korean war in terms of American foreign and domestic policy, see also the articles in Francis H. Heller, ed., *The Korean War: A 25-Year Perspective* (Lawrence, KS, 1977). In addition, consult Walter LaFeber, "Crossing the 38th: The Cold War in Microcosm," in Lynn H. Miller and Ronald W. Pruessen, eds., *Reflections on the Cold War: A Quarter Century of American Foreign Policy* (Philadelphia, 1974), 71–90; John Lewis Gaddis, "Was the Truman Doctrine a Real Turning Point?" *Foreign Affairs,* 52 (January 1974), 386–402; and Arnold Wolfers, "Collective Security and the War in Korea," *Yale Review,* 43 (June 1954), 481–496.

On the period between World War II and the outbreak of hostilities in June 1950, there are a number of fine books and essays that cover such matters as the nature of Korean society, American Korean policy, and the causes of the war. On United States policy toward Korea during World War II, see especially James A. Matray, "An End to Indifference: America's Korean Policy During World War II," *Diplomatic History,* 2 (Spring 1978), 181–196. For the decision to divide Korea at the 38th parallel, see another essay by Matray, "Captive of the Cold War: The Decision to Divide Korea at the 38th Parallel," *Pacific Historical Review,* 50 (May 1981), 145–168. On the importance that Secretary of State Dean Acheson attached to Korea as a source of rice and a market for Japan, see Ronald McClothen, "Acheson, Economics, and the American Commitment in Korea, 1947–1959," *Pacific Historical Review,* 58 (February 1989), 23–53. On Acheson's famous statement to the National Press Club in January 1950, defining America's defense perimeter, see John Lewis Gaddis, "The Strategic Perspective: The Rise and Fall of the

'Defensive Perimeter' Concept, 1947–1951," in Dorothy Borg and Waldo Heinrichs, eds., *Uncertain Years: Chinese-American Relations, 1947–1950* (New York, 1980). In his essay Gaddis points out the fragility of the consensus on the defensive perimeter strategy.

The best study of Korean society in the 1940s can be found in the two volumes by Cumings on the origins of the Korean war, aready cited, in which he brilliantly traces the root causes of the Korean conflict to the civil and revolutionary struggle within Korea during the five years preceding the outbreak of hostilities in 1950. More concise statements of Cumings' thesis are Bruce Cumings, "American Policy and Korean Liberation," in Baldwin, ed., *Without Parallel: The American-Korean Relationship Since 1945*, 39–108; Cumings, "Introduction: The Course of Korean-American Relations, 1943–1953," in Cumings, ed., *Child of Conflict: The Korean-American Relationship, 1943–1953*, 3–55; and Jon Halliday and Bruce Cumings, *Korea: The Unknown War* (London, 1988). Other studies that emphasize the civil nature of the struggle in Korea include Robert R. Simmons, "The Korean Civil War," in Baldwin, ed., *Without Parallel: The American-Korean Relationship Since 1945*, 143–178; John Merrill, "Internal Warfare in Korea, 1948–1950: The Local Setting of the Korean War," in Cumings, ed., *Child of Conflict: The Korean-American Relationship, 1943–1953*, 133–162; and Okonogi Masao, "The Domestic Roots of the Korean War," in Yonosuke Nagai and Akira Iriye, eds., *The Origins of the Cold War in Asia* (New York, 1977), 299–320. Challenging this revisionist review is William Stueck, "The Korean War as International History," *Diplomatic History*, 10 (Fall 1986).

Perhaps the best study in English of the internal development of Korea that does not have as its major purpose an explanation of the causes of the Korean war is Gregory Henderson, *Korea: The Politics of the Vortex* (Cambridge, MA, 1968). Basing his study on Korean and Japanese as well as English language materials, Henderson stresses the homogeneity and centralization of Korean society and argues the need for decentralization of political authority. On the development of Korean nationalism during a critical period, see Michael Edson Robinson, *Cultural Nationalism in Colonial Korea, 1920–1925* (Seattle, WA, 1988). A major study of the Communist movement in Korea is the two-volume work, Robert A. Scalapino and Chong-Sik Lee, *Communism in Korea* (Berkeley, CA, 1972). This should be supplemented by an earlier work, Dae-Sook Suh, *The Korean Communist Movement, 1918–1948* (Princeton, NJ, 1967), which stresses the two conflicting societies that had developed in Korea by 1948. Other books that deal with internal developments in Korea and the growth of Communism are Koon Woo Nam, *The North Korean Communist Leadership, 1945–1965: A Study of Factionalism and Political Consolidation* (University City, AL, 1974); Chong-Shik Chung and Jae-Bong Ro, *Nationalism in Korea* (Seoul, 1979); Byung Chul Koh, *The Foreign Policy of North Korea* (New York, 1969); Chong-Shik Chung and Gahb-Chol Kim, eds., *North Korean Communism: A Comparative Analysis* (Seoul, 1950); Joungwon Alexander Kim, *Divided Korea: The Politics of Development, 1945–1972* (Cambridge, MA, 1975); George M. McCune, *Korea Today* (Cambridge, MA, 1950); and John Kie-Chang OH, *Korea: Democracy on Trial* (Ithaca, NY, 1968). The latter is highly critical of Syngman Rhee, particularly because of his repressive government in the 1940s.

United States policy toward Korea in the five-year period prior to 1950 has received extensive attention. Two important monographs are William Whitney Stueck, Jr., *The Road to Confrontation: American Policy Toward China and Korea, 1947–1950* (Chapel Hill, NC, 1981), and Charles M. Dobbs, *The Unwanted Symbol: American Foreign Policy, the Cold War, and Korea, 1945–1950* (Kent, OH, 1981). In his work, Stueck argues that while the United States did not view Korea as being important in a military sense, the country became increasingly important in terms of America's credibility worldwide— that is, in terms of the United States playing a central role in the world. To maintain its credibility in the world, the United States went to war in South Korea's defense in 1950. Sharing much the same view, Dobbs argues that by 1948 Korea had become a symbol of the United States' determination to defend the free world against Communist aggression; the "loss" of China in 1949 made the symbolic importance of Korea even greater. An excellent essay that emphasizes the errors of policy toward Korea by the big powers in the 1945–1950 period is John Lewis Gaddis, "Korea in American Politics, Strategy, and Diplomacy, 1945–1950," in Nagai and Iriye, eds., *The Origins of the Cold War in Asia*, 277–298. For a somewhat similar view, which maintains that the intrusion of the Cold War into Korea by Washington and, especially, Moscow, was responsible for the failure to reunify Korea after World War II and, ultimately for the Korean war, see James I. Matray, "Cold War of a Sort: The International Origins of the Korean Conflict," in Baum and Matray, eds., *Korea and the Cold War*, 35–62. On the United States' reluctant but growing ties to the Syngman Rhee government by 1948, see Lisle Rose, R*oots of Tragedy: The United States and the Struggle for Asia, 1945–1953* (Westport, CT, 1976). An important essay on the reasons why Truman delayed a settlement of the Korean question in 1945 is Mark Paul, "Diplomacy Delayed: The Atomic Bomb and the Division of Korea, 1945," in Cumings, ed., *Child of Conflict.* For the American occupation of South Korea after World War II, consult E. Grant Meade, *American Military Government in Korea* (New York, 1951). For American assistance in training the South Korean army prior to 1950, see Robert K. Shaw, *Military Advisers in Korea: KMAG in Peace and War* (Washington, DC, 1962). For the bureaucratic struggle between the Department of State and the Pentagon over the withdrawal of American forces from Korea in 1949, see Kim Chull Baum, "U. S. Policy on the Eve of the Korean War: Abandonment or Safeguard?" in Baum and Matray, eds., *Korea and the Cold War,* 63–94.

On the outbreak of hostilities almost all writers attribute the war to North Korea's invasion of South Korea. Two exceptions are I. F. Stone's *The Hidden History of the Korean War* (New York, 1952) and Joyce and Gabriel Kolko's *The Limits of Power: The World and United States Foreign Policy, 1945–1954* (New York, 1972). Based largely on his reading of the *New York Times* immediately before and after June 25, Stone argues that South Korea started the war by attacking north of the 38th parallel. Although conceding that North Korea probably began the war, the Kolkos nevertheless attribute its invasion of South Korea to the military imbalance in favor of South Korea that the United States and the Rhee government had created in 1949 and 1950. The Kolkos also argue that the United States planned to play an active role against Communist expansion even before the outbreak of the Korean war. For a critique of the Kolko thesis and a rejoinder by the Kolkos, see William W. Stueck, Jr., "Cold War Revisionism and the Origins of the Korean Conflict: The Kolko Thesis," and Joyce and Gabriel Kolko, "To Root Out Those Among Them—A Response," *Pacific Historical Review,* 42 (November 1973). Emphasizing the civil nature of the Korean conflict (like other authors already mentioned) and taking a position similar to that of the Kolkos, Robert R. Simmons, *The Strained Alliance: Peking, Pyongyang, Moscow and the Politics of the Korean Civil War* (New York, 1975), argues that contrary to popular opinion (and most historical accounts) North Korea acted on its own initiative and without the approval of the Soviet Union and may have attacked South Korea in anticipation of an early South Korean attack from the other direction. Although taking issue with Simmons' claim that North Korea acted on its own initiative, John Merrill, "The Origins of the Korean War: Unanswered Questions," in Baum and Matray, eds., *Korea and the Cold War*, 95–108, maintains nevertheless that North Korea's invasion of South Korea was a rational response on its part to a growing military and political imbalance on the Korean peninsula in favor of South Korea.

Thanks to the end of the Cold War, the opening of some Soviet archives, and the exchange of information between the United States, the former Soviet Union, and the People's Republic of China, there has been considerable scholarship in recent years on the responsibility of Moscow and Beijing for the Korean war. The most widely held view is that while they knew about Kim Il-sung's plans to invade South Korea and gave their approval to them, both Joseph Stalin and Mao Zedong did so reluctantly because of their concern about a larger war involving the United States. On these points, see Sergei N. Goncharov, John W. Lewis, and Xue Litai, *Uncertain Partners: Stalin, Mao, and the Korean War* (Stanford, CA, 1993), and especially Kathryn Weathersby, "Soviet Aims in Korea and the Origins of the Korean War, 1940–1950; New Evidence from Russian Archives," *Cold War International History Project Working Paper No. 8*, Woodrow Wilson International Center for Scholars (Washington, DC, 1993), and Weathersby, "New Findings on the Korean War," *Cold War International History Project: Bulletin*, Issue 3 (Fall, 1993), 1 and 14–18. For a rejoinder to Weathersby by the Soviet scholar, Adam Ulam, and her response, see *ibid.*, Issue 4 (Fall, 1994), 21. See also William Stueck, Jr., "The Soviet Union and the Origins of the Korean War," in Baum and Matray, eds., *Korea and the Cold War*, 111–124. In contrast to Weathersby, Stueck maintains that Stalin promoted the North Korean venture.

On the responsibility (or lack thereof) of China for the war, consult Jonathan D. Pollack, "The Korean War and Sino-American Relations," in Harry Harding and Yuan Ming, eds., *Sino-American Relations, 1945–1955: A Joint Reassessment of a Critical Decade* (Wilmington, DE, 1989), 213–224; Russell Spurr, *Enter the Dragon: China's Undeclared War Against the U.S. in Korea, 1950–1951* (New York, 1988); Shu Guang Zhang, *Deterrence and Strategic Culture: Chinese-American Confrontations, 1949–1958* (Ithaca, NY, 1992); Hak Joon

Kim, "China's Non-Involvement in the Origins of the Korean War: A Critical Reassessment of the Traditionalist and Revisionist Literature," in Cotton and Neary, eds., *The Korean War in History*, 11–32; Warren Cohen, "Research Note: Conversations with Chinese Friends: Zhou Enlai's Associates Report on Chinese-American Relations in the 1940s and the Korean War," *Diplomatic History*, 11 (Summer, 1987), 283–289; and Michael H. Hunt, "Beijing and the Korean Crisis," *Political Science Quarterly*, 107 (Fall, 1992), 453–478.

The immediate American response to the outbreak of hostilities, almost on an hourly basis, can be followed in Glenn D. Paige, *The Korean Decision* (New York, 1968). See also two articles by Paige, "Comparative Case Analysis of Crisis Decisions: Korea and Cuba," in Charles F. Hermann, ed., *International Crises: Insights from Behavioral Research* (New York, 1972), and "On Values and Science: The Korean Decision Reconsidered," *American Political Science Review*, 71 (December 1977), 1603–1609. An interesting account of why Truman decided quickly to come to the defense of South Korea is Stephen Pelz, "U.S. Decisions on Korean Policy, 1943–1950: Some Hypotheses," in Cumings, ed., *Child of Conflict*, 93–132. Besides considerations growing out of the Cold War conflict between the United States and the Soviet Union, according to Pelz, Truman intervened so decisively in Korea because of his fear of a political attack on his administration at home if he did nothing. Another important account of the first week of the war is Barton J. Bernstein, "The Week We Went to War: American Intervention in the Korean Civil War," *Foreign Service Journal*, 54 (January 1977), 6–9 and 33–35, and *ibid.* (February 1977), 8–11 and 33–35. Bernstein largely substantiates Paige's account of the opening week of the conflict. Ernest May, *Lessons of the Past: The Use and Misuse of History in American Foreign Policy* (New York, 1973), argues that Truman's effort to avoid the mistakes of the past, particularly by not repeating the failed policy of appeasement of the 1930s, influenced his decision to go to war. Alexander L. George, "American Policy-Making and the North Korean Aggression," *World Politics*, 7 (January 1955), 208–232, also agrees that Truman intervened in Korea because he feared the consequences of inaction, believed intervention was necessary to prevent the Soviet Union from other acts of aggression, and was influenced by the Munich syndrome. Morton H. Halperin, "The Limiting Process in the Korean War," *Political Science Review*, 78 (March 1963), 13–39, remarks that the defense of Korea was motivated partly by a feeling in Washington that action was necessary in Korea to convince western Europe that the United States would finally come to its aid if attacked by the Soviet Union. Finally, Yonusuke Nagai, "The Korean War: An Interpretative Essay," *The Japanese Journal of American Studies*, 1 (1981), 151–174, states that the Korean war afforded the United States an opportunity to draw a line of containment against Communism in East Asia.

Besides the Schnabel, Appleman, and Hermes volumes mentioned at the beginning of this essay, which deal with diplomatic as well as with military themes, two other official military histories of the war are James A. Field, Jr., *History of United States Naval Operations: Korea* (Washington, DC, 1962), and Lynn Montrose, Nicholas A. Canonza, et al., *U.S. Marine Operations in Korea* (5 vols., Washington, DC, 1954–1972). For the definitive military history of the war during the critical period from November 1950 to April 1951, see the three volumes by Roy E. Appleman, *Disaster in Korea: The Chinese Confront MacArthur* (College Station, TX, 1989); *Escaping the Trap: The US Army X Corps in Northeast Korea, 1950* (College Station, TX, 1990); and *Ridgway Duels for Korea* (College Station, TX, 1990). In these volumes, Appleman dispels a number of myths associated with the conduct of the war, most notably the argument that the Chinese were able to take advantage of the separation of the Eighth Army from the X Corps following their invasion of Korea in November 1950. He also attributes much of the turnaround in the war in 1951 to the inspired leadership of Matthew Ridgway.

Other histories of military operations during the war include Robert Frank Futrell, *The United States Air Force in Korea, 1950–1953* (New York, 1961); James J. Stewart, ed., *Airpower: The Decisive Force in Korea* (Princeton, NJ, 1957); Walt Sheldon, *Hill or High Water: MacArthur's Landing at Inchon* (New York, 1968); S.L.A. Marshall, *The River and the Gauntlet: The Defeat of the Eighth Army by the Chinese Communist Forces* (New York, 1953); Edwin P. Hoyt, *On to the Yalu* (New York, 1984); Robert Jackson, *Air Power Over Korea* (New York, 1975); Russell A. Gugeler, ed., *Combat Actions in Korea* (Washington, DC, 1954); and U.S. Eighth Army, Historical Office, *Key Korean War Battles Fought in the Republic of Korea* (Seoul, 1972). For the problem of command in a limited war, see D. Clayton James, "Command Crisis: MacArthur and the Korean War," *The Harmon Memorial Lectures in Military History* (United States Air Force Academy, Colorado Springs, CO, 1982). For Canada's military role in the war, consult Thor Thorgrimsson and E. C. Russell, *Canadian Naval Operations in*

Korean Waters, 1950–1952 (Ottawa, 1966), and Herbert Fairlie Wood, *Strange Battleground: The Operations in Korea and Their Effects on the Defense Policy of Canada* (Ottawa, 1966). On Soviet pilots flying Chinese jets during the war, see Steven J. Zaloga, "The Russians in MiG Alley," *Air Force Magazine*, 74 (February 1991), 74–77.

On Truman's decision to cross the 38th parallel in September 1950, consult James I. Matray, "Truman's Plan for Victory: National Self-Determination and the Thirty-Eighth Parallel Decision in Korea," *Journal of American History*, 66 (September 1979), 314–333, and Walter LaFeber, "American Policy-Makers, Public Opinion, and the Outbreak of the Cold War, 1945–1950," in Yonosuke Nagai and Akira Iriye, eds., *The Origins of the Cold War in Asia* (New York, 1977), 43–65. LaFeber maintains that Truman's decision to cross the 38th parallel was made as early as July 1950. On Communist China's subsequent decision to enter the war, see the essays by Pollack and Hunt and the volumes by Spurr and Zhang cited earlier. See also Allen Whiting, *China Crosses the Yalu: The Decision to Enter the Korean War* (Stanford, CA, 1960); Mineo Nakajima, "The Sino-Soviet Confrontation: Its Roots in the International Background of the Korean War," *Australian Journal of Chinese Affairs*, Number 1 (January 1979), 19–47; Bruce Hao Yufan and Zhai Zhihai, "China's Decision to Enter the Korean War: History Revisted," *The China Quarterly*, 121 (March 1990), 94–115; Qiang Zhai, *The Dragon, the Lion, and the Eagle: Chinese/British/American Relations, 1949–1958* (Kent, OH, 1994).

Recent scholarship indicates that following the Chinese invasion and on several other occasions, both Presidents Truman and Eisenhower gave serious consideration to using nuclear weapons against Communist forces. In addition to the two volumes by Foot cited earlier, see Daniel Calingaert, "Nuclear Weapons and the Korean War," *Journal of Strategic Studies*, 11 (June, 1988), 177–202; and, especially, Roger Dingman, "Atomic Diplomacy During the Korean War," *International Security*, 13 (Winter, 1988–89), 50–91. Interestingly, Dingman challenges conventional views (including those in this volume) about the importance Eisenhower attached to the possible use of atomic warfare to end the war even as he makes clear that Truman gave more thought to employing nuclear weapons than previously recognized.

Fear that the United States might resort to nuclear warfare was only one of several issues that exacerbated relations between the United States and its allies (especially Britain) during the war. This is a major theme of Rosemary Foot's two volumes cited earlier, which also make the point that London generally acted as a restraining influence on Washington. On this latter point, see also Foot, "Anglo-American Relations in the Korean Crisis: The British Effort to Avert an Expanded War, December 1950–January 1951," *Diplomatic History*, 10 (Winter 1986), 43–57; M.L. Dockrill, "The Foreign Office, Anglo-American Relations and the Korean Truce Negotiations July 1951–July 1953," in Cotton and Neary (eds.), *The Korean War in History*, 100–119. On the impact of the Korean war on the formation of NATO, see Lawrence S. Kaplan, *The United States and NATO: The Formative Years* (Lexington, KY, 1984), and Walter LaFeber, "NATO and the Korean War: A Context," *Diplomatic History*, 13 (Fall, 1989), 461–477. Kaplan argues that the war was a turning point in the formation of NATO. LaFeber seeks to modify that position by arguing that the transformation of NATO and the American military buildup in Europe began after the Soviet Union successfully tested an atomic bomb, ten months earlier.

On the domestic side of the war there are a number of books and articles. For a narrative on American society in the two weeks following the outbreak of war, see David Detzer, *Thunder of the Captains: The Short Summer in 1950* (New York, 1970). See also John Edward Wiltz, "The Korean War and American Society," in Heller, ed., *The Korean War: A 25-Year Perspective*, 112–158. On the constitutional issues raised by America's undeclared war in Korea, consult Arthur M. Schlesinger, Jr., *The Imperial Presidency* (Boston, 1973). On the breakdown of congressional bipartisanship during the war, see David R. Kepley, *The Collapse of the Middle Way: Senate Republicans and the Bipartisan Foreign Policy, 1948–1952* (Westport, CT, 1988). On the Truman-MacArthur controversy, see John Edward Wiltz, "Truman and MacArthur: The Wake Island Meeting," *Military Affairs*, 42 (December 1978), 168–175; Wiltz, "The MacArthur Hearings of 1951: The Secret Testimony," *Military Affairs*, 39 (December 1975), 167–173; Trumbull Higgins, *Korea and the Fall of MacArthur: A Precis in Limited War* (New York, 1960); Richard H. Rovere and Arthur M. Schlesinger, Jr., *The MacArthur Controversy and American Foreign Policy* (New York, 1951); and especially John W. Spanier, *The Truman-MacArthur Controversy and American Foreign Policy* (Cambridge, MA, 1959). On the impact of the war on American politics, the most complete study remains Ronald J. Caridi, *The Korean War and American Politics: The Republican Party as a Case Study* (Philadelphia, 1968). But see also the appropriate chapters in Robert A. Divine, *Foreign Policy and the U.S. Presidential Elections, 1952–1960* (New York, 1974); H. Bradford Westerfield, *Foreign Policy and Party Politics: Pearl Harbor to Korea* (New Haven, CT, 1955); and Gary W. Reichard, "Divisions and Dissent: Democrats and Foreign Policy, 1952–1956," *Political Science Quarterly*, 93 (Spring 1978).

The definitive biography of Douglas MacArthur is D. Clayton James, *The Years of MacArthur* (3 volumes, Boston, 1971–1985). For the Korean war, see especially volume 3, *Triumph and Disaster 1945–1964*. Also important is Michael Schaller, *Douglas MacArthur: The Far Eastern General* (New York, 1989), which documents the reluctance of the Joint Chiefs of Staff to challenge MacArthur in Korea; in addition, consult William Manchester, *American Caesar: Douglas MacArthur, 1880–1964* (Boston, 1978), and Robert Smith, *MacArthur in Korea: The Naked Emperor* (New York, 1982). Smith describes MacArthur as an impervious individual around whom much myth has been created but who was essentially a downright liar and charlatan. The best volume on Truman is now David Mc-Cullough, *Truman* (New York, 1992), but almost as informative is Robert K. Donovan, *Tumultuous Years: The Presidency of Harry S. Truman, 1949–1953* (New York, 1982). Both are balanced but sympathetic studies. Also good are Donald McCoy, *The Presidency of Harry S. Truman* (Lawrence, KS, 1984), and Cabell Phillips, *The Truman Presidency: The History of a Triumphant Succession* (Baltimore, 1969), whose theme is evident in the book's title. A magisterial biography of Dwight D. Eisenhower is presented in the two volumes by Stephen E. Ambrose, *Eisenhower: Soldier, General of the Army, President-Elect, 1890–1952* (New York, 1983); and *Eisenhower: The President* (New York, 1984). On Eisenhower's efforts to end the Korean war, which points out both his lack of a plan for ending the war when he entered the White House and his willingness to use nuclear weapons against China if Beijing would not agree to an acceptable armistice, see Edward C. Keefer, "President Dwight D. Eisenhower and the End of the Korean War," *Diplomatic History*, 10 (Summer, 1986), 267–289.

Several studies deal with various aspects of the diplomacy during the war. On the role of the United Nations, consult Leland M. Goodrich, *Korea: A Study of U.S. Policy in the United Nations* (New York, 1956). In general, Goodrich is critical of the United States for not following a forceful enough policy with respect to South Korea, politically and diplomatically. India's efforts at mediation are covered in Shif Dayal, *India's Role in the Korean Question* (Delhi, 1959), and Blema S. Steinberg, "The Korean War: A Case Study in Indian Neutralism," Orbis, 8 (Winter, 1965), 937–954. Also worthwhile is J.C. Kundra, *India's Foreign Policy, 1947–1954* (Grunigen, Holland, 1955). A first-rate analysis of Canada's diplomatic role in the Korean war is Denis Stairs, *The Diplomacy of Constraint: Canada, the Korean War and the United States* (Toronto, 1974).

For the armistice negotiations and other matters leading to the end of the war, see Foot, *A Substitute for Victory*, previously cited, and three articles by Barton J. Bernstein, "Truman's Secret Thoughts on Ending the Korean War," *Foreign Service Journal*, 57 (November 1980), 31–33 and 44–45; "Syngman Rhee: The Pawn as Rook: The Struggle to End the Korean War," *Bulletin of Concerned Asian Scholars*, X (January-March 1978), 38–47; and "The Struggle over the Korean War Armistice: Prisoners of Repatriation?" in Cumings, ed., *Child of Conflict*, 261–307. In these essays Bernstein describes Truman's fantasies with respect to the use of atomic weapons and an actual policy of increasing bombing of North Korea in an effort to bring about an end to the war. A fourth essay by Bernstein, "The Origins of America's Commitment in Korea," *Foreign Service Journal*, 55 (March 1978), 10–13 and 34, describes America's dealings with Syngman Rhee, including plans to overthrow the South Korean president, in an effort to win South Korea's acceptance of an armistice agreement, in return for which Washington agreed to a defense pact with the Seoul government. Highly critical of Truman's failure to support the planned coup against Rhee is Edward C. Keefer, "The Truman Administration and the South Korean Political Crisis of 1952: Democracy's Failure," *Pacific Historical Review*, 60 (May 1991), 145–168. On other aspects of the armistice negotiations and final settlement of the war, see Wilfred Bacchus, "The Relationship between Combat and Peace Negotiations: Fighting While Talking in Korea, 1951–1953," Orbis, 17 (Summer 1973), 547–574; Edward Friedman, "Nuclear Blackmail and the End of the Korean War," *Modern China*, 1 (January 1975), 75–91; Ohn Chang-il, "South Korea, the United States, and the Korean Armistice Negotiations," in Baum and Matray, eds., *Korea and the Cold War*, 209–228; John Gittings, "Talks, Bombs, and Germs: Another Look at the Korean War," *Journal of Contemporary Asia*, 5 (1975), 205–217; and Henry W. Brands, Jr., "The Dwight D. Eisenhower Administration and the

'Other' Geneva Conference of 1954," *Pacific Historical Review,* 61 (February 1987), 78–99.

For a comparative analysis of America's involvement in Korea and Vietnam, see Robert J. Donovan, *Nemesis: Truman and Johnson in the Coils of War in Asia* (New York, 1984). On the same subject, see also Alonzo Hamby, "Public Opinion: Korea and Vietnam," *Wilson Quarterly,* II (Summer 1978), 137–141; and Chang Jin Park, "American Foreign Policy in Korea and Vietnam: Comparative Case Studies," *Review of Politics,* 37 (January 1975), 20–47.

Finally, the student of the Korean war is fortunate to have the memoirs and recollections of a number of the participants in the conflict, politically, diplomatically, and militarily. Among the most important of those are Harry S. Truman, *Memoirs: Years of Trial and Hope* (Garden City, NY, 1956); Robert H. Ferrell, ed., *The Autobiography of Harry Truman* (Boulder, CO, 1978); Robert H. Ferrell, ed., *Off the Record: The Private Papers of Harry S. Truman* (New York, 1980); Dwight D. Eisenhower, *Mandate for Change, 1953–1956* (Garden City, NY, 1963); Dean Acheson, *Present at the Creation: My Years in the State Department* (New York, 1969); Douglas MacArthur, *Reminiscences* (New York, 1964); Omar N. Bradley and Clay Blair, *A General's Life* (New York, 1983); Matthew B. Ridgway, *The Korean War* (Garden City, NY, 1967); Mark W. Clark, *From the Danube to the Yalu* (New York, 1954); C. Turner Joy, *How Communists Negotiate* (New York, 1955); Allen E. Goodman, ed., *Negotiating While Fighting: The Diary of Admiral C. Turner Joy at the Korean Armistice Conference* (Stanford, CA, 1978); J. Lawton Collins, *War in Peacetime: The History and Lessons of the Korea* (Boston, 1965); and John M. Allison, *Ambassador from the Prairie or Allison Wonderland* (Boston, 1973).

Other memoirs also contain matters bearing on the Korean war. In Strobe Talbott, ed., *Khrushchev Remembers* (Boston, 1970), former Soviet Premier Nikita Khrushchev comments on the Soviet Union's reluctant approval of Kim Il-sung's plans to invade South Korea in 1950. For George Kennan's efforts in Moscow in 1951 to get negotiations started on Korea, see George F. Kennan, *Memoirs, 1925–1963* (2 vols., Boston, 1967–1972). For the dubious activities of India's ambassador to China to bring about a settlement of the war, consult K.M. Panikkar, *In Two Chinas* (London, 1959). In *Witness to History, 1929–1969* (New York, 1973), Ambassador Charles Bohlen, who was an active participant in State Department discussions on Korean policy, criticizes the United States for overinterpreting the Korean war and overextending its commitments. Although for the most part disappointing, in *Farewell to Foggy Bottom: The Recollections of a Career Diplomat* (New York, 1964), America's ambassador to Korea after November 1952, Ellis Briggs, chronicles Syngman Rhee's opposition to an armistice agreement. In *As It Happened* (New York, 1954), former British Prime Minister Clement R. Attlee remarks on his concern in 1950 and 1951 that the Far Eastern war be confined to Korea. He also describes his trip to Washington in December 1950 for discussions on Korea. Former British Foreign Secretary and Prime Minister Anthony Eden discusses British views on the "greater sanction" statement in 1951 in *Full Circle: The Memoirs of Anthony Eden* (Boston, 1960). Lastly, in *In the Cause of Peace* (New York, 1954), former Secretary-General of the United Nations Trygve Lie discusses some of the diplomacy at the United Nations with respect to the Korean war.

Index

Acheson, Dean, 23, 37, 43, 55, 63, 68, 70, 147–48, 154; and opening of peace negotiations, 119–120, 122; and South Korea as breadbasket for Japan, 22; Atlantic alliance, 41; at MacArthur hearings, 108–109; China 38, 80; defense perimeter speech, 15, 21, 22; demands for resignation of, 38, 55; EDC, 149; Indochina, 211; invasion of South Korea, 18; on MacArthur, 77, 99, 100–101; on Menon resolution, 173–174; on negotiations with the Soviet Union, 26; POWs, 137, 138
Ad Hoc Committee on Korea, 10–11
Adenauer, Konrad, 150
Aldrich, Winthrop, 194
Allison, John, 40
Almond, Edward M., 54
Alsop brothers, 102
Alvarez, del Vayo, 5
American Legion, 76
American Military Government (AMG), 6, 8, 9, 10, 12
Amvets, 76
Anglo-Iranian Oil Company, 125, 147
Appeasement, fear of, see Munich Syndrome
Appleman, Roy, 68, 72, 82

Asia, nationalist movements, 16. See also individual countries
Atlantic alliance, see Western Alliance
Atlantic Monthly, 194
Attlee, Clement, 96, 149, 184; visit to U.S., 70–71
Australia, and UNTCOK, 12

Bacteriological warfare charges, 153–55
Baldwin, Hanson, 92
Bao Dai government, 63
Beria, Lavrenti P., 179
Bevan, Aneurin, 118, 149, 162
BIG SWITCH, 204. See also POWs, final exchange
Bradley, Omar, 47, 64, 70, 73–74, 100, 101, 178; at MacArthur hearings, 107–08
Briggs, Ellis, 185–186
Bundy, William P., on lessons of Korea, 211–212
Burma, 21, 146

Cairo Conference, postwar status of Korea, 4
Cambodia, nominal independence of, 16

Canada, and China, 78–79; and UNT-
    COK, 12
Central Intelligence Agency (CIA), 126;
    on Chinese intervention, 66
Cheju-do Island, guerrilla activity on, 12
Chiang Kai-shek, 10, 13, 24, 46, 55, 79,
    104, 109
Childs, Marquis, 102
China, and Korea, 5
China lobby, 24, 55
China question, 37–38, 79–81, 107,
    108–109
Chosin Reservoir, 68, 72
Churchill, Winston, 2,4, 134–35, 139,
    148–149, 162; Big Four talks, 184,
    203; visit to U.S., 134, 148
Clark, Mark, 157–158, 179, 180, 182–183,
    185–186, 187, 200, 202, 203, 214;
    meeting with Eisenhower, 175–176;
    NNRC, 182–183; on escalation of
    war, 161–163, 164–165; proposed
    coup against Rhee, 159–160. *See also*
    Joint Chiefs of Staff, and Clark
Clausewitz, Karl von, 214
Cleveland, John, 118
Cold War, 1–5, 10–17, 24, 146–148
Collins, J. Lawton, 52, 92, 129, 164
Colson, Charles F., 156
Commonweal, 76
Communist China, *see* People's Republic
    of China (PRC)
Communist conspiracy, *see* Red Scare
Connor, "Bull," 36
Czechoslovakia, and NNRC, 182.

Dean, Arthur, 206
Declaration on Liberated Europe, 2
Defense Production Act (DPA), 44, 72
DeGaulle, Charles, 119
Democratic People's Republic, 12; costs
    of war, 180; invasion of South
    Korea, 17–21; military strength of,
    13
Detroit Common Council, 35–36
Disabled American Veterans, 76
Dodd, Francis, 156
Domino theory, 146

Donovan, Robert, 45
Dulles, John Foster, 178, 203; and Plan
    EVERREADY, 186; European atti-
    tude toward, 184; massive retalia-
    tion doctrine, 177–78; meeting with
    Nehru, 187; on resumption of truce
    negotiations, 180; scolds Rhee,
    195–96, 201; signing of mutual de-
    fense treaty with South Korea, 204

Economist (London), 101
Eden, Anthony, 147, 149, 174; and the
    greater sanction policy, 134; rebukes
    Acheson, 162
Egypt, resentment toward British, 127,
    147
Eisenhower, Dwight D., and MacArthur,
    46–47, 176–177; as NATO comman-
    der, 32, 43, 96–97, 153, 170–171; as
    President-elect, 165, 174; as Presi-
    dent of Columbia University,
    170–171; as presidential candidate,
    165–166, 171–173; draft effort, 170;
    European opinion of, 183–184;
    lessons of Korea, 211; meeting with
    Truman and Marshall, 170–171;
    moves Seventh Fleet, 178–179; on
    Indochina, 211; on "loss" of China,
    171; on nuclear weapons, 177–178,
    187–188; On POWs, 174, 180;
    pledges to go to Korea, 172; reas-
    sures Rhee, 193, 196; resumption of
    truce negotiations, 180; signing of
    armistice agreement, 202–203; trip
    to Korea, 175–176; warning to PRC,
    187; warns Rhee, 181,185, 193,
    195–196, 206
Elections, 1950, 36, 62, 65; 1952, 140,
    151–153, 165, 171–173
England, *see* Great Britain
European Defense Community (EDC),
    134–135, 149–151
European rearmament, *see* Western Al-
    liance; EDC

Faure, Edgar, 150
Formosa, 17, 20, 21, 26, 32

Formosa Straights, Seventh Fleet sent to, 18, 26, 34
France, and German rearmament, 43, 150, 174; Indochina, 17; on Menon resolution, 174; postarmistice political conference, 205; rearmament, 118–119, 150; resentment of American anticolonialism, 174
French Morocco, demands for greater autonomy, 147
Fuchs, Klaus, 23

Geneva Convention (1949), on POWs, 137
Germany, 20, 150; rearming of, 41–43, 96, 134, 149–150
"Get tough policy," 3, 9
Gloucestershire Regiment, 115
Great Britain, and postarmistice political conference, 205; China, 80, 95–96, 117–118, 148; Chinese intervention, 66–67; European rearmament, 42–43, 118, 134–135, 148; greater sanction policy, 134–135, 148–149, 203–204; on bombing of Yalu power plants, 63, 162; on nuclear weapons, 33, 70–71; on Rhee's release of POWs, 194–195; peace initiative (1950), 37–38; on resuming truce negotiations, 127–128, 181, 184; pressures U.S. to conclude armistice agreement, 197; trusteeship for Korea, 4
"Great Debate" (1950–1951), 75–79
Greater Sanction policy, 133–135, 187, 194–195, 203–204
Gromyko, Andrei, 37; at San Francisco Conference, 126

Halsey, William F., 54
Harriman, Averell, 100
Harrison, William K., Jr., 163–164, 200–202
Hastings, Max, 212, 213
Henderson, Loy W.
Hiss, Alger, 23
Hitler, Adolph, 22

Hodge, John, 6, 8, 9
Hoover, Herbert, "Gibraltar" speech, 76–77
Hsieh, Fang, 123
Hukbalahaps, 19, 33
Hurley, Patrick, 109

Inchon landing, 51–54
India, and NNRC, 182–183; and postarmistice political conference, 205; Menon resolution, 173–175; peace initiative (1950), 37–38;
Indochina, 16, 17, 21, 139, 146–147, 153; assistance to, 18, 26
Indonesia, 16
International Red Cross, 154, 179
Iran, nationalization of AIOC, 125, 147; Soviet troops in, 8
Iraq, 127–128
Iron Triangle, 93, 117, 130, 177

Jacobs, Joseph E., 11
Japan, geopolitical importance of to U.S., 20, 21–22, 126, 216
Japanese Peace Conference, *see* San Francisco Conference
Jenner, William, 55, 103
Johnson, Louis, 47, 54
Johnson, Lyndon, 215; lessons of Korea, 211
Joint Chiefs of Staff (JCS), 10, 132; and Clark, 159–160, 162–163, 164–165, 180; and MacArthur, 52–53, 64–66, 73–75, 92, 105, 106–108; and Ridgway, 117, 120–121, 127–128, 132–133, 135–136, 138–139; Chinese intervention, 62, 65, 66; criticism of, 64–65, 94–95, 129, 214–215; greater sanction policy, 133; on crossing the thirty-eighth parallel, 56, 94–95; on POWs, 137 -138; on use of nuclear weapons, 69–70, 71, 163, 164, 187; proposed coup against Rhee, 159–160
Joint Strategic Plans Committee, 164
Joint Strategic Survey Committee, 69–70

Joy, C. Turner, 123, 129, 163; on treatment of POWs, 156

Kaesong, 123, 128; negotiations at, 123, 125
KANSAS LINE, 127
Kelly, David, 37
Kennan, George, 8–9, 40, 119–120, 163
Kennedy, John F., 215
Kim Il-sung, 9, 12, 19–21, 59
Kirk, Alan G., 120
Knowland, William, 184
Koje-do, prison riot on, 153, 155–156
Korea, division of, 5; internal conditions of, 1, 5–8, 11, 12–13, 16; under Japanese rule, 4; Joint Commission on, 8, 9, 10; military importance of, 4–5, 13, 15; occupation of, 6, 8–10; postwar conference on, 205–207; trusteeship for, 4, 8. *See also* Democratic People's Republic; Republic of Korea (ROK)
Korean Communist Party (KCP), 7
Korean Democratic Party (KDP), 6
Korean Military Advisory Group (KMAG), 14
Korean People's Republic (KPR), 6
Korean War, and Vietnam, 210–212; constitutional issues, 44–45, 77–78; military engagements, 17–19, 33–35, 47–54, 60, 65, 67–68, 72, 81–82, 89–93, 115–117, 130, 131–132, 160–161, 162–163, 177, 198–200, 210, 213; military stalemate, 129–131, 145; mobilization for, 96; political objectives of, 39; significance of 213–214, 215–217; signing of armistice agreement, 202. *See also* DPA; *individual battles and operations*

LaFeber, Walter, 37
Laos, nominal independence of, 16
Lawrence, David, 102
Lehman, Herbert, 36
Lie Trygve, 97
Life, 75, 76, 78, 148, 178

LINE NO NAME, 116
Lisbon meeting, 149–150. *See also* EDC
LITTLE SWITCH, *see* POWs, exchange of sick and wounded
Lodge, Henry Cabot, 103, 170
Lovett, Robert A., 11, 63, 99
Lyuh Woo-hyung, 9

MacArthur, Douglas, 18, 19, 32, 45–46, 92, 214; appointed UN commander, 33; European attitude toward, 69, 71, 95, 101; growing criticism of, 69; Inchon landing, 51–54; on bombing of Yalu bridges and Manchuria, 63–64; on Chinese intervention, 63, 66, 70, 73–75; on Formosa, 46; on peace initiative (1951), 97–98; recall, 99–110; visit to Formosa, 57–58, 59. See also Joint Chiefs of Staff and MacArthur; MacArthur hearings; Truman-MacArthur controversy; Wake Island conference
MacArthur hearings, 104–109
McCarran Internal Security Bill, 36
McCarthy, Joseph, 23–24, 62, 143, 152; attacks British, 184; attacks Marshall, 152; Bohlen appointment, 183; European view of 183–184; on Korean War, 35, 152. *See also* Red Scare
McCarthyism, *see* Red Scare
McCleod, Scott, 183
McMahon, Brien, 106
Makins, Sir Roger, 194
Malaysia, 21, 147
Malenkov, Georgi, 179
Malik, Jacob, 111, 119
Mao Zedong, 13, 16, 20, 59, 213
Marshall, George, 10, 73, 101; appointment as defense secretary, 54–55; at MacArthur hearings, 107, 110
Marshall Plan, 10, 24
Martin, Joseph, 99–100
Massive retaliation doctrine, 216
Menon, Krishna, 173
Menon resolution, 173–175
"MiG Alley," 131
Molotov, Vyacheslav, meeting with Truman, 3

Morocco, *see* French Morocco
Morse, Wayne, 152
Moscow Foreign Ministers Conference
(1945), 7–8
Muccio, John, 122, 159
Munich Syndrome, 22
Murphy, Robert, 163
Myers, Francis, 93

Nam Il, 123, 200, 202
Nation, 73, 103
National Security Council (NSC), 13,
181; on armistice agreement, 180; on
Chinese intervention, 66–67, 68–69;
on release of POWs, 195. *See also in-
dividual NSC papers*
Nehru, Jawaharlal, 320
Neutral Nations Repatriation Commis-
sion (NNRC), 181–183, 188, 196,
205–206
New Republic, 41, 103, 110
New Statesman and Nation, 80
New York Times, 104, 128
North Atlantic Treaty Organization
(NATO), 32, 41–43, 96–97, 149–150
North Atlantic Treaty Council, 148, 149
North Korea, *see* Democratic People's
Republic
NSC-68, 17, 33, 43–44, 48
NSC-81/1, 40, 56
NSC 118/2, 133

Office of Defense Mobilization, 72
Old Baldy, battle of, 198–199
OPERATION STRANGLE, 131
OPERATION THUNDERBOLT, 90

Pace, Frank, 101
Panikkar, K.M., 57, 59
Panmunjom, negotiations at, 127–137,
156–157, 163–164, 176, 177, 181–185,
188, 200; signing of armistice, 202
Pelz, Stephen, 22
People's Republic of China (PRC), 16,
20, 81–82; air force of, 118, 124, 131,
145–146, 162–163; costs of war, 127,
154, 179–180, 213; intervention of,
57–59, 61–68; on opening of peace
negotiations, 129; on prisoner exchange, 179–181; proposed bombing of Manchuria, 117; proposed
embargo against, 117; recognition
of, 37, 71; resumption of peace negotiations (1953), 181; Rhee's release
of POWs, 196; U.S. perceptions of
57, 59–60, 65. *See also* Bacteriological
warfare charges; POWs, exchange
of sick and wounded
Philippine Islands, 146; assistance to
18–19, 26
Plan EVERREADY, 186
Poland, and NNRC, 186
Policy Planning Staff (PPS), 40
Porkchop Hill, battle of, 199
Postarmistice political conference,
205–207
Potsdam Conference, 3–4; postwar status of Korea, 4
POWs, 136–139, 157, 163, 173–175, 188;
exchange of sick and wounded, 179,
180–181; final exchange of, 204–205;
release of by Rhee, 194–196
Preventive war, 38–39, 76
Prisoners of war, *see* POWs
Pusan perimeter, 33
Pyun Tai Yung, 201

Quirino, Elpidio, 146

Rassemblement du Peuples Francais,
119
Red Cross, 121
Red Scare, 23–25, 32, 35–37, 151–153,
172, 183, 212; European reaction to,
183–184. *See also* McCarthy, Joseph
Republic of Korea (ROK), establishment
of, 12; internal conditions, 121, 158;
opposition to cease fire and truce
talks, 121–122, 124, 181, 193–194; security pact with U.S., 196–198,
200–202, 204. *See also* Postarmistice
political conference

Reston, James, 69, 104
Rhee, Syngman, 6, 9, 10, 11–12, 23, 82;
    agrees to armistice, 198–201; Ameri-
    can attitude toward, 9, 11–13, 15–16,
    158–160; elected president of ROK,
    12; government coercion, 15,
    158–160; in post-armistice period,
    206; institutes martial law, 160;
    meeting with Eisenhower, 175–176;
    on American assistance, 14; opposes
    cease-fire (1951), 121–122, 124; op-
    position to armistice agreements,
    181, 182, 185–186, 193–194, 196–198,
    200–202; political opposition to,
    15–16, 21, 158–159; proposed coup
    against, 159–160; release of POWs,
    194. See also Plan EVERREADY;
    Postarmistice political conference;
    Republic of Korea, security pact
    with U.S.
Ridgway, Matthew, 89, 90–91, 120, 124,
    125; greater sanction policy, 135; on
    escalating war, 161; on limited war,
    211; on POW question, 138; opposes
    cease-fire (1951), 120–121; proposes
    bombing Manchuria, 117–118; suc-
    ceeds MacArthur, 101. See also Joint
    Chiefs of Staff, and Ridgway.
Robertson, Walter, mission to Korea,
    195–198
Roosevelt, Franklin, 2, 24; and Korean
    trusteeship, 4–5
Rovere, Richard, 55
Rusk, Dean, 61, 63, 99
Russell, Richard, 104, 109
Russia, see Soviet Union
Russian Civil War, 1
Russo-Japanese War (1904), 4

Saltonstall, Leverett, 103
San Francisco Conference, 125–126
Schine, David, 184
Scott, Hugh D., Jr., 56
Sherman, Forrest, 52
Sino-Japanese War (1894), 4
Sino-Soviet Treaty, 57, 60
Smith, H. Alexander, 44

Smith, Oliver P., 72
Soviet Union, 56, 57; and postarmistice
    conference, 205–206; and strategic
    importance of Korea, 7; atomic
    bomb, 23; German neutralization
    proposal, 150, 179, 203; negotiations
    with, 25–26; "peace offensive"
    (1953), 179; relations with U.S., 1–4,
    8–9. See also Cold War
Stalin, Joseph, 2,4, 19–20, 179
Stassen, Harold, 76
Stevenson, Adlai, 172
Strategic Air Command (SAC), 70, 136
Stratemeyer, George E., 70
Suiho, attack on, 161
Sulzberger, Arthur, 102
Survey Research Center, 172
Sweden, and NNRC, 182
Switzerland, and NNRC, 182

Tae Han Youth Corps, 159
Taft, Robert, 36; as presidential candi-
    date, 151–152, 153, 165; and the
    "great debate" (1950–1951), 76–78;
    on constitutional issue, 44, 77–78;
    on Marshall, 55
Taylor, Maxwell, 199–200, 215
Tehran Conference, 4
Thirty-eighth parallel, crossing of,
    39–40, 47–48, 55–57, 60; recrossing
    of, 93–95
Time 39, 90, 146–147
Times (London), 151
Truman Doctrine, 10, 24
Truman, Harry, 3, 10, 37, 43–44, 53, 63,
    174; decision to cross thirty-eighth
    parallel, 56–57; Declaration of Na-
    tional Emergency, 72; influence of
    State Department on, 5; meeting
    with Molotov, 3; on Chinese inter-
    vention, 34, 62, 66, 68; on consulta-
    tion with Congress, 44–45, 78; on
    Eisenhower-MacArthur meeting,
    176–77; on nuclear weapons, 33–34,
    47, 69–71, 100, 135–136, 161, 216; on
    peace negotiations, 132, 133–134,
    135–136, 163164; peace initiative

(1951), 97–99, 119; personality of, 23, 47, 102; POWs, 137–139; proposed coup against Rhee, 159–160; rejects new approaches to Communists, 163–164; response to North Korean invasion, 18–19, 21–27, 212; unpopularity of, 101–102, 110–111, 161; warns Rhee, 124, 159. *See also* Truman-MacArthur controversy; Wake Island conference
Truman-MacArthur controversy, 32, 45–47, 74, 98–110. *See also* MacArthur, Douglas, recall
Tunisia, 147

United Nations (UN), aggressor nation resolution, 79–81; and post-armistice conference, 205–206; efforts at peace, 71–72; response to North Korean invasion, 21, 47
United Nations Temporary Commission (UNTCOK), 11, 12
United Press International (UPI), 155
United States, and occupation of Korea, 6; political climate of, 38–39, 55, 75, 76, 82, 95, 96–97, 101–104, 110–111, 115, 121, 125, 146–153, 161, 165, 172–173, 183–184, 197, 202, 212. *See also* Red Scare
U Nu, 146

Vandenberg, Hoyt, 33, 108, 145
Van Fleet, James, 116–117, 128, 165, 199
Veterans of Foreign Wars, 47, 61, 76

Vietnam, 210, 214, 215
Vietnam War, compared to Korean War, 212
Vishinsky, Andrei, 173, 175
Voice of America, 184

Wake Island conference, 60–61
Walker, Walton H., 54, 68, 89
Washington *Post*, 103
Western Alliance, 40–43, 48; divisions within, 78–81, 95–96, 118–119, 149–151, 173–175, 184–185, 203, 214. *See also* North Atlantic Treaty Organization.
Western Europe, on Big Four talks, 79, 161–162; on bombing of Yalu power plants, 161–162; on Eisenhower administration, 183–184; on McCarthy, 194; on peace negotiations, 119, 121, 183–184; on release of POWs, 194–195; on use of nuclear weapons, 69–71, 178
Weyland, Otto P., 131, 165
Wherry, Kenneth, 44, 78
Wherry Resolution, 78
White Horse Hill, battle of, 177
Wilson, Charles E., 186
World Health Organization, 121

Yalta Conference, 2
Yalu power plants, bombing of, 161–162
Yu Chan Yang, 201

Zhou Enlai, 57, 181